W9-BRY-556

The Complete Illustrated
WOODWORKING COURSE

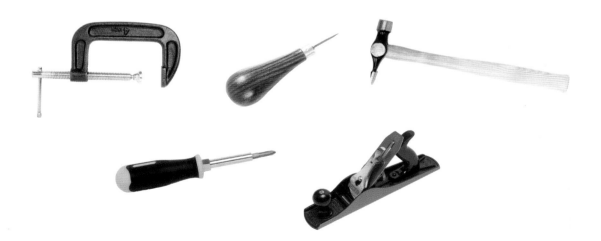

The Complete Illustrated
WOODWORKING COURSE

A Step-by-Step Guide to Basic Techniques and Skill-Building Projects

Nick Gibbs

Reader's Digest

The Reader's Digest Association, Inc.
Pleasantville, NY/Montreal/Sydney

A READER'S DIGEST BOOK

This edition published by The Reader's Digest Association, Inc., by
arrangement with Collins & Brown, an imprint of Chrysalis Books Group
plc The Chrysalis Building, Bramley Road, London W10 6SP, England

© Collins & Brown 2005
Text copyright © Nick Gibbs 2005
Photography copyright © Collins & Brown 2005

All rights reserved. Unauthorized reproduction, in any manner, is
prohibited.

Reader's Digest is a registered trademark of The Reader's Digest
Association, Inc.

FOR COLLINS & BROWN
Project Editor: Miranda Sessions
Copy Editor: Phil Hunt
Photographer: Michael Wicks
Designers: Caroline Hill and Bet Ayer

FOR READER'S DIGEST
U.S. Project Editor: Marilyn J. Knowlton
Canadian Project Editor: Pamela Johnson
Consulting Editor: David Schiff
Senior Project Designer: George McKeon
Executive Editor, Trade Publishing: Dolores York
President & Publisher, Books & Music: Harold Clarke

Library of Congress Cataloging-in-Publication Data:
Gibbs, Nick,
    The complete illustrated woodworking course : a step-by-step guide
to basic techniques and skill-building projects / Nick Gibbs.
        p. cm
    Includes index.
    ISBN 0-7621-0572-0
1. Woodwork—Textbooks. I. Title

TT180.G53 2006
684'.08—dc22

                                    2005044409

Address any comments about *The Complete Illustrated Woodworking
Course: A Step-by-Step Guide to Basic Techniques and
Skill-Building Projects* to:
        The Reader's Digest Association, Inc.
        Adult Trade Publishing
        Reader's Digest Road
        Pleasantville, NY 10570-7000

For more Reader's Digest products and information, visit our website:
        www.rd.com www.rd.com   (in the United States)
        www.readersdigest.ca   (in Canada)
        www.readersdigest.au   (in Australia)

Printed in Singapore

Contents

CONTENTS

Introduction

Some furniture makers are fortunate enough to find their vocation early in life and receive full-time training that prepares them for any task. The rest of us may have learned some basic skills at school or from our fathers but spend the next 20 years forgetting everything we were taught.

Wood is the most remarkable material, which anyone with an interest in making things will want to use, not just because it is beautiful, strong, and sustainable, but for the challenge of taming its qualities and flaws. To do so successfully, you need skills and tools, but you'd be surprised, what can be achieved with only a limited range of both.

So, unlike most woodworking books, we will start at the beginning with only a few tools, wood from home center stores, a portable workbench and the ambition to make some simple projects. I still use the same set of chisels I chose when I first became a carpenter in the 1980s, and the same tenon saw and the same mallet, which is looking a bit worse for wear but is an old friend now.

Gradually we will introduce you to tools and techniques that will enable the learning woodworker to take on ever more complicated projects. The aim is to become self-sufficient, able to choose the right joint, the right lumber, and the right glues, abrasives, and finishes. You will find useful advice to help you buy the most suitable machines and power tools, and tips on maintaining and using your equipment.

At every stage there are projects to test your skills and techniques. During Term One these are essentially simple, using ready-planed materials and basic joints. Term Two introduces the backbone of woodworking joints that you will be using again and again, as well as showing you how to make or buy a workbench and the best machines to pick first. With Term Three come the confidence and advanced skills to take on any project. By the time you reach the end, you will have the abilities and equipment to achieve whatever you want and, I hope, the journey will have been both challenging and enjoyable!

—Nick Gibbs

Learning
the Basics

What you will find in this section

What to Expect

Tools

Fortunately, novice woodworkers need only a few key tools to get going, and it is those we will study in this first section. Working with prepared lumber, little more than a good saw and combination square are needed to make a basic birdhouse, but soon you'll need a plane, some chisels, mallet, and basic marking tools. We will be showing you what to buy, and how to judge what is good and bad, with tips on sharpening and using tools effectively and safely.

Materials

Any lumber yard has a supply of prepared softwood boards ready to be converted into projects. There is no better place to start for a novice woodworker because the wood is generally dry and easy to use. As your skills improve, we will be introducing some common hardwoods, explaining what to look out for and how to overcome the challenges of using less forgiving lumber. There will be sections on sheet materials, and on the glues, finishes, and abrasives you will need to enhance projects.

You will be using the measuring gauge for all of the projects in this section (see page 44).

You will learn how to treat wood with a stain to create impressive results (see page 49).

Discover how to sharpen and hone a plane blade (see page 27).

Find out how to stop knots from weeping (see page 49).

Discover how to use a chisel, to pare a joint and to scribe an accurate shoulder (see page 46).

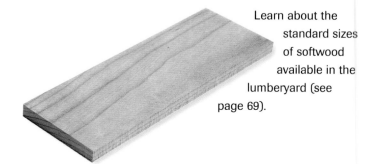

Learn about the standard sizes of softwood available in the lumberyard (see page 69).

Techniques

More often than not, the key to successful woodworking is in preparing pieces of lumber for jointing together. From the initial cutting of boards to length accuracy is essential, and subsequent operations will never be easy if the first cuts are poor. In this section we will be learning the most basic techniques for holding tools, starting and completing cuts, and good preparation.

Cutting to length with a simple saw is an essential skill you will learn (see page 13).

You'll be drilling holes in cabinet doors (see page 35).

Planing wood is a highly satisfying technique (see page 64).

Projects

These are the eight projects in this first section, Getting started. As you will see, these projects increase in complexity, and they all incorporate key techniques that you will be learning along the way.

Birdhouse **p. 18**

Bookends **p. 60**

Toy truck **p. 30**

Knife block **p. 70**

Shoe rack **p. 38**

Bulletin board **p. 80**

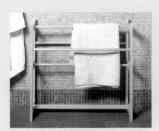

Towel rail **p. 50**

Wall cabinet **p. 90**

Lesson 1
Cutting to Length

Getting started

With so much pre-prepared lumber sold in home centers, you can make many projects with only a very few tools, cutting boards to length by hand and joining them with screws or nails. You need only a saw and the ability to cut cleanly and accurately, though the most important lesson to learn is that successful woodworking relies entirely upon a flat, solid surface on which to work. Fortunately, this can be a folding workbench, of which there are many versions. I worked for many years on site with no more than the simplest portable workbench, which I still own and still use occasionally.

Accurate cutting also relies on good marking out and careful cuts, so we will be studying how to prepare well and I will be explaining how to start and finish a cut without damaging the board. We will be introducing the simplest of joints, the butt joint, which depends only on glue and screws or nails to hold it together. It requires little by way of preparation, but if cut inaccurately, it will be very weak.

I am assuming that most people aiming to start woodworking will already own a few tools for doing tasks around the home, and these will help for many jobs. There's no need, for instance, to buy a new drill until you choose to expand your tool kit with specialist woodworking equipment. However, you will soon learn that the heavy claw hammer that works so well around the house and garden isn't easy to use for tapping in fine molding pins for a woodworking project.

Marking out to cut

First you must check that the board you are using has straight and square edges. This is even true of sized-four sides (S4S) boards you buy from a home center or lumberyard. Use the combination square or a try square with the stock against an edge and blade across the face to check that the edges and faces are square to one another. Look for any thin shafts of light between the

Start by marking across the face of the board, creating a clear line you can see easily.

Lesson planner

Key techniques	Key tools and materials
• Basic marking out: checking and marking • Holding a saw • Starting and finishing the cut • Surveying the cut • The butt joint: when to use, pros & cons, how to cut	• Handsaw • Tenon saw • Combination square • Portable workbench • Small C-clamp • Pencil, ballpoint, or knife • Small hammer • Adjustable square • Combination screwdriver • Countersinking bit • Nails and screws • Wood glue

blade and the face. If the piece isn't square, you'll need to plane it (see page 64).

Once satisfied, use the square to mark a line across a face, with the stock against the edge. Then mark a line across that edge, holding the stock against the face you've just marked. Work your way around the board from those lines, and if all's well, the lines will meet in the far corner. Always hold the stock against either the edge or the face where you started.

Holding a saw

By cutting straight, woodworkers can save themselves considerable time, since the wood will not need to be cleaned up with a block plane or abrasives. To do this well, you need control of the saw blade, which is achieved by holding the saw properly. When you grip the saw, extend your index finger along the handle to help guide the cut by using the rigidity within the tendon that runs from the knuckle along the forearm. Many people hold planes and power tools in the same way, and I've even tried holding a shotgun this way, firing with my middle finger.

Always hold the stock of the combination square against the first face and mark up the edges.

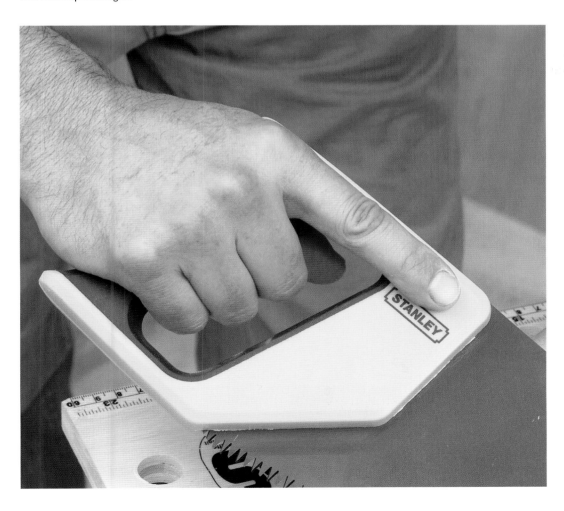

By extending your first finger along the handle of the saw, you gain more control through the tendons in your arm.

Starting the cut

A board can easily be damaged when you cut it, with the result that you may have to repair an edge or face, wasting both time and wood. To start a cut, rub the saw blade against the thumb or index finger of your other hand, keeping the teeth away from your flesh, and with the saw resting on the far corner of the board. Make sure the teeth are to the waste side of the line, rather than cutting straight down the center of your mark. Holding the saw at a low angle, gently draw the blade toward you until you've made a shallow groove and can increase the stroke, potentially cutting on both the push and pull. Notice how smaller teeth damage the fibers less, but cut more slowly.

Surveying the cut

When cutting a board to length, you need to follow marked lines across the top face and the nearest edge, even though to start, you will often mark lines around all four sides of a workpiece. Once you have started cutting along the line across the top, you'll need to cut down the edge nearest you to ensure the cut is square. With time you will do this automatically, from muscle memory, but to start, you need to follow both lines carefully. Once you've made the cut down the nearest edge, you can use the groove as a guide and extend the cut down the back edge. Some woodworkers actually start their cut at the near corner, which is more awkward, but it makes it easier to follow the two lines.

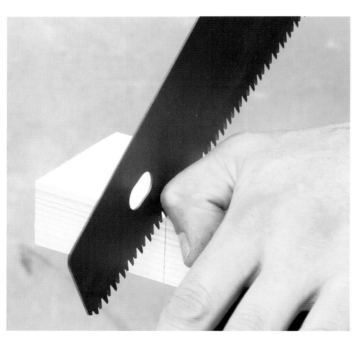

Either use the tip of your first finger or your thumb joint to guide the saw.

Trade secret

Don't push the saw

The traditional maxim is to let the weight of the saw do the cutting, and it is certainly best not to force the teeth into the wood. It's better to use the full length of the blade in long, gentle strokes than to make hurried, short efforts. When you get near the end, more damage can be done by the waste falling away and tearing the board. The safest way to resolve this is to clamp the board to a sawhorse or bench and then use your spare hand to hold the waste as you cut it off.

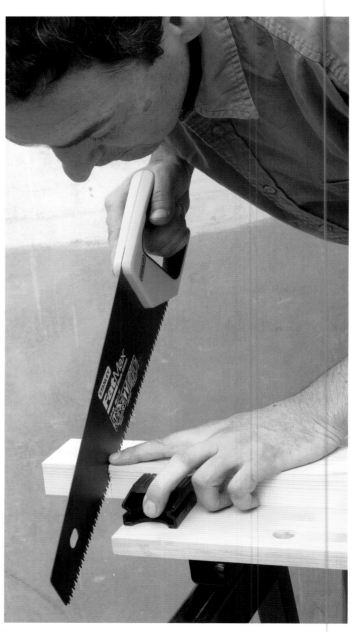

Don't remove your guiding finger until the cut is well under way.

Uses for the butt joint

• To fix two boards together edge to edge to produce a wider board or panel. This joint is glued and sometimes reinforced with biscuits or dowels (see pages 54 and 138).
• Boards fixed at 90 degrees to one another, usually using glue and nails or screws for security. This joint isn't very strong and tends to be employed for basic projects or utility jobs around the workshop. It is also often used when joining sheet materials and can be reinforced with biscuits or dowels (see page 85).

Pros

• Simple and quick to cut and assemble
• Efficient, since it requires no interlocking pieces

Cons

• Weak without reinforcement
• Can be difficult to tighten
• Any inaccuracy in cutting will be conspicuous

Use a combination drill bit and countersink to drill holes to fix the battens.

How to cut the butt joint

The simple rule is that the meeting edges or face and edge must be smooth, straight, and square. If there is any inaccuracy, the joint will wobble and assembly will be difficult. The easiest way to join pieces at 90 degrees is to hold one piece with the edge flush with the top of a work surface. Then smear glue along the edge and screw or nail the second piece to the edge.

With the batten held in the portable workbench, screw the "table" of the bench hook to the batten.

Trade secret

The weakest of joints

The strength of the butt relies largely upon the accuracy of cutting. It is very important that the mating surfaces are flat and true; otherwise there is a high risk of movement however well reinforced the joint is. It is a real test of hand skills to cut a board squarely across the end, but this is essential for a good butt joint. A tenon saw—with its reinforced back—will cut more accurately than a hand-saw. Professionals will use a table saw (see page 218) or disk sander (see page 224) to get a superb finish to end grain.

Tools

It doesn't matter if you only have a small collection of tools, as long as they are all useful and of good quality. Though there are more sophisticated alternatives to most of the tools listed here, the ones I've chosen to get you started will always be handy and don't require too much initial outlay. The idea is to gradually build up a tool kit, adding new equipment as your horizons or budget widen.

Handsaws

Saws are divided into those with or without a reinforced spine or back. Most woodworkers start off with a tenon saw for cutting small items or for cutting accurate joints and a handsaw for cutting wider boards. Backsaws, of which the tenon saw is the most common example, have a restricted depth of cut, so they can't be used for cutting wide boards and certainly not thicker boards. They are also shorter, so cut less per stroke, and they have smaller teeth for fine but slower cutting. However, the reinforced back keeps the blade square and improves accuracy.

Most people start with a medium tenon saw, about 10 inches (254 mm) long and with about 13 teeth per inch (tpi). It's worth buying a saw with hardened teeth, which can cut any material and is thrown away once blunt. As your confidence and skills develop, you can buy traditional saws that you can sharpen yourself, though I tend to favor Japanese saws, which cut on both the push and pull strokes. Fortunately, even the most basic tenon saws and handsaws are available with what are known as triple tooth-form teeth, which can also cut both ways.

For a handsaw I also recommend hardened teeth, with 8 tpi and a blade about 20 inches (508 mm) long. Check the blade. If it's too flimsy, it will bend as you cut. Both these and the tenon saws are designed for cutting across the grain rather than with it. Few woodworkers cut boards along the grain by hand, since you ideally need a special rip saw and plenty of energy (see pages 109 and 212).

Combination square

Though you can, of course, buy a dedicated try square, a good compromise is the combination square. This provides you with
a straight edge, which can be removed from the stock, usually a spirit level, and 90 and 45 degrees angles for marking up. Some even have variable angles in between. Check the accuracy of the combination square by holding the stock against the edge and drawing a line along the blade. Then flip the square over so the stock is pointing the other way and draw another line beside the first. The two lines should be parallel.

Portable workbench

A surface on which to work is essential for successful woodworking, and you can get going well enough with a portable workbench, like the Workmate. Various manufacturers make these, but my recommendation is to go for something simple. I have owned a few of them over the years but always tend to return to the very simplest Workmate I bought when I started woodworking. Characterized by its crossed legs at each end, it has a small work surface and not much flexibility in the vise, but I like it for being easy to erect and having no pieces that can fall off. Choose something solid, and it will last for years.

Small C-clamp

They say you can never have enough clamps, and for assembling projects just with glue, you will need a number of them. Initially, a couple will do, mainly for holding a board to the work surface while you cut joints or clean up edges. Choose 4-inch (102-mm) C-clamps, but always go for quality items, as they should last a lifetime and cheap clamps are a nightmare to use. A quality lightweight clamp is far better than a cheap heavyweight version.

Pencil, ballpoint, or knife

Find a marking tool that you're happy with as soon as possible. Some favor a ballpoint pen, saying that it has a finer line for greater accuracy, though pencil-lovers tend to believe that the ink can leach into the fibers. Few woodworkers use a carpenter's pencil for fine work because the lead is too wide, so a good HB or H pencil is more suitable. The mark of a pencil with hard lead can be difficult to see, while softer pencils will smudge. Other people use a craft knife or box cutter for marking, but the consequences of a slip are more serious.

Small hammer

I love small hammers and have a few of them in my shop, ranging from about 3.5 ounces (99 grams) to 6 ounces (170 grams). I'm not fussy

about them having a ball pein or wedge-shaped cross pein, but I like the hammer to be nicely balanced for tapping home nails.

Combination screwdriver

You probably own a variety of screwdrivers for working around the home, but I've discovered that I prefer having one good-quality combination driver that always returns to the same place in the shop. I find it useful to have dedicated drivers for the car, the kitchen, and the workshop. The trick is to match the screws you use to your screwdrivers. Mine has two slotted and two crosshead bits.

Countersinks

Assuming you already have a power drill, cordless or otherwise, you will need a countersink for tidy screwed joints. Some screws have sharpened heads that will self-countersink beautifully, but the best solution is to buy a couple of combination countersink/counterbore units, with a fluted collar attaching to a drill bit with a set screw. Don't go for a cheap set, as the set screws tend to fail, buy a couple of good-quality sizes that suit the screws you use (see page 36).

Nail set

To sink nail heads below the surface, you will need a nail set. You can always make do with a nail with a flattened tip if you don't have, or don't want to buy, a dedicated hole punch. I thoroughly encourage you to start creating your own tools and solutions, as it can save you money and it will help you to develop an open-mindedness to woodworking.

Materials

Screws or nails

I rarely use nails for woodworking, preferring the certainty of screws. The disadvantage of a screw is that it is more expensive, needs more preparation in the drilling of a clearance hole and a pilot hole, and takes up more room with its head, which may need to be hidden with filler or a bung. On the plus side, it is more secure than a nail, and you don't necessarily need any glue. Nails are quick to install and are ideal for small components as long as the wood doesn't split.

Which screws?

Though I tend to use flathead brass slot screws for hinges and other fittings, I tend to favor Phillips-head screws for all

other purposes. I buy them by the box and always have a good range of sizes and lengths. I tend not to keep old steel screws unless they are exceptionally large or long, since the slots are usually damaged and will cause as many problems being inserted as a new one would cost. I generally have 2 inch, 1½ inch, 1¼ inch, and 1 inch (8 gauge); 1 inch and ¾ inch (6 gauge); and ½ inch and ⅜ inch (4 gauge). Purchasing sets of screws can be good value, and I particularly like those that have a serrated tip for catching the grain faster.

Which nails?

I keep a very limited range of nails, with 2 inch, 1½ inch, and 1 inch in both ovals and flatheads, plus a few boxes of molding nails, panel nails, and escutcheon nails, which I've bought for specific projects. You don't need many to get going.

Wood filler

You can buy all sorts of wood filler, but a general rule is to use filler that's a bit darker than the wood you're working on. Though filler will take a stain, darker filler tends not to show up as much, but as in all cases, the best thing to do is experiment first and make up your own mind which works best.

Buying softwood

You pay for softwood by the foot or by the inch, in what's known as a linear price. It will usually be referred to by its nominal size; that is, after it has left the saw and before it is surfaced. What you buy, surfaced (planed) on all four sides, may be referred to by its nominal size, but in fact, it is thinner and narrower and is the dressed size.

Standard sizes of softwood

Lumber dimensions up to 2 in. thick are often referred to in quarters, with 1½ in. for instance, often labeled as ⁶⁄₄ in.

Nominal		Dressed	
1 x 1 in.	1 x 2 in.	¾ x ¾ in.	1½ x ¾ in.
1 x 2 in.	2 x 2 in.	¾ x 1½ in.	1½ x 1½ in.
1 x 3 in.	2 x 3 in.	¾ x 2½ in.	1½ x 2½ in.
1 x 4 in.	2 x 4 in.	¾ x 3½ in.	1½ x 3½ in.
1 x 6 in.	2 x 6 in.	¾ x 5½ in.	1½ x 5½ in.
1 x 8 in.	2 x 8 in.	¾ x 7¼ in.	1½ x 7¼ in.
1 x 10 in.	2 x 10 in.	¾ x 9¼ in.	1½ x 9¼ in.
1 x 12 in.	2 x 12 in.	¾ x 11¼ in.	1½ x 11¼ in.

Project **Birdhouse**

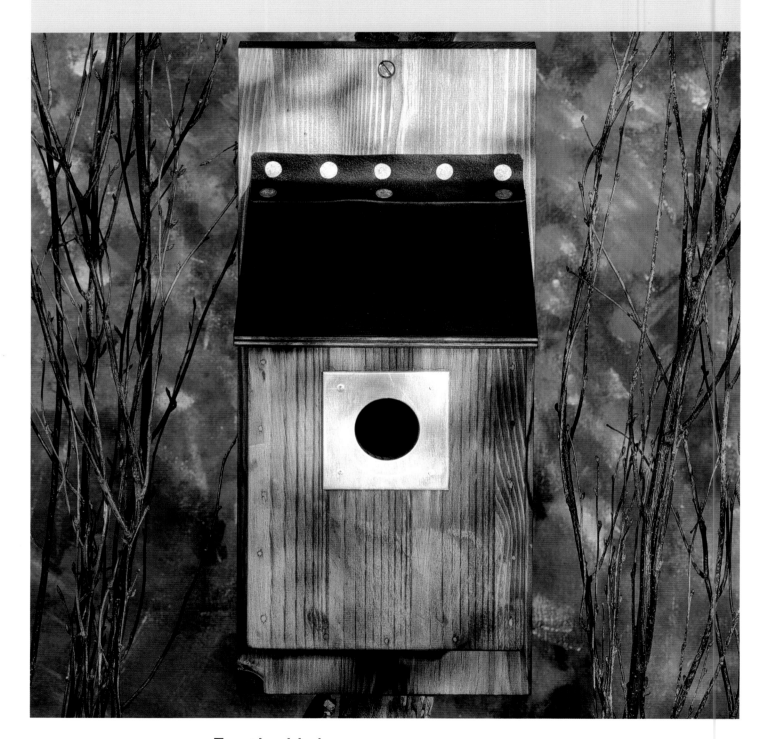

For the birds

This birdhouse is designed for small birds and should be fitted high up on a wall, in a tree, or on a post, but make sure it is safe from cats and other predators. It is designed to be waterproof, so use waterproof adhesive and galvanized nails.

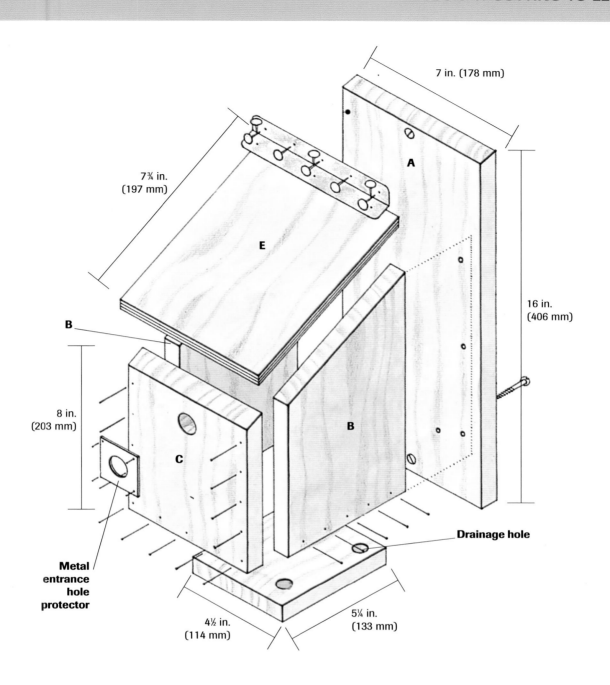

7 in. (178 mm)

7¾ in. (197 mm)

A

16 in. (406 mm)

E

B

B

8 in. (203 mm)

C

Drainage hole

Metal entrance hole protector

4½ in. (114 mm)

5¼ in. (133 mm)

Cutting list

Part	Material	Quantity	Dimensions thickness, width, length
A Back	softwood	1	¾ x 7¼ x 16 in. (19 x 184 x 400 mm)
B Sides	softwood	2	¾ x 5½ x 10 in. (19 x 133 x 254 mm)
C Front	softwood	1	¾ x 5½ x 8 in. (19 x 140 x 203 mm)
D Base	softwood	1	¾ x 4 x 4¾ in. (19 x 102 x 121 mm)
E Top	plywood	1	½ x 6 x 7¾ in. (13 x 152 x 197 mm)

Shopping list

Bill of materials

Hinge tough leather or webbing, roughly 7¾ x 2 in. (197 x 51 mm)
Entrance hole protection 2½ x 2½ in. (63 x 63 mm) thin metal sheet
Nails to assemble birdhouse 1½ in (38 mm) nails
Galvanized tacks for hinge ½ in. (13 mm)
Screws for fixing back to box ten 1¼ in. (32 mm) no. 8 flathead
Wood filler for nail-head holes
Exterior varnish for exterior finishes
Drill and bits for making the drainage holes in the base of the box. Drills, see page 185
Flat bit 1-in. (25-mm) diameter for the entrance hole
Sliding bevel to mark up angles of any degree
Protractor for marking up angles for this project

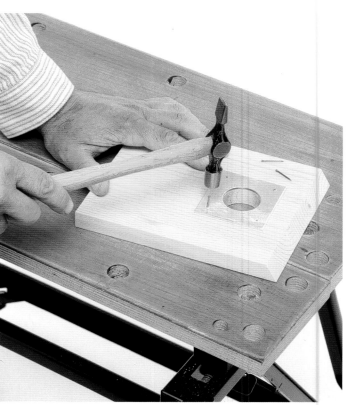

1 Cut the back (**A**) to length and then mark out the board for the sides. Use a protractor or combination square to mark up a 60-degree angle on the sides (**B**) and all components to length. When it comes to cutting the front (**C**), remember to angle your saw to 60 degrees to match the angle of the roof. This will save you time cleaning up later.

2 Drill the front for the entrance hole, centered and about 1½ inches (38 mm) from the top edge. When using a flat bit, make sure you drill into a piece of waste wood underneath to reduce tearing. You may need to get the hole in the metal protection sheet drilled by an engineer, since metal can be difficult to drill with a flat bit. Nail it to the front of the birdhouse front (**C**).

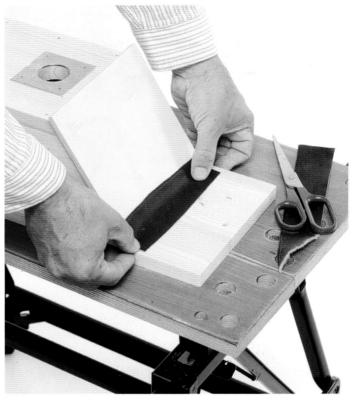

3 Drill ventilation/drainage holes in the base. Position the box sides (**B**) on a flat work surface, with the front edge facing upward. Spread glue along those edges, and place the house front on top. Use your fingers to align the front with the sides, and then nail the front to the sides. Before the glue dries off, apply some glue to the front and side edges of the base and insert inside the front and sides. Then nail in place.

4 Once it is set, offer the house construction to the back, and mark up where the fixing screws should go. Drill these holes in the back, and holes for screws to fit the birdhouse to its home. Then screw the back to the house. Tap all the nail heads below the surface with a hammer and nail set. Cut out the top from a piece of scrap plywood, and use the galvanized nails to fix the hinge. Fill the nail-head holes with filler and sand the whole project. Finish with an exterior varnish.

Lessons learned

- Notice how joining the front to the sides is made much easier because the edges are straight and square. In this case, you didn't need to join the cut edges because they were already planed, but imagine how the quality of your cut would have implicated the quality of a joint.

- How did your cuts start and finish? Did you need to sand back any tears on the corners? Practice will improve that.

- When you drilled, did the wood tear? This is a common problem and is only solved at the back by drilling into waste wood and at the front by using quality drill bits and a good drill or drill press (see page 185).

- You can save a little lumber by carefully cutting the sides from a board. Because the top edges are angled, you can overlap them a little from the board, and you'll want to use this technique frequently in the future to save wood.

Lesson 2
Sheet Materials

Getting started

When I was editing a woodworking magazine some years ago, I was asked to comment about medium-density fiberboard (MDF) on a television program, as I'd just written a column stating how much I disliked the stuff. My dislike of this heavy, dusty, lifeless material remains, and I will not allow it in my workshop. That's not true, however, of all sheet materials.

Birch plywood is one of my favorite of all materials, and is used in Europe in place of maple-faced ply. It cuts well, the edges can be planed really smooth, and the surfaces are fine. Its smell is particularly distinctive. This sort of high-quality plywood is easy to use because it cuts so well and is ideal for projects of all sizes and shapes. Plywood generally is a very good place for novices to start because the thickness is consistent and all you need to do is cut out the shape to suit your needs. It isn't as heavy as MDF—you feel as if you're almost using real wood. You can even buy certified ply these days (though it can be hard to find), which is guaranteed to have been harvested from a sustainable source.

Sheet materials of all types are extremely useful to have around the workshop. Even odd little pieces can prove to be invaluable, so don't throw the offcuts away. Each type of sheet has its own special uses, and even exterior sheathing ply can be useful for more functional jobs.

Cutting plywood

Plywood is a superb material for newcomers to woodworking, but it isn't always easy to work with, especially if you buy it in large 4 X 8 feet (1219 X 2438 mm) sheets. Fortunately, home centers sell it in smaller sizes and lumberyards are usually willing to make a couple of cuts for free. All other cutting can be done with a handsaw.

The challenge when working with plywood is cutting it without tearing the grain. Here are five tips for cutting plywood effectively.

Lesson planner

Key techniques	Key tools and materials
• Cutting plywood • Cutting sheets • Cutting shapes • Planing plywood and end grain	• Sawhorses • Jigsaw • Coping saw • Large drill bits • Block plane • Rasps and files • Plywood • Varnish • Craft knife

1 Thin plywood will often chatter as you cut. Clamp it to the workbench with the cut line very close to the edge to reduce the amount of flex and give you more control.

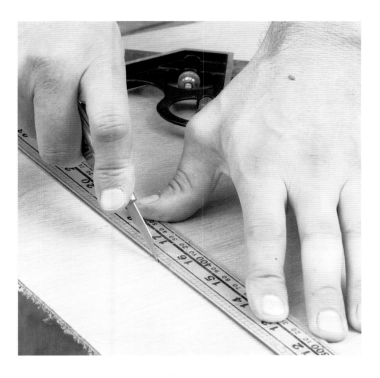

2 Mark the cut line with a pencil and score it with a craft knife to break the fibers along the cut. This should reduce tearing, especially when cutting across the grain.

3 If tearing is a real problem when cutting across the grain, you can try laying masking tape along the line. This reduces the tear-out and also means that you don't have a pencil line to clean up afterward.

4 Use a fine-toothed handsaw (up to 12 points per inch) for cutting plywood if tearing is an issue. If you are using a jigsaw, turn off the pendulum action and fit fine-toothed blades.

TIP: Buy a band saw. Though a band saw's throat limits the width of cut, you can achieve superb results (see page 218).

Planing plywood and end grain

Obviously, you don't need to plane the surface of plywood, though if you do, it can reveal superb shapes and colors. The best tool for smoothing the edges is a block plane because the low angle of the cutter is designed to deal with end grain. The block plane is also easy to use one-handed in case you need to support a wobbling piece of ply with your other hand. Another option is the modern Microplane, which is a bit like a cheese grater but designed for wood.

Even when you are following the grain of the face layers of the ply, you will be planing end grain of some core layers. There is a risk that at the end of the cut, the end grain will break out because the fibers are easily split there. The same is true for solid wood. There are a couple of ways that you can avoid this.

1 Plane first from one end, then reverse the workpiece and work from the other end.

As a slight adaptation, plane a very angled section at the beginning of the board down to the finish line, then plane down to it from the other end.

2 Clamp a sacrificial piece of scrap wood to the end of the board to reduce the splitting. This is difficult to do on thin ply, though one tip is to tape the scrap in place and then hold it firmly in the vise.

Ultimately, a fixed disk or belt sander (see pages 118 and 224) is ideal for cleaning up the edges of plywood.

A coping saw is a great first woodworking tool and useful for cutting shapes in plywood. Twist the blade in the frame as you work your way around a curve.

Cutting shapes

One of the most significant advantages of plywood is that it can be used very effectively for cutting shaped components because the alternating grain direction provides strength where solid wood might snap. That's why it is so good for toymaking. If you get into making jigsaw puzzles or lots of toys, you will probably eventually want to buy a powered scroll saw (see page 58). For now, a coping saw will do. Obviously, you need to drill an access hole through which to feed the blade if you are making internal cuts. Clean up the cuts afterward with a rasp, metal-working file, or a Microplane.

Tools

How does a plane work?

A plane is no more than a chisel (known as the cutter or iron) held within a wooden or metal body. The adjustments help you fine-tune the cut, and differences in the shape and style of the body are designed for specific woodworking jobs. In most planes the cutter is actually inverted, with the bevel facing downward so that there is metal behind the edge to support it as it cuts.

On some planes (particularly block planes) the opening (mouth) through which the cutter protrudes is adjustable. This is because the sole ahead of the edge stops the shaving tearing from the board. For fine cuts the mouth needs to be smaller because the shaving is thinner. The cutter sits on the frog of the plane, at an angle to the sole. A cap iron above the cutter curls the shaving out of the plane, rather than it getting jammed in the mechanism. The cap iron must be adjusted nearer the edge for finer shavings, with the distance varying between ¼₄ inch (0.4 mm) and ¹⁄₁₆ inch (1.6 mm). The block plane is almost identical except that the bevel faces upward because the angle is lower and there's less stress on the edge. The bevel does the curling of the shaving.

Block planes

Over the years, I've advocated the short block plane—usually about 6 inches (152 mm) long—as being essential for woodworking. It is certainly a useful tool, especially if you work as a jobbing carpenter and need to tidy up bits here and there. As a woodworker, with an established workshop, I find myself needing it less and less as a short plane, but it is useful for cleaning up end grain. I would spend a little more than normal and buy a low-angle block plane designed for working with end grain, which is harder to cut than long grain and less likely to tear. There are other features you should consider:
• Lateral adjustment enables you to line up the cutter edge with the sole.
• Depth control offers fine adjustment and is much easier to work than the cheaper block planes that you have to tap to control the depth of cut.
• An adjustable mouth helps you control the shaving, closing it up tightly for fine cuts and opening it to give more space for a thicker shaving.

Sharpening a block plane

To sharpen a block plane, you will need an oilstone and a honing guide, which helps you keep the bevel of the cutter level on the oilstone as you sharpen. The same tool is used

1 The block plane is very simple, with the cap iron holding the cutter in place.

2 To sharpen a block plane, use a straightedge to line up the bevel in the honing guide.

for sharpening chisels (see page 48). Use a straight edge to line up the bevel in the honing guide, then run it back and forth over the oilstone, which has to be primed with honing oil. Once the single bevel is smooth, adjust the cutter in the honing guide so that the bevel is at a slightly higher angle. This produces the honing bevel, which can be sharpened more quickly and more easily. Then work the back a little on the oilstone.

3 Lubricate the oilstone with oil.

4 Holding the honing guide firmly with your fingers around the front of the blade, place it on the oilstone and run it back and forth.

5 Once the bevel has been sharpened, tidy up the back on the oilstone.

6 When reassembling the plane, look down it to make sure that the cutter doesn't project, even by a fraction.

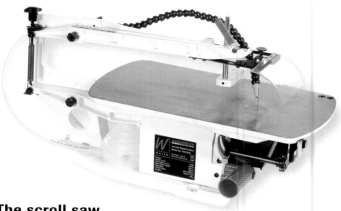

Larger drill bits

Anyone who owns an electric drill will already have a collection of drill bits, probably in anything from moderate to atrocious condition. When you start buying them for woodwork, try keeping them only for that purpose or they'll soon get ruined. For removing the waste from mortises, you will need some larger bits than you find in the average set, which are usually limited to ⅜ inch (10 mm) maximum diameter. The best solution is to buy flat bits when you need them. Use a file to sharpen their edges and to make sure the point is centered. Later we will discuss more advanced types of drill bit, but most of these are only worth considering once you have a drill press (see page 185).

The scroll saw

The scroll saw is one of the first tools young woodworkers try because it is safe and fun to use. Twisting the handle tightens the blade, which can be positioned to cut on the pull or the push stroke and can be fed through an access hole for internal cuts. A slight refinement of the scroll saw is the adjustable piercing saw, with a system for shortening the amount of exposed saw blade for more controlled cutting of thin material (see page 58).

Files, rasps, and Microplanes

There have always been rasps and files for cleaning up edges, especially curves, and for many years the Surform range of planes and files were considered to be the best. I remember being given a Surform block plane as a child and loving it. But for serious woodworking you will find them quite frustrating. There is, however, a new kid on the block, the Microplane rang, which is superb and cuts brilliantly for cleaning up.

The flat bit needs to be sharp, or it will tear the grain.

Make sure the point of the flat bit is ground centrally.

Trade secret

Buying a jigsaw

After a drill, the jigsaw is often one of the first power tools a woodworker buys. They are quite useful around the home and can be used for all sorts of cutting, especially curves. There is no harm in owning one, it is not an essential tool in the workshop. In the long term, you will find a band saw a much more useful piece of equipment, and it can often make the jigsaw redundant.

When I was working as a site carpenter, I bought a very expensive jigsaw, with lots of power and weight. It has survived well and has been used extensively. However, now that my woodworking is limited to a workshop, I hardly ever use it, and I could happily cope with a much cheaper model for the one or two occasions a year it's needed. If you only plan to use a jigsaw from time to time, like I do, I recommend you choose something solid but inexpensive and without too many features. Always pay for good blades, though—ideally tungsten carbide, as they last longer.

Sawhorses

For cutting sheets of plywood and long lengths of wood, you need a pair of sawhorses. Many woodworkers are encouraged to make these as their first project. Personally, with limited space, I favor buying a pair of foldable plastic sawhorses that can be tucked away most of the time.

Materials

Sheet materials

Using sheet materials is an ideal way for woodworkers to get going, as they are stable, a consistent thickness, and don't have the challenges associated with movement (see page 166). After a while they become frustratingly uniform, but they are a valuable resource, especially as small sizes. Usually sold in 2-foot (610-mm) intervals, they are available from home centers.

Increasingly, sheet materials are sold in metric thicknesses, certainly in Europe. In our projects in this book, some caution has to be paid to the thickness of plywood, as the conversions will not always be consistent from one source to another. You may need to use plywood as close as possible to the measurements that we have given and adjust the plans accordingly.

Plywood

In my opinion, plywood is the king of sheet materials, and whenever possible, I pay a little extra for birch ply. It tends to be more dense than ply made with tropical hardwoods, and I have a little more faith that the birch comes from a sustainable source. If you want a guarantee of this, you will need to buy FSC certified plywood, but I'm not sure any exists yet (see pages 168–69)!

I always try to have some sheets or offcuts of ¼-inch (6 mm), ⅜-inch (10-mm), and ½-inch (13-mm) birch ply around the workshop. I also like the ¹⁄₁₆-inch (1.6-mm) microply, which is really useful for making templates and writing lists but is not so easy to find! Modelmaking shops sometimes stock it.

Fiberboards

Some people love medium-density fiberboard (MDF). I hate the stuff because it's heavy, dusty, and blunts your tools. It has very little strength and given the opportunity will bend. The health scares that it is carcinogenic are the least of my concerns, though you must wear a respirator or dust mask when using MDF, and indeed for any dust-producing operations with wood and other sheet materials. I try not to have any in my workshop, though it does have its uses for very specific purposes, particularly when you want to rout a profile on the edge. Similar to MDF, chipboard has larger chips of wood and isn't as dense, but it is even weaker than MDF and can't be routed along the edge easily. I have used it for work surfaces in my shop, but I'd prefer to use plywood any day (see page 136).

Clear finishes

Clear finishes are used to protect the surface and enhance the color and pattern of wood. There is a wide range of options, but here are some you might consider. I favor oils for furniture and shellac/wax for smaller, more decorative pieces. Varnish is good for utility jobs and for outside surfaces.

Varnish and wax

The most common type of finish in home centers is generically termed varnish, but it applies to various mixes of resin and oil or water. You're likely to find polyurethane in water- and oil-based versions, and in matt, gloss, and satin finishes. The water-based finish dries faster and is easier to use. After a couple of coats I usually rub the surface with wax, using a flexible abrasive pad, then buff with a soft cloth. However, I don't use polyurethane very often, as it tends to dry very hard and is very difficult to repair if it deteriorates.

Oils

I often use oil finishes because they are so easy to apply and produce a more natural effect. Some are pure, like linseed and tung oils, while others such as Danish and teak oils are mixed with resins to produce better protection. You can wipe oils on a surface, and when they start to lose their luster, you simply add another layer, but this does mean they need long-term maintenance.

Sanding sealer and wax

The quickest finish I know is to use a sanding sealer and then polish with wax. Sanding sealer is similar to varnish and can be brushed or wiped on. It is either shellac- or cellulose-based, and you can dilute it with thinners to suit your needs. I prefer the cellulose product because it is slightly less messy. Both types dry very quickly, and you can then apply wax as for varnish. However, they do not offer much protection, and the wax finish will need additional coats in the future.

Project **Toy truck**

For playtime

Toys are superb projects for home woodworkers—
my children still play with the plywood garage my
father made me when he took up the hobby. The joy
of this truck is that it is made almost entirely from
birch plywood, and there is also plenty of room to
customize the design.

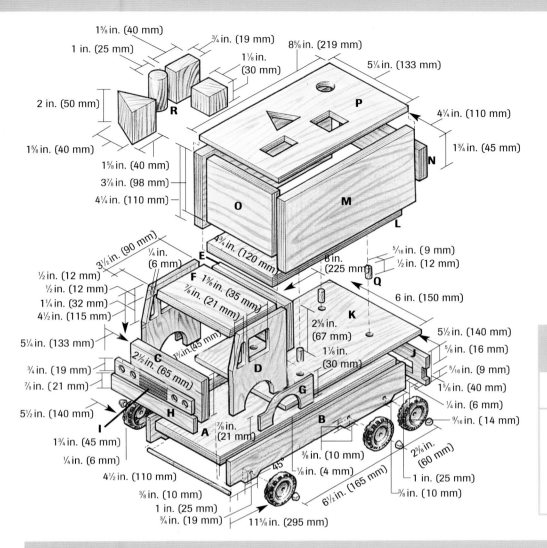

Shopping list

You will also need

Axles 3, ⁵⁄₁₆ in. (5 mm)
Plastic wheels 6
Spring hubcaps 6
Glue and **molding pins**
Ideally ¾ in. and 1 in. (18 mm and 25 mm)

Cutting list

Part	Material	Quantity	Dimensions thickness, width, length	Part	Material	Quantity	Dimensions thickness, width, length
A Chassis	birch ply	1	¼ x 1¾ x 11⅝ in. (6 x 45 x 295 mm)	**J** Tailgate	birch ply	1	¼ x 1⅝ x 6 in. (6 x 41 x 152 mm)
B Chassis side	birch ply	2	½ x 2½ x 4¾ in. (12 x 64 x 121 mm)	**K** Flatbed Sorter box	birch ply	1	¼ x 6 x 8⅞ in. (6 x 152 x 225 mm)
C Cab front	birch ply	1	¼ x 3½ x 4½ in. 6 x 89 x 114 mm	**L** Base	birch ply	1	½ x 4¾ x 8⅝ in. (12 x 120 x 219 mm)
D Cab side	birch ply	2	½ x 2⅜ x 4¾ in. 12 x 59 x 121 mm	**M** Side	birch ply	2	½ x 3⅞ x 8⅝ in. (12 x 98 x 219 mm)
E Cab back	birch ply	1	⅜ x 3 x 4¾ in. (10 x 76 x 121 mm)	**N** Back	birch ply	1	½ x 1¾ x 4¾ in. (12 x 45 x 120 mm)
F Cab roof	birch ply	1	⅛ x 2 x 3½ in. (4 or 3 x 51 x 89 mm)	**O** Front	birch ply	1	½ x 3⅜ x 4¾ in. (12 x 85 x 120 mm)
G Wheel arch	birch ply	1	¼ x ⅞ x 5½ in. (6 x 21 x 140 mm)	**P** Top	birch ply	1	¼ x 5¾ x 8⅝ in. (6 x 146 x 219 mm)
H Bumper	birch ply	1	¼ x ⅞ x 5½ in. (6 x 21 x 140 mm)	**Q** Sorter fixing	dowel	4	⅜ x ⅜ x ½ in. (10 x 10 x 12 mm)
I Lights/rad	birch ply	1	¼ x ¾ x 5½ in. (6 x 19 x 140 mm)	**R** Shapes			Each shape is 2 in. (50 mm) long and cut to suit the holes you make in the roof. Cut these from whatever offcuts you have.

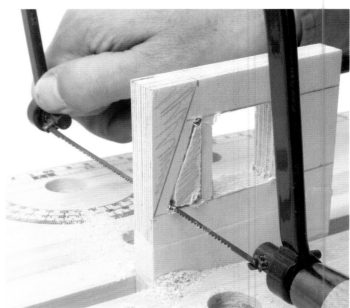

1 Cut out all the parts for the chassis. Drill the holes in the sides (**B**) for the axles, then glue and nail the sides (**B**) to the chassis (**A**).

TIP: When it comes to cutting shaped parts, you may find it easier to cut the shaped windows and other parts before cutting each from the plywood sheet.

2 Cut out the cab sides (**D**) and cut the window and wheel arch shapes using a coping saw (see page 58).

3 Cut the wheel arches to suit the wheels you have bought. Nail and glue the cab sides to the chassis sides, making sure the front edge of the cab side is flush with the front edge of the chassis side.

4 Cut out the cab front (**C**) and back (**E**) and roof (**F**) to fit within the cab sides. This should be a snug fit, but must not push the side outward. Use a block plane or rasp to angle the leading edge of the roof to match the angle on the front edge of the cab sides.

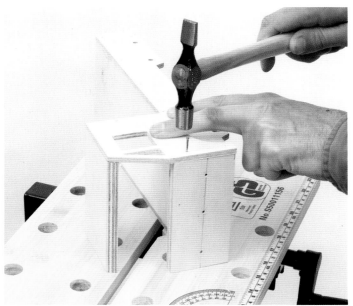

5 Use a nail set to tap all the nail heads below the surface for filling later. Nail and glue the cab front, back, and roof in place, and while the glue sets, cut out the bumper (**H**) and lights and radiator piece (**I**). Once again you may find it easier to drill the light holes and cut out the grille before cutting the piece from the sheet of ply. Cut out all the sort box parts, making sure the front (**O**) and back (**N**) are exactly as long as the base (**L**) is wide. Cut out the shapes in the top. Also cut out the flatbed (**K**). Position the sort box base on the flatbed, and temporarily attach with sticky tape so that you can drill the locating holes for the sorter nails (**Q**).

6 Nail and glue the sides (**M**) to the base, then the front and back in place, and finally the top (**P**). Leave the glue to set between steps.

Make the blocks to fit the holes you've cut in the sort-box top, then sand and clean up all the parts and apply the finish of your choice, which must be child-friendly. Finally, add the wheels and perhaps some stickers to personalize the truck.

Lessons learned

- **TIP:** If you don't have the right length of trim nail, or think a nail will protrude through the wood, snip off the excess from a 1-inch (25-mm) nail before insertion.

- This is the ideal opportunity to discover how many components can be nailed and glued in one operation. Too many, and it will go awfully wrong. You may also have found that clothespins or bulldog clips are useful temporary clamps to hold pieces in position while you nail them in place.

- Gradually a project becomes increasingly sturdy as you add more parts.

- The dimensions of one component may have a significant impact on the fit of that one or another. Look out for components that have identical measurements or those that are critical to the construction. In this project, for instance, the relationship between the width of the chassis sides (**B**), the length of the cab sides (**D**), the width of the cab back (**E**), and the thickness of the cab roof (**F**) is absolutely critical to the success of that part of the project.

Lesson 3
Drilling Basic Joints

Getting started

The round hole is about as simple as it gets in woodworking terms, and yet it remains one of the most effective tools for joining pieces of wood together. Where you use the hole for screws or for a dowel rod, it is easy to position accurately and is quick to cut.

1 Use an awl to mark the position of the hole.

In fact, the introduction of the cordless drill has been one of the most dramatic revolutions for woodworking over the last 20-odd years. The router and its multitude of cutters and jigs have led to a greater leap in terms of opening up new techniques and methods to all woodworkers, but battery technology has made life so much more convenient. I can't remember the last time I used a brace and bit. Certainly not since the development of the more powerful cordless drills.

Though drilled joints have been superseded by biscuits and other modern approaches, it is still an important technique to learn, since it is extremely versatile and often strong. In this lesson we will also be looking at the use of softwoods and how you have to watch out for movement in wood and be able to adjust your work accordingly.

Drilling holes
Drilling a hole is certainly one of the easiest woodworking tasks, but take my word for it, things can go wrong, and there are some key tips for successful drilling.

2 Drill slowly to start while the bit settles. Keep backing out every ¼ inch (6 mm) or so to remove the waste and stop the bit from burning.

Lesson planner

Key techniques	Key tools and materials
• Drilling • Cutting with the grain • Holding stuff on the bench • The bench hook	• Cordless drill • Types of drill bit • Tenon saw • Dowel rod

3 You can buy collars to fit drill bits to set the depth, or you can create a depth stop for the drill bit. This can be done with a piece of tape, but the drill or the hole or both can end up getting clogged. A better solution is to drill through a short piece of narrow dowel that you can push up or down the drill bit as a depth guide or stop, but watch that it doesn't mark the wood. Take care using flat bits, as the point is long, and you can easily drill through the workpiece accidentally. You won't be able to use one for the Shoe rack project, for instance, because the bit will break through the sides.

Drilling for screws

When joining two pieces of wood with screws, you need to drill two different holes. In the guest piece—the one being held by the screw—you need a clearance hole through which the screw slips. In the host piece you need a pilot or thread hole into which the screw bites. It makes screwing easier and reduces the risk of splitting. Sometimes, for soft woods that aren't likely to split, you can get away without a pilot hole or perhaps just a very thin one. In fact, modern screws are designed to be self-tapping, without a pilot hole, and many have serrated tips to cut their way into the wood. Cordless drills also make it simpler, but there is still a risk of splitting.

Cutting with the grain

To create the shoe rack in this lesson, you have to make an angled cut along the grain, known as ripping. You will soon discover this is harder going than cutting across the grain. This is because the fibers tend to tear more cutting with the grain, and these larger particles get clogged up in the saw's teeth. The handsaw you bought for Lesson 1 may be tough to use for this job, as it is designed for cutting

Choosing a drill bit for screws

You may want to reduce the diameter of the pilot hole for softer species.

Screw gauge (or diameter)	Clearance hole	Pilot hole
2	0.095 in. or ⁶⁄₆₄ in. (2.5 mm)	0.058 in. or ¹⁄₁₆ in. (1.6 mm)
4	0.110 in or ⁷⁄₆₄ in. (3 mm)	0.065 in or ³⁄₃₂ in. (1.65 mm)
6	0.140 in. or ⁹⁄₆₄ in. (3.5 mm)	0.085 in. or ³⁄₁₆ in. (2 mm)
8	0.175 in. or ¹¹⁄₆₄ in. (4.5 mm)	0.095 in. or ⁶⁄₆₄ in. (2.5 mm)
10	0.200 in. or ¹³⁄₆₄ in. (5 mm)	0.110 in. or ⁷⁄₆₄ in. (3 mm)

When cutting with the grain, use a wedge to stop the blade binding in the cut.

across the grain and is further proof that buying a table saw is a good idea (see page 251).

To rip a long board in half, it's best to place it on a pair of sawhorses and then move it when you are likely to cut one of them. For shorter pieces, as in the shoe rack, clamp the board to the workbench, overhanging to one side. You will need to plane the sawn edge afterward, with the block plane doing this perfectly.

Making a bench hook

A useful addition to any workbench is a homemade bench hook to hold a board as you cut. It is very simple to make, but can be adapted to suit your needs. A batten at the front underneath holds the bench hook securely against the front edge of the working surface, while another batten along the top at the back is used as a fence against which to hold the lumber.

Most people use these for cutting thinner pieces of wood, with the waste not heavy enough to tear the corner as the cut finishes. But notice how the table extends beyond the end of the back fence, both to support the waste and to reduce tear as the saw cuts through the bottom of the board. A simple bench hook can be customized to include precut grooves for cutting at 90 or 45 degrees, or other regularly used angles.

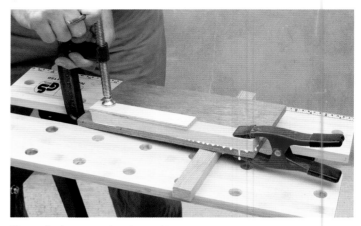
Clamp the batten to the plywood base.

Run a glue bead along the batten.

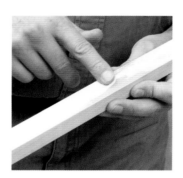
Spread the glue with a brush or finger.

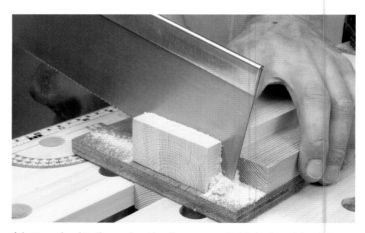
A batten glued to the underside allows you to hold the bench hook in a portable workbench or vise.

Tools

The cordless drill

We've assumed, up to this point, that you can make do with the electric drill you use around the house for drilling operations as a woodworker. That may continue to be the case, but I'd also recommend you look at buying a cordless drill. There is no need for a hand drill or a brace and bit (unless you want to try chairmaking or like the crunch of the bit and the waste wood peacefully emerging from the hole).

The big decisions if you are in the market for a cordless drill are the power and whether you buy one with hammer action. A really powerful, 18 volt hammer-action cordless drill is superb for drilling into masonry. But in the workshop you can probably make do with something smaller, say 9 volt or 12 volt. Make sure it has a chuck you can tighten and loosen by hand, and forward and backward. You don't need many speeds, but torque control can help if you are inserting delicate screws (though I have to admit I've never used it).

Drill bits

There are two main types of drill bit for home woodworkers, though there are many other specialized bits we will come to later. Both main drill bits can be fitted with a countersinking collar so that you can drill and countersink a hole in one operation (see page 17).

Twist bits

This is the most common drill bit and is used for drilling into both wood and metal. It works perfectly well for woodworking, but the point isn't always that easy to position. You can buy twist bits up to almost any size, but few sets go beyond ⅜ inch (10 mm), and you will have to buy those larger bits separately.

Lip and spur bits

A better bit for drilling wood is the lip and spur, sometimes referred to as the dowel bit. This has a central point, and is much easier to position on a mark. It is also less likely to wander than a twist bit. These are a bit more expensive than twist bits, but worth buying and keeping to one side for woodworking. If you regularly use dowels of a particular diameter, as for the Shoe rack project in this lesson, it is worth buying a special dowel bit to suit. You can buy sets up to ½ inch (13 mm) in diameter.

The bradawl

You will use an awl time and time again. A cheap one will do, or you can even make one yourself by knocking a nail  into a piece of dowel and sharpening the point if you have a grinder. Considering they cost so little, I'd buy one.

The tenon saw

Saws are divided into those with or without a reinforced spine or back. Most woodworkers start off with a tenon saw for cutting small items or for cutting accurate joints and a handsaw for cutting wider boards. Backsaws, of which the tenon saw is the most common example, have a restricted depth of cut so they can't be used for cutting wide boards easily and certainly not thicker boards. They are also shorter, so cut less per stroke, and they have smaller teeth for fine but slower cutting. However, the reinforced back keeps the blade square and improves accuracy.

Most people start with a medium tenon saw, about 10 inches (254 mm) long and with about 13 teeth per inch (tpi). It's worth buying a saw with hardened teeth, which can cut any material and can be thrown away when blunt. Once your confidence and skills develop, you can buy traditional saws that you can sharpen yourself, though I tend to favor Japanese saws that cut on both the push and pull strokes. Fortunately, even the most basic tenon saws and handsaws are available with what are known as triple tooth-form teeth, which can also cut both ways (see page 212).

Materials

Dowel rod

Prerounded lengths of wood are known as dowel or doweling, commonly available in a few standard sizes, in steps from about ⅛ inch (3 mm) to 1½ inch (38 mm). Dowel is, however, notoriously inaccurate, with one length fractionally bigger or smaller than others supposedly of the same diameter. This can lead to sloppy joints and great frustration. So once you find a supply that suits your drill bits, buy plenty and stick to it.

Dowel is supplied in softwood or hardwood, with the former being far cheaper. More often than not, softwood dowel will do the job, and you are more likely to find FSC-certified supplies of this than of hardwood doweling, which can be of uncertain origin (see pages 60 and 168).

Problems with wood

Any project incorporating wood has to be designed with the material's inherent instability in mind, acknowledging that the material expands and contracts depending on the ambient humidity of its surroundings. We will look at how this affects designs later in the book (see page 60).

When you buy wood, you will notice that it is not always flat and straight. A board that is curved or bowed along its length shouldn't present too many problems for the woodworker, as you are likely to be cutting it up into shorter lengths. Boards that are twisted along their length should, however, be avoided because you will lose much of the material in trying to flatten them.

Cupping across the width is the most common problem, but it isn't difficult to resolve, and projects should be designed with the risks of further cupping in mind. If you look at the end of a board, you'll notice the growth rings of the tree. By cutting through those rings to produce a flat board, the level of tension on the two sides will be different, and the growth rings will try to flatten themselves. This actually forces the board to cup, rising at the edges.

How to solve cupping

Cupped boards can easily be planed flat and used to make a project, just like the Shoe Rack this lesson. But move the rack from the workshop into a warm bedroom, and the moisture content and tensions in the wood will change. The sides of the rack may not be able to bow or twist, because they are held by the front and back rails and by the dowel. They could, however, cup.

The effects of cupping are more likely to be noticed on wide boards than thin boards because the tensions are amplified, since the difference between the two sides is greater. One way to avoid this is to use quarter-sawn boards, but you won't find much softwood lumber milled this way. The solution is to glue up wide boards from a number of thin strips, alternating the direction of the growth rings to minimize the consequences of cupping (see page 212).

Strip wood

You can buy wide boards of thin strips that will help you make projects before you own the machines or have the skills to glue panels from narrow boards. Strip wood reduces the risks of cupping but is more expensive than plain-sawn boards, even those surfaced on all four sides (S4S in the United States and PAR in Europe).

Project **Shoe rack**

For your bedroom

Using strip wood reduces the risks of the sides of the shoe rack cupping. This project relies on accurate drilling of the holes for the dowel racking and straight cutting of the notches at the back.

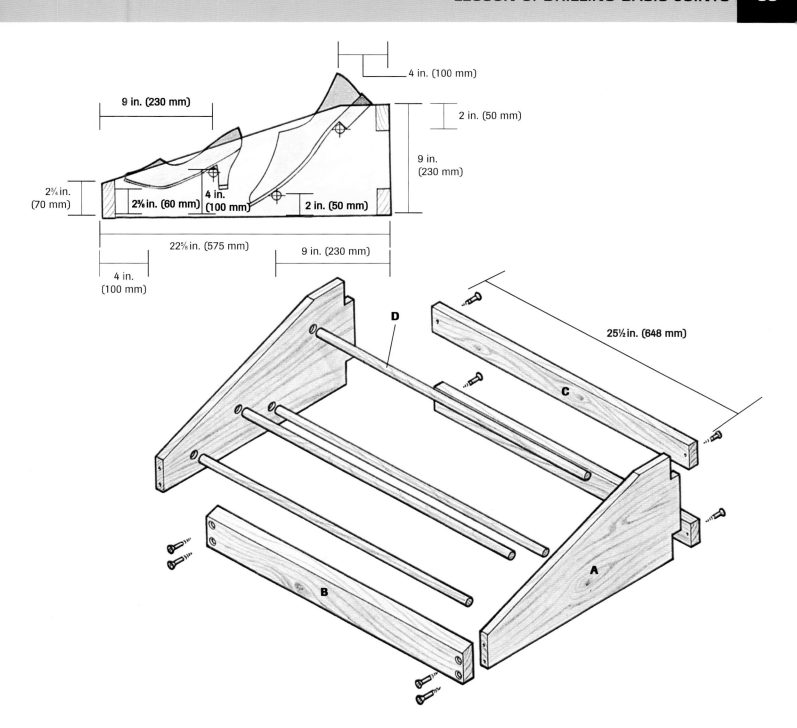

Cutting list

Part	Material	Quantity	Dimensions thickness, width, length
A Side	strip wood	2	¾ x 9 x 21⅝ in. (19 x 229 x 549 mm)
B Front rail	softwood	1	¾ x 2½ x 25½ in. (19 x 63 x 648 mm)
C Back rail	softwood	2	¾ x 1½ x 25½ in. (19 x 38 x 648 mm)
D Shoe rail	dowel	4	¾ x ¾ x 24½ in. (19 x 19 x 622 mm)

Shopping list

Extra tools for the job

Screws No. 8 1¼ in. (32 mm)
Flat bit ¾ in. (19 mm) to drill the dowel holes or
Suitable twist bit, since you'll get a better finish and can drill the holes deeper for more stability

1 Cut the sides (**A**) to length and mark up the tapers with a straight edge and pencil. Cut the tapers and clean up with a block plane.

2 Mark out the positions for the dowel holes, making sure the sides are paired and you don't end up drilling the inside face of one and the outside face of the other.

3 With a twist bit or flat bit, drill the dowel holes, making sure you use a depth stop or mark on the bit so as not to pierce the sides. Check the fit of the dowel after you've cut one hole, then do the rest.

Cut the notches at the back of the sides with a tenon saw, using the back rails (**C**) themselves to mark out the notches.

Use the sliding bevel I introduced in Lesson 1, and set it to the angle of the taper. Then mark the ends of the front rail (**B**) to that angle and plane the top edge with a block plane.

4 Drill and countersink the ends of the rails for inserting screws. Place the rails up to the sides and use screws to mark where you need to drill pilot or thread holes in the sides. If you don't drill pilot holes in the sides, you are likely to split the wood.

Do a dry run, and when you are satisfied, apply glue, using the screwed rails to hold it all together. If you are worried about the amount of gluing you are doing in one go, glue the dowels in place initially, but use screws for the rails. Once the glue for the dowels has set, you can carefully undo the rails one by one and glue them in place.

Clean up and apply a finish; varnish is an ideal choice.

Lessons learned

- Screws inserted into thin softwood are likely to split the wood.

- Flat bits tear wood fibers, and twist bits are far better if you can afford them.

- Wood will cup over wide boards unless you take precautions.

Lesson 4
Interlocking Joints

Getting started

Though there are plenty of ways to join pieces of wood with metal fasteners and other connectors, the most satisfying method is to create interlocking joints from the lumber itself. These rely upon the fit and glue to varying degrees, with truly mechanical joints like the drawer-bored mortise and tenon requiring no adhesive at all.

The first type of joint to try is the lap joint, which is used for simple constructions. The shoulders on the joint provide good lateral support, to stop twist, but the lap joint relies largely upon glue, though a good fit will improve its longevity. The good thing is that in learning how to cut the lap joint, you have to develop skills with tools that will help with all future woodworking. In particular, you will have to master the marking gauge for marking up joints, the tenon saw for cutting shoulders, and the chisel for paring back the cheeks of joints.

This lesson's project, the Towel rail, employs various types of lap joints, between pieces of softwood and plywood. What you will discover is that this technique may be simple, but everything about the joint is on show, so any mistakes are on display. Other joints, later on, hide the link more cleverly but are more complicated to cut.

Lesson planner

Key techniques	Key tools and materials
• When to use the lap joint • Marking up the lap joint • Cutting the lap joint • Setting the marking gauge	• Chisels Selecting a chisel isn't the hardest choice you'll have to make as a woodworker, but these are tools you will use for years, and they'll also need regular sharpening. • Marking gauge • Kitchen or child-safe finishes • Dealing with knots

Trade secret

Gluing end grain
Glue does not take well to end grain, because it is unable to grip into the fibers. Any joint that relies on the end grain being glued is vulnerable. Instead, we try to make sure that any glued joint has a section of long grain meeting long grain. This is known as the gluing area. The larger the gluing area in a joint, the better the chances of survival.

How to choose a joint
One of the most important skills to develop is learning which joint to use and when. While it is tempting to rely on glues and metal fasteners to join two or more pieces of wood—as are employed in knock-down furniture—the strongest long-term solution is to produce a mechanical joint with interlocking wooden components. Which joint you select depends on the dimensions of the stock you are using, the tools and equipment you own, and the stresses and tension exerted on the finished project.

Since a chair has to cope with severe pressure in many directions, it needs a particularly strong joint—so the value of the mortise and tenon is that the male part slots deeply into its partner for strength. A box, on the other hand, suffers only from the risk of the sides bowing and breaking the corner joints, so for that purpose we use dovetails that lock the boards in an embrace that cannot easily be broken. A picture frame needs very little strength, but must look good, for which the miter is ideal. And then there are simple projects, especially around the workshop itself, that don't need much strength and for which speed is the key. Here the halving joint is functional and quick.

When to use the lap joint
Up to now we have largely used butt joints and drilled joints to assemble our projects. The time comes, though, when you need to join square or rectangular section

components with some strength. Though it's not particularly strong itself, a very simple introduction to joint-cutting is the halving or lap joint.

The principle of this joint is that components overlap one another, often by reducing the thickness of each by half—hence the two names often associated with this joint. It is ideal for joining two pieces of identical section at right angles. The shoulders of the joint help to align the pieces, and there is plenty of long grain to long grain to glue.

Types of lap joint

There are numerous variations of the lap joint. Though it is usually the case, the components don't have to be cut at 90 degrees to one another, and angled versions of all these joints can be used.

• **The end lap.** Very quick to cut, the end lap is used in frame corners but has very little sideways strength. Often it will be screwed or pegged to reduce the risk of breaking.

• **The center lap.** Otherwise known as the cross-halving joint, the center lap is surprisingly strong and can be cut very tightly. The shoulders stop any twist, but there is very little margin for error in cutting, as a loose joint looks sloppy and is weak.

• **The T lap.** Very similar to the center lap, but one component ends in the "housing," making it an end lap for one part and center lap for the other.

• **The full lap.** The components are of unequal thickness, with the full depth of one part fitting into a housing or lap on the other.

• **Dovetailed lap joint.** A version of the T lap, with the male and female parts cut to a dovetail shape. This is particularly useful if you have no way of holding a frame together while it is being assembled and the glue is setting.

Marking up the lap joint

The quickest way to mark up the lap joint is to offer one component up to the other and use it to mark the shoulder lines. Remember, though, that this marks the outside of the joint, so the shoulders have to be cut to the inside of the lines or the joint will be sloppy.

Once the position is finalized, you can set the depth for the joint to be cut. You do this with a marking gauge. The idea is to scribe a thin groove along the sides (and across the end grain on an end or T lap). This groove should mark the midpoint of the thickness, assuming both components are the same. You will cut down the shoulders to this mark and then use it to guide the chisel.

Cut the pieces roughly to length; it doesn't matter if they are a little long.

Use one piece to mark up the shoulder line on the other board.

Then mark around the board, using a knife and combination square.

Using a marking gauge

To use a marking gauge, at least to start, it's best to hold the workpiece in a vise or the jaws of a portable workbench, though with practice you can hold it by hand, resting one end of the board against your leg or the bench. Grasp the marking gauge with your fingers around the stock and hold the stock against the board, resting on the shaft. Twist the marking gauge till the point breaks the surface and move from around the joint. If you push, you get a better view of the pin and line, but I find pulling gives you better control even if the visibility is worse. Try for yourself. A few gentle passes are better than one heavy one, which might slip and damage the surface.

Set the marking gauge by marking with the stock held against each face.

Marking across the end grain can be more awkward.

Cup the marking gauge in your hand and run it down the grain.

Trade secret

Setting the marking gauge

The marking gauge must be set accurately if you are going to be able to use it repetitively for all your joints. Take the board and set the stock roughly half the board's thickness from the pin. Hold the stock against the board and make a light puncture. Do the same from the other side. Now adjust the stock to position the pin exactly between your first two holes. For fine adjustment, release the locking nut on the stock a fraction, then knock the gauge shaft on the bench.

Cutting the halving joint

How you cut the joint depends a little on which type of lap you are forming, though the initial steps are the same for all. The guiding principal is that you cut the shoulders with a saw, and remove the waste and clean up the joint cheek with a chisel.

1 Cut the shoulders down to the depth mark, with the wood held in the jaws. Once you get the knack, this can easily be done with a bench hook to speed up the process. Make sure you cut to the waste side, and you follow the lines you've squared around the sides as well as across the top. Ideally, cut exactly to the line you want, or you'll have to do some boring chisel work.

2 For an end lap you can remove the waste by using the chisel from the end, with the grain. Don't try to remove all the waste in one go, as you don't know how the grain is running and you may find a split chases down below the depth mark. For cleaning up the joint, discard the mallet and use gentle pressure.

3 Once you have cleaned up the joint cheek, use the corner of the chisel to cut through the shavings and to clean up the bottom corner of the shoulder. The face of the shoulder should be clean from the saw cut.

4 For a center lap or T lap, you have to chop away the waste across the grain. The end-lap process of working your way down applies, but you have to work from both sides, making sure the final cuts along the edge are tidy, since that is where any mistakes will be seen.

Tools

Your first mechanical joints can be cut with a few tools, but the lessons learned in using and maintaining chisels, in particular, will reinforce most woodworking you will do in the future.

Choosing a chisel

Chisels are produced in various forms, but initially you'll only need a few bevel-edged types, either bought in a set or individually. You can buy plenty of specialized chisels from secondhand stores.

● **Bevel-edged chisels.** As you might expect, these chisels are wasted toward the edges to make them easier to get in and out of mortises, but they offer little lateral control and can easily wander.

● **Straight-sided chisels.** The standard version of the bevel-edged chisel, but without the wasting, is called the firmer chisel, which offers more control and a bit more strength to the chisel. The mortise chisel is even thicker to provide more power in removing waste from mortises. You need these only if you are planning on doing a lot of hand mortising, though I do love the old firmer chisels I've acquired over the years.

Singles or sets?

You can usually save a little money by buying chisels in sets of anything from three upward. Personally, I think between three and six is enough to start, but only if you get exactly what you require—don't waste money on chisels you don't really need. My ideal set of bevel-edged chisels would include an ⅛ inch (3 mm), ¼ inch (6 mm), ⅜ inch (9 mm), ½ inch(12 mm), ¾ inch (18 mm) and 1 inch (25 mm).

Alternatively, I'd be more creative, bearing in mind I don't use either the ⅛-inch (3-mm) or 1-inch (25-mm) chisels very often, and do use the ¾-inch (19-mm) chisel most of the time.

So if my budget was limited, I would buy a bevel-edged ¼ inch (6 mm) for awkward jobs and a ¾ inch (18 mm), for general paring and cleaning up. I would then plan to buy ⅜ inch (9 mm) and ½ inch (13 mm) firmer chisels for mortising and other chiseling.

Most of my chisels have wooden handles, but I'm not a purist on this subject, and as long as they are comfortable, plastic handles are just as good (if slightly less friendly to the environment). Eventually you can make your own handles once you have acquired a lathe (see page 248).

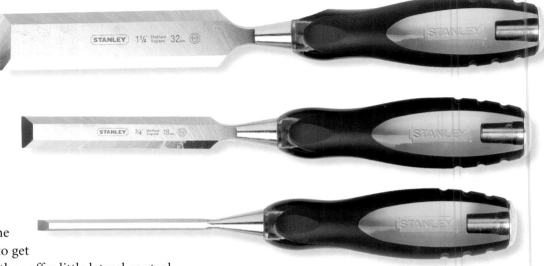

Top: 1-inch bevel-edged chisel; center: ½-inch bevel-edged chisel; bottom: ¼-inch bevel-edged chisel.

How to use a chisel

Developing skill with a chisel takes time and really is a question of touch, though the job is always made easier with a sharp tool. There are various ways of using a chisel.

1 **Paring** Hold the handle with your stronger hand, using this for the power, and then guide it by cradling or covering the blade with your other hand, a bit like a pool player holds a cue. Sometimes you'll use the thumb of your weaker hand to push the chisel.

2 **With a mallet** For more power, and sometimes more control, tap or hit the chisel with a mallet, usually holding the chisel by its handle. You can position the chisel bevel up or down. With the bevel facing downward, you raise the handle for better access and potentially a deeper cut, but it is slightly less easy to control this way.

Trade secret

Paring with a chisel

When you come to cleaning up the cheek of an end lap, for instance, you pare, using the flat base of the chisel to guide the edge that you push gently by hand. Paring is often done in a sweeping motion to keep the shavings very thin and to cope with the changing grain.

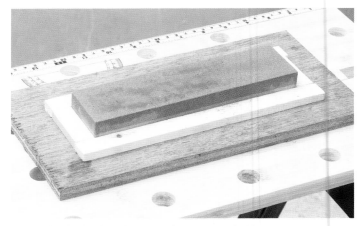

Make a holder for the oilstone so that it can be held in a vise.

When is the chisel blunt?

Initially, woodworkers fear sharpening a chisel, often seeing it as a waste of valuable woodworking time and anxious that they'll ruin the edge of a new chisel. I've always believed it's a good idea to assume tools are blunt when they arrive, so any sharpening of your own will improve the tool and you will have stamped your mark upon the tool. It's important to believe that you can improve anything you buy (from a kettle to a shirt) and don't have to rely upon someone else's design and production.

A chisel is blunt when it doesn't cut as well. It is blunt when you carefully rub your thumb across (but not along) the edge and it doesn't feel any resistance. It is blunt when you can see the edge, rather than it blurring into infinity.

Sharpening a chisel

It's best to assume the angle of the chisel's bevel is about right, so doesn't need regrinding unless you dropped it while taking it from the box. I recommend you buy an oilstone and honing guide to start with, possibly as a kit. Choose a medium-grit oilstone, since this will always be versatile and you may want to move on to more sophisticated sharpening systems for fine or coarse work (see page 119).

The honing guide I prefer has a roller underneath and clamps on each side designed to hold chisels or plane irons. Use your 6-inch (152-mm) rule to line up the bevel and roller, then run it back and forth over the lubricated oilstone. Once the edge is sharpened, loosen the guide and raise the bevel a couple of degrees to sharpen a strip about $\frac{1}{16}$ inch (1.6 mm) along the edge. This is known as the honing bevel and means you have to work only on a small area of steel each time the chisel needs sharpening until you need to regrind the chisel (see page 120).

Once the honing bevel is glinting beautifully, polish the chisel back on the oilstone to ensure the edge is perfect and the chisel can glide smoothly over the wood.

Use a steel ruler to adjust the chisel in the honing guide.

You should see a fine shaving of metal still attached to the edge.

Tidy up the chisel back on the oilstone, holding it flat with your fingers.

A honing guide helps you keep the bevel at the right angle.

Materials

Coloring wood

There are a number of ways to add color to your work. You can use a stain or precolored varnish, applying it with a brush or cloth.

1 If you want to retain the patterning of wood, you can apply a colored stain to the sanded surface and then protect it with a varnish once it has dried. Spirit-based stains are really the best because they bite hardest into the wood and they don't expand the fibers.

2 Apply a precolored varnish, which will either be water- or oil-based. These are quicker to apply than stains, but the color tends to lie on top of the surface rather than soaking down into the grain. You may not notice this to begin with, but you will see the difference later.

Use a normal wood paint, priming the surface first with a primer and undercoat. Make sure it is safe for children and food to be in contact with the paint if you are using it for toys or in the kitchen. This probably gives you the widest range of colors. Milk paints are a specialized solution—these are only available from limited suppliers in a small range of colors, but the effect on wood is superb.

Dealing with knots

Knots in wood are a serious issue for a number of reasons. Some species, especially softwoods, suffer more from them than others. In the United States, softwood grading guarantees you knot-free lumber if you're willing to pay for Select or Superior Finish boards. In the United Kingdom, grading never seems to be as certain, and the best advice is to visit the yard and choose boards for yourself.

There are a few problems with knots that you have to consider. You might need to buy blemish-free boards or be able to just place the knots carefully in the project. In many ways knots add character to projects, so don't worry about keeping them, as long as they don't undermine the function of the piece. Some problems include:

● Knots can seep resin, particularly in softwood species. The effects of this bleeding are most conspicuous when you paint the wood, since a dark mark may show through. The solution is to paint the knot with shellac before finishing.

● Knots can weaken thin components, so you should avoid any such defects on lengths of wood less than 1 inch (25 mm) square in section. Molding is particularly vulnerable.

● Knots may break out, leaving a hole. Loose knots can be glued in place using cyanoacrylate glue or epoxy, and holes can be filled with filler or another knot. (I have a stock of old knots.) If you use filler, make sure it is darker than the surrounding wood so it resembles a knot.

● Knots can make planing very difficult because the grain is deflected in all sorts of directions and tears. Equally, that grain can look superb if you can control the cut.

Shellac seals the knot and stops any resin bleeding.

Project **Towel rail**

A practical bathroom accessory

This towel rail consists of a pair of end frames joined together by rails. It does not have to be very robust; just take care when you mark out the positions of the joints and dowels. The components should fit easily.

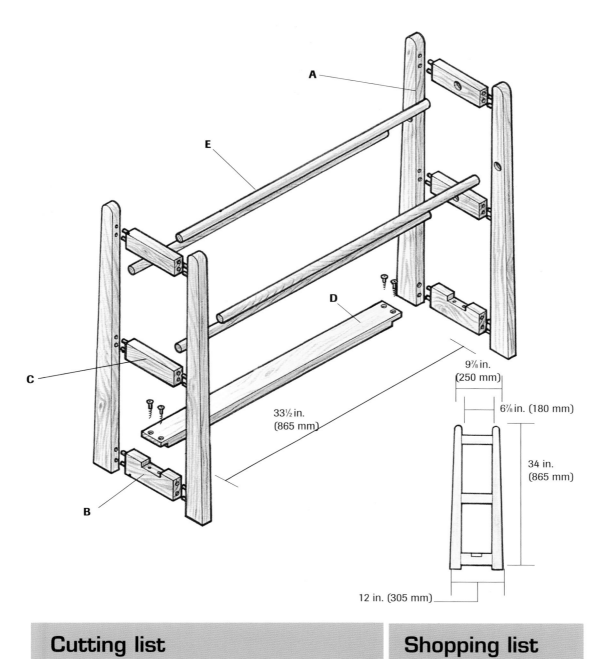

A

E

C

B

D

33½ in.
(865 mm)

9⅞ in.
(250 mm)

6⅞ in. (180 mm)

34 in.
(865 mm)

12 in. (305 mm)

Cutting list

Part		Material	Quantity	Dimensions thickness, width, length
A	Posts	softwood	4	1 x 3 x 34 in. (25 x 75 x 865 mm)
B	Bottom rails	softwood	2	1 x 3 x 7 in. (25 x 75 x 178 mm)
C	Mid-rails	softwood	4	1 x 2 x 7 in. (25 x 50 x 178 mm)
D	Connecting rail	softwood	1	1 x 2 x 34 in. (25 x 50 x 865 mm)
E	Hanging rails	softwood	4	1 x 33 in. (25 x 840 mm)
F	Dowels	softwood	24	2 x ⅜ in (50 x 10mm)

Shopping list

Bill of materials

Screws four 1¼ in. (32 mm)
No. 8 brass countersunk
Straightedge and **try square**
Ripsaw or **panel saw**
Tenon saw
Bench plane and **block plane**
Sash cramps
Dowel pins
Power drill and **bits**
Chisel ¾ in. (19 mm)
Bradawl
Screwdriver

1 Make a template for the posts from spare sheet material—³⁄₁₆ or ¼-in. (5 or 6-mm) MDF is ideal. Draw the template full size and cut it out. Round off the top of the template and then use it to mark out wood for the four posts.

2 Lightly cramp the posts together in line and mark the positions of the three end-frame rails across all of them. Mark the end of each rail for a pair of dowels and mark the drilling centers with a sharp bradawl. Drill the holes, which should be slightly deeper than half the length of a dowel. Slot doweling pins in the holes in the ends of the rails and position the rails against their marks on the posts. Drill out the dowel holes in the posts, making sure that they are only slightly deeper than half the length of a dowel. Apply waterproof adhesive to the dowels and their holes, and then assemble the posts and rails to complete the construction of the two end frames. Use sash cramps to hold the frames together until the glue dries. If necessary, smooth down both sides of each join with a bench plane.

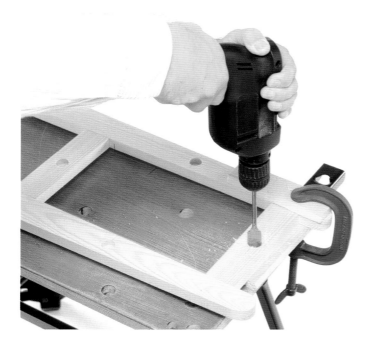

3 Mark the connecting rail slightly overlength and shape it to the correct width and thickness with a bench plane. Mark the shoulder lines for the halving joints on the connecting rail. The distance between the shoulder lines should equal the overall length of the towel rail minus the thicknesses of the two end frames. Mark out the halving joints at both ends of the connecting rail and at the two midpoints of the bottom rails on the end frames. Cut the waste from the joints with a tenon saw. Clean up the joints with a ¾-in. (19-mm) chisel and make sure the faces of the joints are flat and square.

4 Next, drill two countersunk clearance holes at each end of the connecting rail and dry-assemble the joints. Make sure the two joints fit together tightly and then mark the bottom rails through the clearance holes with a bradawl. Once assembled drill the holes for the dowel rod. Using screws, fix the connecting rail to the bottom rail of one of the end frames. The connecting rail holds the assembly together, so fix one end first, and only once the hanging rails are ready should you attach the other end of the connecting rail to the other frame. Notice how the connecting rail is notched into the frame rail.

5 With the dowel rails all cut to length and the connecting rail screwed to one frame, apply glue to the end of the hanging rails and assemble the towel rail. Make sure you remove any excess glue with a damp cloth, and then complete the piece with a waterproof finish, preferably polyurethane varnish.

Lessons learned

- Lapped joints may be simple to cut, but the shoulder lines are very visible, so they must be cut accurately. As you will discover, tenon-and-mortise joints may look more complicated, but actually the joint is easier to hide.

- It can be very difficult to get a good fit with a dowel in a hole. Test the fit first. The dowel joint is relatively strong but can be difficult to line up.

- It is always worth assembling a project as complicated as this towel rail in sections, one frame at a time. In this case, you need to assemble the end frames individually and then join them together with the hanging rails and the connecting rail.

Lesson 5
The Versatile Dowel

Getting started

In the 1960s and '70s, with the advent of the cheap electric drill and a boom in home improvement, special jigs for accurately drilling dowel holes were popular, and the dowel joint was used extensively for the making of home-built cabinets, chests, and bookshelves. A revolution in the 1980s brought the introduction of the router and the decline in the popularity of the dowel or drilling jig. Even the dowel joint is used less often now.

There was a time when it seemed that every piece of furniture included a dowel joint. Now the biscuit jointer and router dominate, but the dowel shouldn't be ignored, since it can be a very effective means of joining pieces of wood. The key benefit of the dowel joint is its versatility, with the dowel rod employed to reinforce restoration jobs, or as a quick solution to strengthen butt joints. These days there has been a revival of the joint, with some furniture makers using stainless steel threaded rod instead of wooden dowel for joints. The challenge is lining up holes for drilling, and if you aren't using a jig of some sort, the problem of the drill bit wandering is always an issue, especially when drilling into end grain.

Using the dowel joint

One of the simplest mechanical joints for fixing two pieces of wood together is to use short lengths of dowel rod, drilled into each component. This technique has been used for decades, if not centuries, in the mass production

of chairs and furniture. With the right equipment and jigs, it is relatively easy to create this joint accurately and do so over and over for repetitive joints.

Even though the router has superseded the dowel jig, the joint still has value, especially for reinforcing a simple butt joint, with two boards meeting at right angles. One advantage of the dowel joint is that it is very easy to set out and mark up, and the dowel is a versatile way to strengthen a joint. You can mark up the joint quickly as a one-off, use marking gauges for repetitive setting out, or use a jig to produce many joints quickly and accurately.

The joint itself is relatively strong, and the glue area is pretty wide. One of the problems is finding a balance between using enough dowels and weakening the component. You must also consider that drilling into end grain, as is very likely to happen for at least one part of the joint, is not easy, and the drill bit may wander unless you are using a bench drill and the component is held against a fence. Checking by eye using two set squares is possible but tricky, and any discrepancy will severely weaken the joint and make assembly difficult.

Lesson planner

Key techniques	Key tools and materials
• When to use a dowel joint • Marking up and drilling the dowel joint • Using dowel centers • Making a sanding block	• Buying and using a scroll saw • Child-safe paints • Geometric marking tools • Drilling jigs

Marking up the dowel joint

There are a couple of ways to mark up the dowel joint, but the simplest is to use a marking gauge. Let's assume you are planning to joint two identical boards at a right angle, as is being done in the project this lesson. The plan is to use three dowels to reinforce the joint between the two pieces. It is the best joint for the job, but later you'll find that a biscuit will do this as well. You could screw one board to the other, but in doing that, you will need to screw into the end grain of one board, and screws rarely hold well into end grain, because the fibers split around the screw. Nor can you rely on the glue, as end grain never bonds very well. You need some form of mechanical connection strengthened with glue.

1 Lay out the two boards end to end, with the inside face of each facing upward. Gently mark that these are the meeting faces with a soft pencil. Also mark the positions for the holes to be drilled across the width and put one board up to the other to repeat this. If you have a number of joints to cut, you could keep one piece as a template and use it for repetitive marking. Set the marking gauge to half the thickness of the board.

3 It's a bit confusing, but you must make sure you place the stock against the correct face when marking across the end grain of the other piece. Although the gauge should be set central, there may be some discrepancy, so make sure the stock is against the outside face and not against the inside face that you marked earlier. This positions the line correctly. You can square across the positions for the holes at this stage if you haven't done so already. The two boards should now be ready for drilling.

2 With the stock against the end of the board, mark across one component.

Trade secret

Pin or Knife?

The marking gauge we are using here uses a sharpened knife to score the line, rather than the pin you often find in cheaper models. The advantage of the knife is that it cuts more easily through the fibers, but it leaves a beveled edge to the groove on one side, whereas the pin produces a V-groove, which is more suitable for marking out mortises-and-tenons.

Drilling a dowel joint

Assuming you don't have a drilling machine, I'm going to explain how to make a dowel joint using a cordless or electrically powered drill. This technique relies upon good marking up and the ability to drill accurately and square into the two components.

1 Mark up the two components as described on page 55. In my opinion, there is greater risk of inaccuracy when it comes to drilling into end grain, so I would do that first. If necessary, you can then adjust the drilling of the second piece. It is often difficult to keep the drill bit still when starting the cut into end, and there may be a tendency for it to be deflected by the grain. Some people use a very thin drill bit first to guide the larger bit, but if the "pilot" hole is too large, the proper one will not sit accurately, so practice first.

3 Dry-assemble the joint first to check the fit. Then apply glue to the dowels and tap them into one component with a hammer. They should be a snug fit, with some glue oozing out around the edges through the grooves. Bring up the other component and tap home using a rubber mallet. Check for square and wait for the glue to dry. It should not need clamping, which is another benefit of this joint.

2 Hold the second piece on the bench, ideally over some scrap and held down with a toggle clamp or similar. You can use a bench hook for this, but only if you don't mind the board being ruined by drill holes. You will need to use a depth stop to ensure you don't drill right through the lumber.

TIP: It's a good idea to countersink all the holes a little, as this will help guide the dowel rod into place when you assemble the joint.

4 There's a good chance that you'll need to tidy up the outside of the joint. Ideally you want the end grain to protrude, as this is easier to plane back than having to reduce the thickness of the other piece. Use a block plane for paring back the end grain, but watch out for splitting the end of the board. By clamping a piece of scrap against the end, you can reduce the risk of this happening.

Using dowel centers

A quick way to mark up a dowel joint is to use dowel centers. These fit into a drilled hole and have a point for marking the partner piece. They are superb for one-off jobs.

1 Mark up and drill one set of holes in a component—it doesn't matter where, just as long as they are drilled in straight.

2 Fit the dowel centers in the holes and bring the piece up to its partner or vice versa. You may want to hold the piece with the dowel centers in a vise; otherwise the centers might fall out as you bring the piece up.

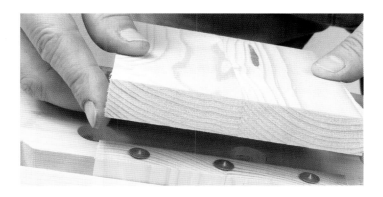

3 Once you are satisfied with the alignment of the two pieces, gently push down to make the marks. Ideally you need to get this right the first time, so make sure all three marks have been made. Now you can drill the holes as you would normally.

Making and grooving your own dowel

You can buy pregrooved dowel rod, cut to length, beveled at the ends, and grooved to let the excess glue escape. Without the grooves there is a risk that the excess glue will get compressed at the bottom of the hole and then force the joint apart when you remove any pressure or when your back is turned.

With screws scoring the dowel, you can adjust the grooves that will allow adhesive to escape from the joint.

With a steel dowel plate, you can produce your own dowel.

Knock the dowel through the jig using a medium hammer.

If you don't have any pregrooved dowel, it is easy to make your own by drilling an appropriate hole in a piece of scrap and inserting nails or screws through the side of the hole to make the grooves. Screws are best, since they can be adjusted more easily. Tap the dowel rod through the groover, cut to length, and bevel the ends for easy insertion.

You could also make your own dowel by drilling appropriate holes in a piece of mild steel or by buying a dowel plate. Harder steel will produce a better surface, but desperate situations require desperate measures. Some people even use a very hard species of wood for the dowel plate, but it isn't as effective and can "polish" the surface of the dowel rod too much and reduce its adhesion.

Cutting out shapes

Toys make great projects in the early stages of woodworking. One of the most popular approaches is to cut out shapes using a scroll saw and make them into mobiles, bookends, or just animals to play with. There are many books with scroll-saw patterns, or you can use a copier to enlarge or reduce images you come across, though don't ignore the copyright laws if you start selling your work. The simplest technique is to stick copies to the workpiece with spray adhesive, but be sure that you do so in a well-ventilated space or outside, since the fumes can irritate.

Trade secret

Making a sanding block

However well you plane a board, everything can be ruined by turning over the corners with uneven sanding at the end. The best solution is to use a sanding block for finishing. This spreads the pressure and reduces the risk of sanding too much away around the edges or in dips. Though you can buy various types of sanding block, with the abrasive held by pins or by Velcro, a quick and cheap solution is to make your own.

Find an offcut block about ¾ inch thick (38 mm), 2½ inches wide (63 mm) and 3½ inches long (89 mm), around which you can fold paper or cloth-backed abrasive. Beveling the edges can help with the folding and increase the life span of the abrasive.

Tools

Buying and using a scroll saw

The scroll saw wouldn't be the first machine I'd buy, as I'd always favor a band saw, but many woodworkers get going with this versatile tool. It can't be used for cutting up boards, but the scroll saw is ideal for beginners who want to dabble with toymaking and create jigsaw puzzles and other gifts.

Essentially, the scroll saw is no more than a mechanized coping saw, with a table to hold the lumber you are cutting. Though there are varying designs, the blade always cuts on the downstroke, and because it is so thin, you can cut tight corners and curves to produce shapes. By stacking thin boards one on top of the other, you can create multiple designs. Some scroll saws will cut up to 2 inches (51 mm) thick, but there is a tendency for the blade to wander and bend at these extremes, with a loss of accuracy.

There aren't many things to look out for when buying a scroll saw, and the amount you pay depends on how much you expect to use it. Some scroll saws have a longer throat than others, so check the distance between the blade and the back of the frame. Others have variable speeds, which is useful, but to be honest, I've never used it on my machine (which is always set on fast). The table will invariably tilt, but this only needs to be one way. Check out the extraction before you buy, though, since some have nozzles that blow the dust away from the cut line. Personally, I prefer those that suck up the dust rather than blast it around.

Another issue is the blade-holding device and tensioning mechanism. Test a few of these out first, since some are more awkward than others and you may end up using this feature.

Tips for using a scroll saw

Fixing the blade in the frame is an important part of preparing the scroll saw. Make sure the blade is centered in the holders; otherwise they will be pulled off-line as you tighten the frame and you'll shorten the life of your blades. Test the tension by flicking the blade with your finger (obviously with the saw turned off) until it sings. Experiment until you find a tension that suits your work.

My dislike of scroll saws has always been based on the tendency for the workpiece to jump and clatter on the table if you don't hold it securely. Small pieces are particularly susceptible. You can buy hold-down devices, but I prefer to use my hands and just remember to maintain the pressure. A magnifier and light can make cutting much easier.

Internal cuts require a piercing hole, through which the blade is fed for cutting. Some scroll saws are supplied with a flexible drive and drill for drilling this tiny hole as you sit at the saw. This is a good option if you are planning to do a lot of complicated cutting with lots of internal cuts, but personally, I rely on a cordless drill or bench drill.

Choosing blades

The thinner the scroll-saw blade, the more likely it is to break, and you will go through a fair number. The best idea when you start scroll-sawing is to buy a multipack of blades of different size and tooth configuration. On most blades all the teeth face downward, but more modern configurations have a few teeth pointing upward for a finer cut. I prefer the simple blades, since I've found they give me better control. Whatever you do, make sure you make a note of which blades you are using and which you like for particular tasks. Then buy a bulk order of them and clearly label them so you know which is which.

Drilling jigs

Some years ago I threw away my last drilling jig for making dowel joints because I so rarely use this technique. It coincided with the purchase of a bench drill. However, jigs can be very useful in the manufacture of cases, like kitchen cupboards, and there are some very good ones on the market.

One extremely useful drilling jig that I do use regularly is the pocket-screw jig. This device guides a special stepped drill bit to produce an angled hole in the side of a board that you use for attaching screws to another piece. Effectively a reinforced butt joint, it isn't the strongest, but it is good enough for many quick jobs.

Marking out shapes

If you get into scroll work and start designing your own shapes, you will want to buy a few geometry marking tools. These include plastic sheets of circles or other shapes, rubber rules that you can bend to a specific shape, and the French curve, which has an ever increasing radius to suit whatever shape you want to produce. Many of these can be bought at a stationery store and are provided in children's pencil kits. I've been using a pair of the cheapest compasses for years to scribe curved lines on shelves to fit into alcoves or against awkward walls.

Materials

Dowel rod

Buying dowel rod can be one of the most frustrating tasks for a woodworker. Rarely are the diameters consistent, and any variance will result in a sloppy joint or unexpected tightness that splits the wood. The most common dowel rod is made from softwood, but you can also purchase hardwood dowel from various species.

Personally, I prefer to make my own dowel using a dowel plate I bought some years ago at what seemed like a high price for seven holes drilled in a piece of steel. It has proved to be invaluable, since I can now produce whatever dowel rod I desire.

Child-safe paints

If you are making toys, it is important to check that any finishes are child safe. This should be displayed on the label, and if it isn't, you'd better use something else. When making toys, it is also important to remember that small parts can be swallowed.

Project **Bookends**

For their favorite storybooks

The teddy bear bookends are a good introduction to
the world of scroll-sawing and to the challenges and
benefits of the dowel joint. Though these are made
from softwood, you could use plywood or another,
more exotic wood.

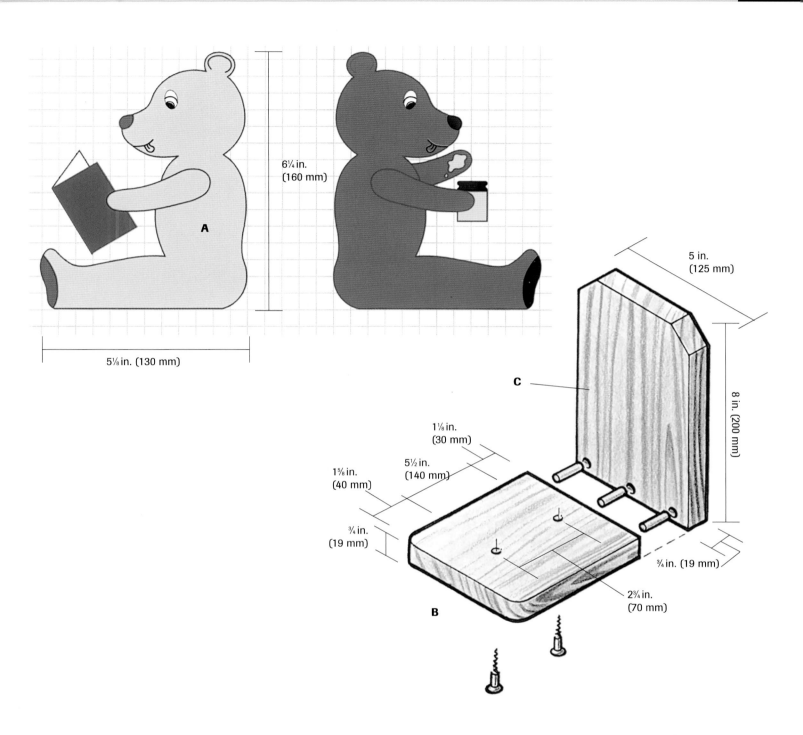

6¼ in.
(160 mm)

5 in.
(125 mm)

A

8 in. (200 mm)

C

1⅛ in.
(30 mm)

5½ in.
(140 mm)

1⅝ in.
(40 mm)

¾ in.
(19 mm)

¾ in. (19 mm)

2¾ in.
(70 mm)

5⅛ in. (130 mm)

B

Cutting list

Part	Material	Quantity	Dimensions thickness, width, length
A Bear	softwood	1	½ x 5⅛ x 6¼ in. (13 x 130 x 159 mm)
B Base	softwood	1	¾ x 5½ x 5½ in. (19 x 140 x 140 mm)
C Upright	softwood	1	¾ x 5½ x 8 in. (19 x 140 x 203 mm)

Shopping list

Extra tools for the job

Screws two No. 6 screws,
1½ in. (38 mm) long for attaching
the bear
Dowel rod ⅜-in. (10-mm)
diameter

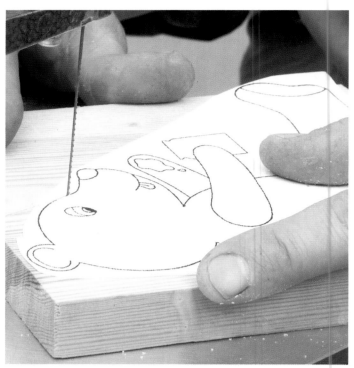

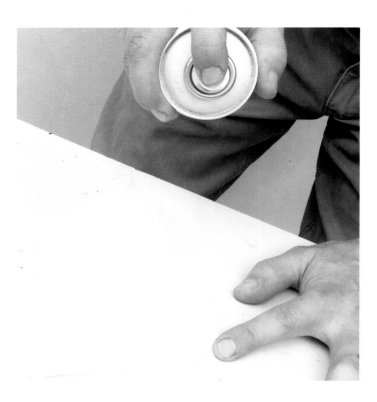

1 Copy the bear shape (**A**) to fit and fix it to the board with spray adhesive.

2 Cut around the outside with a scroll saw or with a coping saw. One of the advantages of a scroll saw is that it gives a superb finish that usually requires very little extra finishing. Try to keep the piece moving steadily with as few jerks as possible, and don't panic if you wander off the line. Your mistakes are unlikely to be noticeable later, once the pattern has been removed.

The base (**B**) and upright (**C**) are made from 1 x 6-inch nominal boards, dressed to ¾ x 5½ inches. Cut the pieces to length and clean up the ends with a block plane to make sure they are square. It is particularly important that the end of the base that joins the upright is square for the joint to work.

3 Mark up and drill three holes in the end of the base for dowels, using an appropriate bit. Check the fit of the bit and the dowel in waste end grain and long grain first.

Using three pointed dowel-markers, transfer the position of the dowels from one piece to the other. Drill the holes, using a depth stop.

Glue the dowels and knock the joint together, having first drilled pilot holes for screws in the base. Once dry, clean up the joint, paying particular attention to the underside where the end grain of the upright is unlikely to be entirely flush with the bottom of the base. Use a block plane to clean up the joint.

4 Sand and finish, rounding over any edges and corners. Then screw the bear in place.

5 Paint the surface of the wood with high-gloss paint and add any final decorations to complete the bear.

Lessons learned

- If you learn anything from drilling holes for dowel joints, it's that you can rarely overcome mistakes made in drilling the holes at an angle or in the wrong place. They invariably end up sloppy if you try to rectify problems, though you can resolve some errors by inserting a dowel in the hole and starting again.

- I hated using scroll saws initially, but plenty of practice has improved my technique. The wood doesn't jump so often, and I can cut to the line accurately. In fact, I often find cutting can produce a more flowing line than a pencil can, and I often leave the original mark when a better line presents itself.

Lesson 6
Planing as Preparation

Getting started

The plane is no more than a chisel held within a metal body, with various adjustments to help control the cut. Understanding the principles of planing and developing the dexterity to handle a plane effectively are the foundations of most woodworking and probably the most important skills you will learn. After all, almost every woodworking task and project requires flat, mating surfaces, and any inaccuracy is punished when you come to assemble the piece.

When it comes to successful planing, so much depends on developing what's sometimes referred to as muscle memory: It used to be called practice. How you hold the plane, how you stand, and how you transfer weight and pressure determine how easily you achieve the results you expect.

There are many types of plane to choose from. This lesson we'll discuss some of the options, what to look for, and why I'm recommending a bench plane. This is likely to be the most expensive tool you will have bought so far, so it's worth investing in something that will last and is versatile.

The moment you start planing, you discover the true challenge of working with wood, for you have to understand and deal with the way wood grows and the effect grain has on your work. I will be outlining some of the principles of wood technology and introducing some of the most common hardwoods.

Holding the bench plane

Once the plane is sharp and set up properly, it's time to give it a go. There is nothing finer in woodworking than the sound of shavings hissing from a plane, curling their way off the bench, and scattering across the floor. To do so successfully, you need to hold the plane firmly but not too hard: You certainly don't need white knuckles.

Hold the rear handle with your stronger hand, extending your index finger along the side of the cutter, just as you do with a saw, and for the same reasons. Your other hand holds the knob at the front or in some cases actually clasps the side of the plane, but we will look at this later. Your rear hand does most of the pushing, with the front one adding power, guiding the plane, or being used for downward pressure (see page 13).

Get your weight well over the plane, with pressure applied at the front.

Extending your first finger around the plane iron gives you more control.

Lesson planner

Key techniques	Key tools and materials
• Holding the plane • How you stand • Transferring weight and pressure • Holding the wood • Marking up the wood for width and thickness	• Choice of hand planes • Sharpening a plane iron • What is grain? • Why does grain matter? • Is texture an issue? • Some common hardwoods • Simple abrasives

How you stand

Whether you are using a bench plane or a machine jointer (see page 156), the principles of stance are pretty much the same. Place the workpiece in the vise so that it is horizontal and free from obstruction. Assuming you are right-handed, position your right foot near the start of the board and your left foot a comfortable step forward, but pretty much in line with the board so that your shoulders are twisted parallel to the board.

The planing starts pretty much level with your body, which feels natural, and you then extend the plane as far as you can. If the cut is longer than you can reach comfortably (and planing is all about finding what works for you), move your right foot up to your left and then take another step forward with your left foot.

All about pressure

In theory, a plane can cut with no downward pressure. The flat sole should keep the plane level, with the cutter engaging the wood and the weight of the plane maintaining the cut. More often than not, though, you will need to press down to keep the cut going and ensure you produce a flat surface. There is a tendency to remove more wood at the start and end of the cut because the back of the plane will tend to dip at the beginning and the front will drop as it leaves the board.

To avoid this, you need to compensate by pressing down on the front knob at the start until the length of the plane is on the board. Then you can spread the pressure to both handles until the end of the board, when you must push down at the back a bit harder. The only way to learn this is to experiment on some softwood, producing loads of shavings. (This can be useful as kindling for a fire!)

Practice planing

To practice planing, you need a piece of wood at least 2 feet (610 mm) long, but no more than 3 feet (914 mm), to give you a good stroke without having to overextend. The best board is about 1½ inches (38 mm) wide, to give the plane good lateral support. It is often more difficult to learn on narrow pieces, since the plane tends to tilt one way or the other and then it mysteriously stops cutting. Wider boards are just plain too hard to work. (Please forgive the pun.)

A piece of softwood will do, but make sure it is free of knots. You are looking for something without conspicuous growth rings and a fine, even texture. Some hardwoods are worth trying, like cherry, whitewood, and hickory. The grain pattern will guide the direction of planing. Imagine they are contours on a map, and you are planing downhill. It can help to look at the edge of the board to see which way you should plane, as if you're stroking a dog to smooth its fur (see page 69).

Notice how the plane is following the grain (shown by a "V").

On this board you would plane from left to right to avoid tearing.

Holding the wood

Assuming your workbench is a portable one, hold the wood in the jaws, making sure the pressure is even along the length. One of the problems with these benches is that the jaws can damage boards. This doesn't matter when you are practicing, but to make a project, you will need to check the jaws for sharp edges and pimples. It is a good idea to replace the existing jaws with 1-inch (25-mm)-thick softwood jaws if you intend to use the bench for woodworking over a long period of time.

Of course, anyone who has a solid workbench can hold the piece in the bench vise, parallel to the front edge. Make sure the jaws are lined with softwood so as not to damage the workpiece. Hold the board so that it is parallel with the bench top (and presumably the floor), with the top edge high enough above the bench so that your plane doesn't hit anything but with enough in the vise for good support.

Flattening the edge

Before you plane, check the straightness of the board by looking along its edge. This is done to choose which face of the board to plane first. Ideally, you want to start with an edge with high ends and a hollow at the middle. This way the plane cuts at the beginning and end of the stroke, and then gradually the cuts increase toward the center. When the high point is at the middle, the plane will tend to rock and it is much more difficult (though not impossible) to fashion a level edge. You'll know the edge is flat when the shaving is uninterrupted from start to finish. You'll also know that you can plane.

By planing the concave "hollow" edge, you will remove the ends first and work into the hollow.

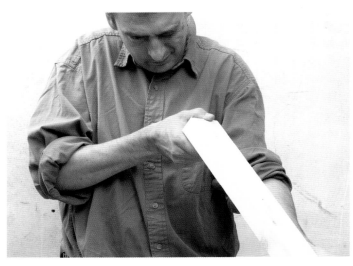

Sight down the board to find out which edge is concave and which is convex.

If you try to plane a convex edge, the plane is likely to rock and you won't achieve a flat surface.

Trade secret

Guiding the plane

It is one thing to flatten the edge of a board along its length but quite another to ensure the edge is square to the face. To stop the plane from tilting to one side or the other, hold the front of the plane with your thumb behind the knob and your fingers curled underneath, running against the board. This has the added advantage of keeping the plane centered on the board, which is important because the cutters on many planes are sharpened with a very shallow curve along the edge to cut a fraction deeper at the center. Do be careful, though, to keep your fingers away from the blade, and make sure there are no protruding splinters in the wood (see pages 68, 120, and 122).

Planing a wider board

Most woodworkers will end up planing boards to thickness by machine or buying it ready-measured from the yard. Planing a wide board flat is tricky enough and in my opinion not a skill that's worth spending much time perfecting in the early stages of woodwork. You have to learn how to move the cutter around the board, often using angled strokes to find and level the high points. It reduces the friction on the cutter and improves the cut, though you will always want to finish parallel to the grain.

Planing a board to width

Given that the board is thicknessed, smooth on both sides, and one edge is planed square to the best face, you will need to plane the second edge to produce parallel edges. Ideally you need to have cut the board roughly to width before planing, but if the edges are far from straight, you may need to straighten one edge first. The best way to mark up a board for width is with a marking gauge, which is very similar to a mortise gauge, but with only one point, not two (see pages 99 and 101).

Set the stock to the width of the board you want. Holding the stock against the best edge, use the point to mark both the best face and the other side. Use a couple of light runs with the marking gauge rather than trying to push the pin in hard once. Now you can plane the edge, working down to the tiny grooves. You will notice the shavings narrow a fraction just as you hit the groove, and this is your clue that you've reached the right level.

If the edge isn't flat, move the plane over toward the "high" side and remove narrow shavings until the edge is level.

Use a marking gauge once you have planed one edge.

As you reach the scored line, you will notice the shaving narrows.

Trade secret

Face and edge

Almost all woodworking starts by creating two adjacent surfaces at 90 degrees or, as we say, square to one another. As most components have one side wider than the other, these are known as the face and edge. Sometimes referred to as the best face and best side, these are the surfaces you plane first.

You start by planing the wider side, or face, until it is flat. This can be very slow work and is more often than not done by machine these days. At this stage I'll assume it has already been done at the yard. In the future, you can do this by using a jointer (see page 157).

Once you have chosen the best face, you need to identify it with a pencil mark. You do this by also determining the best edge, which is usually the one easiest to plane first, with the ends higher than the center. I make a small V sign on the face, pointing toward the best edge. Once the edge is planed, I mark a corresponding sign on that, pointing toward the best face. This face and edge have become your reference for most future work on the project and are normally the sides that are seen.

Tools

Bench planes

I've made do with two planes for the last ten years, using a power jointer and power planer to do most of the surfacing and thicknessing. I love planing by hand and occasionally will make a project without machines for fun, but surfacing isn't a job that I enjoy enough to do by hand. Bench planes are defined, more often than not, by their length, with nomenclature depending on where you live.

My favorite bench plane is a jack plane, sometimes referred to as a No. 5 bench plane. It is about 14 inches (356 mm) long, with a 2-inch (51-mm) cutter. It is the ideal compromise for planing edges, and occasionally the face, without being too short or too long. You can spend as much or as little as you like on this, but I'd probably look to pay about $40 (£60) to get something that will last and you will enjoy using.

Setting the plane

To get a plane to shave well, you need more than just a sharp blade. As you set the depth of the cutter, the

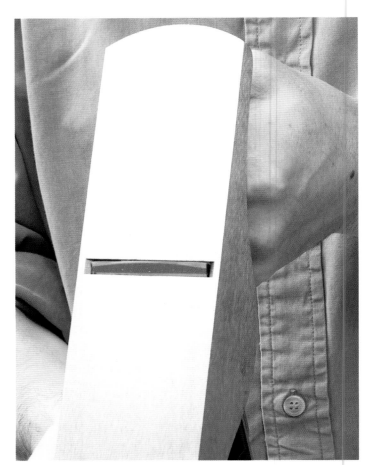

edge will protrude through the mouth. Look along the sole to watch it arrive. Use the lateral adjustment to get the blade level with the sole, and away you go. Drop the cutter farther if you need to remove more wood, and then check that the shaving isn't getting caught in the cap iron.

Loosen the chip-breaker nut and remove from the cutter before sharpening.

Look down the length of the plane sole to check that the cutter is protruding and level.

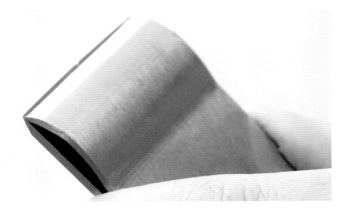

The curved part of the chip breaker directs the shaving out the plane mouth.

It is important that the plane is free of any dirt or dust when you put the cutter back in position.

Materials

What is grain direction?

Just as stroking a cat is easier in one direction than the other, planing is easiest when it is done with the grain, with the fibers either parallel to the sole or pointing downward. Fibers pointing up toward the plane are more likely to tear.

Unfortunately, you can't guarantee that even in the most ideal situation a board will be cut from the tree with the fibers all flat. More often than not, the grain isn't entirely straight, with some species having notoriously spiraling or interlocking grain that can suddenly veer off in all directions. Around knots and defects, grain will often wander and make planing especially difficult.

The grain direction is usually indicated by the patterning of dark and light bands (growth rings) that is common to most species, though to a much lesser and greater extent depending on the type of tree and local conditions. It is almost absent in some species. The lighter bands signify the growth in springtime, when the fibers are used to carry nutrients and moisture to the growing tree. The darker, denser latewood is added over the summer and supports the new growth. The contrast in density of latewood and earlywood can further challenge the woodworker trying to plane against the grain.

Is texture an issue?

The texture of wood varies greatly from one species to another. Oak, for instance, has a coarse texture. When it is planed, open pores are exposed. This can be seen as an asset by people who like the tactile effect or as a nuisance by those who like their finish perfectly flat. Wood with fine texture is usually more easily smoothed, though this doesn't mean the grain direction isn't awkward and the fibers won't tear.

Neither is texture consistent within wood. Those species that have even or uniform texture, be it coarse or fine, tend to be easier to work than those that are described as being uneven. Generally speaking, woodworkers prefer grain that is straight in direction and even in texture. These are certainly the best species for beginners to try.

Some common hardwoods

It won't take a new woodworker long to want to work with hardwood and sample its amazing range of color, texture, and patterning. Here are a few of the best hardwoods to start off with because they are relatively easy to use and widely available.

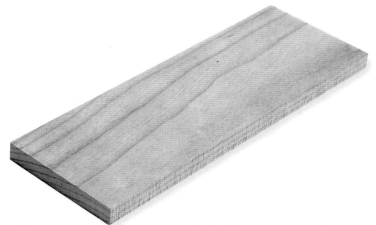

Cherry (*Prunus serotina*) Described as black cherry in the United States and American cherry in the United Kingdom, this lumber is now ubiquitous, offering many of the qualities of mahogany. It has an even texture and a straight grain.

White oak (*Quercus alba*) Straight grained and with few defects, white (or American) oak is good and hard to give you sharp corners and details, but it has a coarse texture for character and great patterning.

Red or soft maple (*Acer rubrum*) Easier to work than its hard cousin (hard maple, *Acer saccharum*), soft maple has more interesting color but fine and even texture.

Simple abrasives

The best abrasive for woodworking, at least initially, is cloth-backed aluminum oxide, which can be bought on rolls and that way you can tear off what you need. When you sand, you start coarse and, grade by grade, work down toward the finest grits. You can get by with rolls of 120, 220, and 320. I also recommend you buy some flexible abrasive pads or take them from the kitchen, where they are used for scouring. Though you can buy all sorts of holding block systems for abrasive, wrapping it around a wooden block is pretty good and will help you keep it flat.

Project **Knife block**

For your kitchen knives

If you buy surfaced boards to make this knife block—and I suggest you do unless you already own a jointer and planer—you will need a plane only for cleaning up after assembly. The construction is simple. You take three boards, cut knife-shaped slots in two sides, and then glue them all together (see page 157).

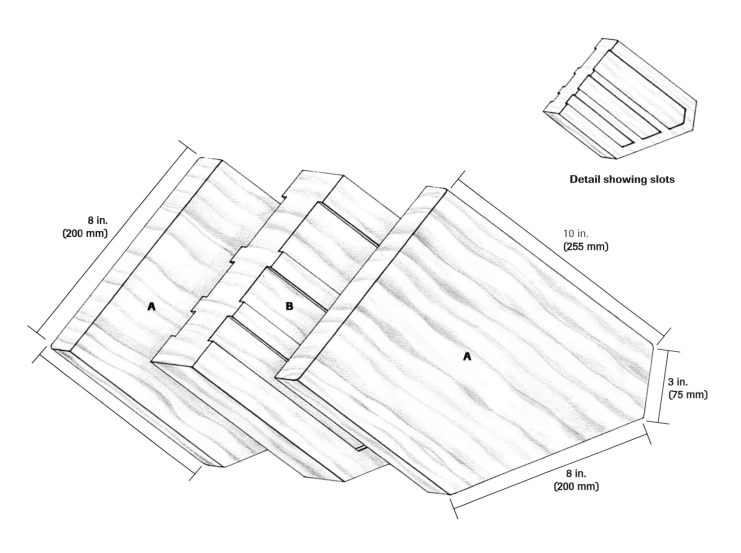

8 in.
(200 mm)

10 in.
(255 mm)

A

B

A

3 in.
(75 mm)

8 in.
(200 mm)

Detail showing slots

Top plan

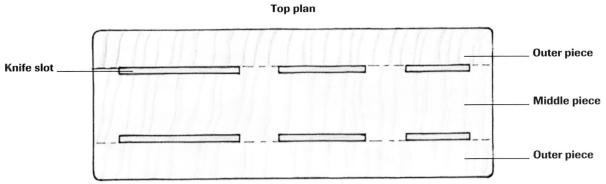

Knife slot

Outer piece

Middle piece

Outer piece

Cutting list

Part	Material	Quantity	Dimensions thickness, width, length
A Outer piece	hardwood	4	1 x 8½ x 12 in. (25 x 216 x 305 mm)
B Inner piece	hardwood	2	1½ x 8½ x 12 in. (38 x 216 x 305 mm)

Shopping list

Extra tools for the job

C-clamps You'll certainly need two and ideally four.

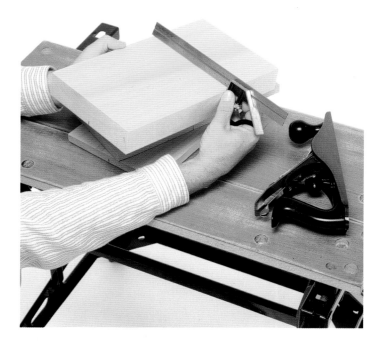

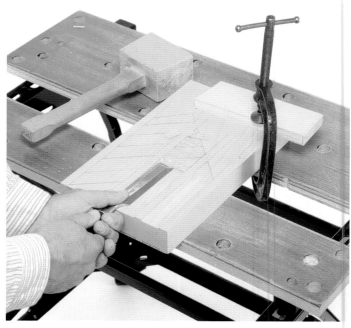

1 Cut your parts to length, with a little excess on each. Don't worry about cutting the angles yet.

Check how well the boards fit together by clamping them together without glue and by checking their flatness with the straight edge on your combination square. Unless there are bumps on the surface, the clamps will probably draw up any gaps, but it's good to test first.

If you have to plane the surfaces flatter, do so very carefully, only take a very little off each time, and always check to see that you are removing just the high points. It is as easy to cause more problems than you'll solve with this sort of flattening, but it is also a good test of your ability to use a plane and to identify where the problem lies.

2 Mark out the knife slots on the central or outer piece, depending on how you buy your lumber.

Chop down vertically around the knife slots, but not too deeply. The slots won't be seen but will be visible where they are cut across the top, so try to be as tidy as possible there. Perhaps leave that section till last when you have learned some lessons on how the grain is behaving and how it's best to work.

Chisel out the slots using a mallet and chisel, with the bevel facing downward if you find it easier. Notice how chiseling in different directions is affected by the grain direction, with tearing more likely one way than the other.

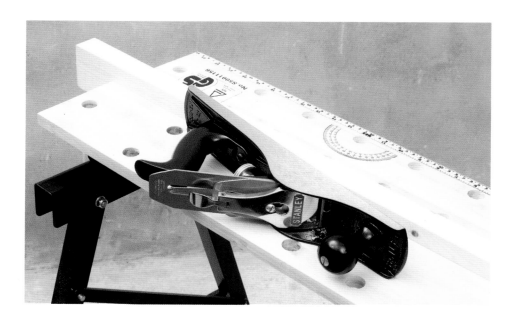

TIP: When your bench plane is not in use, it is sensible to store it on its side on your bench to prevent damaging or blunting it.

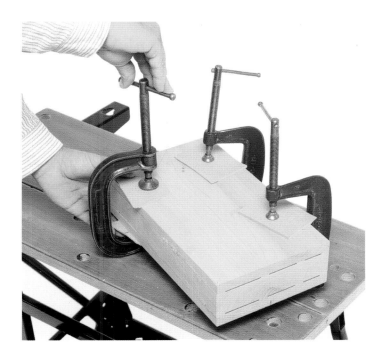

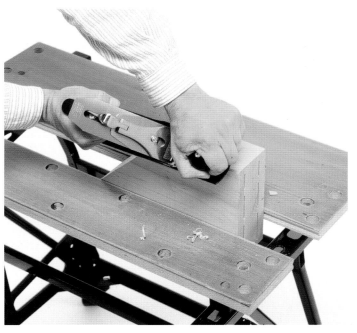

3 Do another dry assembly with clamps to check the fit and get the clamps right; then spread waterproof wood glue on the mating surfaces and assemble.

Once the glue has set (probably overnight), remove the clamps and tidy up the edges with a bench plane. Leave the ends for the moment.

Mark the shape of the final block on one face and cut with your handsaw. One day you'll have a band saw to do this! Holding the block in your vise, tidy up the ends. If you can, use a block plane, since this is suited to working with end grain (see pages 24 and 109).

4 Chamfer the edges with a plane; then use abrasive around a small piece of wood to clean up the block. Finish with a vegetable oil like Salad Bowl Oil, which is safe around food and available in woodworking catalogs.

TIP: When planing a block that has been glued up from boards, first chip away any excess adhesive, since this can damage the edge of your plane cutter.

Lessons learned

- You can clamp boards tightly to overcome some gaps, but if they are too great, you will never resolve the problem and you will need to do further planing.

- It's very difficult to align components when you are gluing with clamps. A dry run helps, but the glue still changes the situation, especially with parts more likely to slip. A good tip is not to overtighten the first clamp and use that only for positioning. And don't expect to get it exactly right—you're better off expecting to do some tidying up afterward.

Lesson 7
The Dedicated Miter

Getting started

One of the first tools I tested as a young journalist on a woodworking magazine was a Nobex miter saw. I'd previously relied upon homemade miter boxes, which guide a standard tenon saw in grooves cut at angles (usually 45 or 30 degrees) to the fence, against which the wood is held. I'd always found cutting accurate miters something of a challenge and was intrigued to see how a dedicated miter saw might improve my joint-cutting.

The measure of the tool's excellence is that I still have it and use it somewhere in the gray zone between regularly and occasionally. No powered option has come near to its accuracy, and that is what the miter joint demands. There is no hiding from inaccuracy when you cut a miter. Even the tiniest of slip or misjudgment is amplified when it comes to assembling the frame. I consider it one of the most difficult joints to cut and am often amazed that so many woodworking books place it as one of the earliest techniques. I would have liked to introduce it later, to be honest, but I just couldn't hold off any longer!

The miter isn't a particularly strong joint, with end grain meeting end grain, but it is tidy and quick. It is invaluable when it comes to joining molded profiles, and for many of the decorative additions you may want to add to your projects. The miter can't be avoided, so you'd better practice the techniques thoroughly.

Lesson planner

Key techniques	Key tools and materials
• When to use a miter joint • Marking out a miter joint • Cutting miters • Assembling a mitered frame • Reinforcing a miter joint	• Buying and using a mitered frame • Clamping miter joints • Glues for miters • Molded profiles • Glues • Choosing abrasives

The miter joint

Accurately cutting a miter joint requires a fair amount of practice and will doubtless involve many mistakes along the way. Done well, it is a beautiful joint, with a neat line at the corner and the profiles or moldings meeting at the joint and then gracefully moving on. In fact, the line of the joint can help to emphasize the shape of a profile or molding.

Unless reinforced with wooden splines across the corner or metal staples in the back, it isn't a strong joint. In fact, normally the miter depends on the glue, and therein lies the problem because the joint is almost end grain to end grain—the most unsatisfactory arrangement in woodworking. The glue doesn't have long fibers to grip when applied to end grain, just as it's difficult to pick up a match by its tip.

The basic four-sided frame employs 45-degree cuts as miters, with more sides lowering the angle. Miters tend to be used for joining relatively thin stock, like picture frames, but are also chosen for boxmaking and interior trim using wider boards. However, the longer the miter, the more opportunity there is for a mistake and for gaps to appear in the join line. However, the miter is a very clean solution for boxes, since there's no end grain to disrupt the lines of the design, and it is excellent for making frames of more than four sides.

Marking out the miter joint

Mitered frames are generally easy to mark out, since you need do little more than cut the pieces to length. It is, however, easy to mess up by cutting a profile the wrong way, producing an external miter when you need an internal one. I've wasted many lengths of picture framing doing that. It is for this reason that I often, unnecessarily, mark up all miter joints even when I'm using a jig, just to remind myself which way to make the angled cut.

More often than not, miters are cut in some form of jig, so you won't usually need to square the whole way around each piece. If you are doing a lot of them, it might be worth buying a miter square for 45-degree angles, but I have one and rarely use it, picking it up occasionally to set the angles on machines.

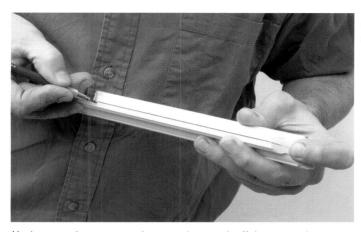

Having cut miters on one piece, use it to mark off the cut on the next one.

Trade secret

Cutting in pairs

The key to a successful mitered frame is that all the components, or at least pairs of components, are exactly the same length. The quickest way to do this is to cut one and use that to mark up others. When cutting complex moldings, it can sometimes be difficult to line up the saw blade with the highest point, so you may need to use the combination square or miter square to mark the highest point on the profile, where the saw blade will touch first.

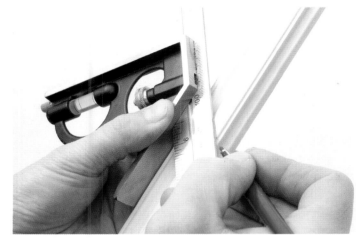

If you are cutting without a miter saw, use a combination square to mark up.

Hold the molding against the fence when using a miter box.

Miter angles

The angle of miter you cut depends on the number of sides to the frame. The simple calculation is to divide 360 degrees by twice the number of sides.

Four sides	45°	Seven sides	25.7°
Five sides	36°	Eight sides	22.5°
Six sides	30°	Ten sides	18°

Cutting the miter joint

Though you can obviously make an angled cut by following a line, most woodworkers quickly learn the benefits of using a guide of some sort to hold the workpiece and direct the saw. The simplest version of this is the miter box, but there is much benefit in buying a dedicated miter saw.

The miter box is very simple to make yourself, either with a single fence at the back, as I have, or with one at the front as well. The saw runs in slots cut across the box. Unfortunately, with time the grooves widen, though it helps if you use Japanese saws or those without a kerf.

The slots in a miter box usually wear after a few years and lose accuracy.

There are countless ways to cut a miter, all of them based on the principle of the lumber being held against a fence. Either the fence or the saw moves to cut the miter. Bench disk sanders can also be used effectively to produce very accurate miters.

Assembling a mitered frame

Another of the challenges of using mitered joints is assembling the frame. Though I will later show you how to cut a locked miter joint, the main problem is that the miters will tend to slip, especially once you've applied glue.

Picture framers have special clamps to hold each corner while a special staple is inserted in the back of the joint. For less specialized woodworking, the best approach is to use one of the many frame-clamping systems developed for the purpose.

Obviously you must do a dry run first, and it is particularly important with the mitered frame to have a flat surface. It is a good idea to keep a plywood board, say 1 inch (25 mm) thick, that you use for assembling frames. Polish and wax it so that dried glue can be knocked off easily.

The slightest inaccuracy in the length or angle of cuts can put the frame out of square, so you must check it before gluing up. The simplest technique is to use a pair

With the frame clamped, use a pair of pointed battens to check diagonals.

of thin offcuts, pointed at one end of each to check the diagonals. If the diagonals are the same, you can be sure the frame is accurate. Overlap the pointers, extend them into the corners across a diagonal, and mark one of them. Try the other diagonal and see if the pointers line up on the mark again.

If the diagonals are wrong, it may just be that the frame is slightly skewed, and a nudge to one corner will put it right. Otherwise the chances are one component is longer or shorter than its pair and you may need to start again. If they are all the right length but the angles are wrong, you should be able to get the diagonals right, but there will be gaps in the joints. Solution: Cut the miters again!

TIP: If you find the miters are difficult to align and keep falling over, a simple trick is to lay them out in a line with the miters facing downward. Then stick them together temporarily with sticky tape, ideally a type that comes off easily later. You will then be able to assemble the frame with ease. This works particularly well for wider miters—say, for making boxes or drawers.

Reinforcing a miter joint

Modern glues are often enough for mitered frames. Picture frames will often survive this way, and boxes with mitered corners are sometimes supported by the top and bottom and the internal framework.

A quick way to reinforce a miter is to cut thin slots across the joint and insert veneer splines or thicker wooden keys. You can do this with a contrasting species for good effect, and it can be done before or after the joint has been glued, but I think it's easier with the miter glued, unless you are prepared to make a special clamping device to hold the joint while you make the cut.

You need only a piece of plywood with a 90-degree corner to make a jig.

Fix the plywood block with glue to a larger piece to make a holding jig.

Making a simple cutting jig to reinforce glued miters is very simple. To a piece of plywood or lumber fix a smaller block, the corner of which you know to be 90 degrees (or whatever is appropriate for the frame). Hold this in a vise, and rest the joint on the block so that you can cut the spline slot. Cutting can be a little tricky, since you will be working against the grain, so be steady and use a fine saw. Practice first.

Once the slot is cut, insert one or more pieces of veneer with glue, and tap home. The grain should run across the joint. Once the glue is dry, pare back the veneer spline with a chisel. When using miters on boxes you can use a series of splines and angle them to mimic dovetails.

If you don't want to see the splines but need reinforcement, you are going to need to insert a loose tongue, dovetail, or spline inside the miter joint. This is not very easy to do by hand and tends to be used for larger miters on cases, for which the biscuit jointer is a good option.

You can use veneer for the splines, the number of pieces depending on the width of the cut.

Hold the miter on the jig to cut the slot for a spline.

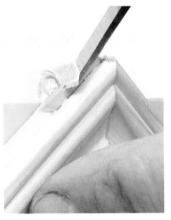

Trim back the veneer spline after the glue has set.

Try using a contrasting spline for added effect.

Tools

The miter saw

For many years, until I bought a band saw, my miter saw was the only guided saw I owned. They are extremely useful for cutting miters, naturally, but also for cutting any piece of lumber to length. The finish can be excellent, and when used carefully, they are very accurate. The best ones can cut slices of wood so thin they are translucent up to a light.

Check that the rear fence is at 90 degrees to the table or bed of the saw on which you rest the lumber. In the past I have lined both the fence and the table with plywood, thinking it would give a better cut, but I'm not convinced it helps and it certainly reduces the depth and width of cut. One benefit of a wooden lining is that it supports

short lengths better. Another advantage is that you can add stops for repetitive cutting more easily, and the lining protects your workpiece.

Some miter saws have end stops you can adjust for repeat cuts. I've never much favored these, since they tend to get in the way and the sharp point of the miter is so delicate that it's easy to align it incorrectly, but I have often used the integral clamps that come with some saws. Most of the time I keep a versatile 24 tpi blade on the saw for speed and reasonable finish.

Using a miter saw

A good miter saw should have stops for the most common angled cuts. You will use 45 and 90 degrees most often, but the others will be useful. Make sure

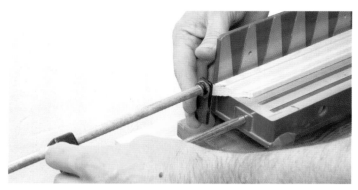

You can set a stop on some miter saws for repetitive cutting.

I have in the past fixed a wooden fence to my saw, but it can restrict the cut.

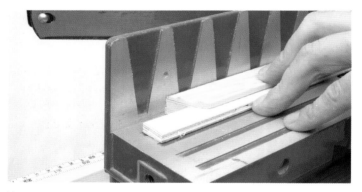

Use a piece of scrap ply to support a picture-framing profile.

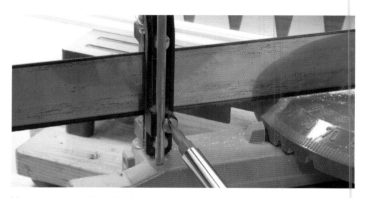

You can even adjust the depth of cut on good miter saws.

these are accurate to the saw. There may also be a clamping device that holds the blade to its set position. A depth stop should ensure the blade doesn't cut into the table and should also allow you to make stopped cuts, if, say, you are using the miter saw for cutting through housing joints or dados.

It is important to hold the saw firmly in the folding bench, or clamp it to a work surface, since it isn't the heaviest thing and will tend to wander as you cut. Line up the cut with your marked line and cut gently, holding the workpiece tightly against the fence. If you can clamp the

lumber to the fence or table, it's a good idea. Otherwise it can easily move halfway through the cut.

If you are cutting moldings for picture framing you may need to support the rabbet with a piece of scrap to stop the piece falling over and ruining the cut. Plywood is good for this job, and you can use the same pieces to adjust a router for cutting the rabbet if you are making your own profile.

Miter clamping systems

One of the most common systems for clamping miters is the string or band clamp that envelops the frame, with

You will often need to support the parts of a frame during assembly.

The string-frame clamp is simple but very effective and easy to make.

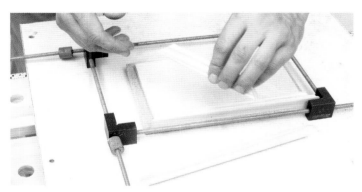

Another popular clamp uses a threaded rod and corner blocks.

blocks at the corners tightening the joints. These can be bought or made. With an L-shaped block at each corner, you simply tighten the string with a tourniquet, but I think the shop-bought version I'm using here is difficult to beat, especially for small frames.

An alternative system is to use a threaded rod instead of string to draw the blocks together. The Veritas version of this works well because the blocks sit so firmly on the work surface, though I've found you often need to raise thinner stock off the surface to get even pressure. It is also a good idea to place a false board in the center of rabbeted frames so that they don't collapse inward as you assemble the components.

Materials

Glues for miters

On-site, carpenters tend to use a two-part adhesive for gluing miters quickly before fixing in place. These combine a cyanoacrylate liquid and spray catalyst that speed up the bond. They are amazingly strong but tend to be brittle, so can't be relied upon for long-term strength.

Specialist cyanoacrylate adhesive can quicken the bonding process.

Moldings

Home centers sell many types of applied molding and profiles in softwood and hardwood. Ideally, you should look out for hardwood moldings that are certified as being supplied from a sustainable source. Once you have a router

table up and running, there won't be as much need to buy moldings, but they are extremely useful for woodworkers looking to add some decoration to their work. Most applied moldings are flat-backed, but some are already rabbeted, especially if you go to a picture-framing product supplier.

Doors can be improved with creative use of applied moldings, mitered at the corners. The best way to attach just profiles is with finishing nails and glue, using a nail set to tap the nail heads below the surface. Tidy up with filler.

Velcro-backed abrasives

Increasingly, abrasives are attached to power tools, sanding blocks, and sanding machines with Velcro. I always hold on to old disks and sheets for some time because a used coarse abrasive can become a perfectly good fine-grade one once the grit has been dulled.

Old pieces can also be used to make small sanding blocks for curved surfaces or for getting into awkward spots. You can buy self-adhesive "hooks" and stick them to whatever you like for sanding. I once made a detail sander this way from an electric toothbrush.

Cork tiles

Cork is a superb material that we should be encouraging because it is produced sustainably. Producers have suffered terribly in recent years with the move to plastic stoppers for wine bottles, which may be recycled but are unlikely to be from a sustainable source. I refuse to call such items corks, as it's an insult to the cork woodlands that have an uncertain future.

I believe woodworkers have a special responsibility to our forests and woodlands, depending as we do on lumber to fuel our hobby or career. I would encourage everyone to question the source of the materials they use and encourage the development of sustainable forests that maintain biodiversity and protect a proportion of old-growth forests until new specimens mature to the age of the veteran trees that are so difficult to replace.

You can buy cork tiles in various states. Some have a peel-off back for quick fixing, and you can buy the tiles sealed or unsealed. It is easy to cut and a pleasure to use.

More on glue

The two-part miter glue is just one of many specialized adhesives the woodworker will collect. I always have some contact adhesive ready for sticking down fabric covering or tiles, and slow-dry cyanoacrylate for quick fixes. This is much more useful, I find, than normal "Super Glue," since it is slightly thicker for a stronger bond, and you have about 45 seconds to make the joint.

Project **Bulletin board**

For notes and photographs

The mitered frame on this bulletin board is actually no more than applied decoration and requires no reinforcement, but it sets off this useful project very well. Don't be fooled by the simplicity of the miter, it is a difficult joint to cut accurately.

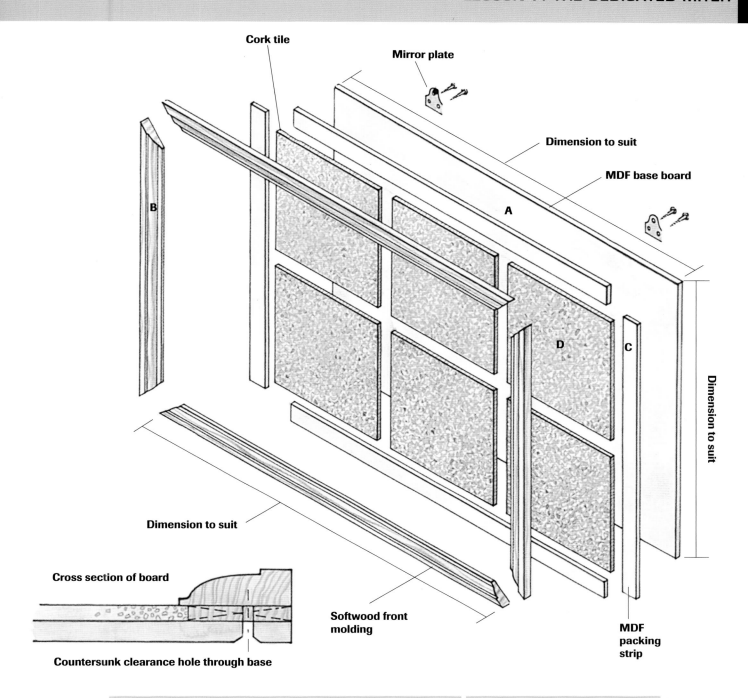

Cork tile

Mirror plate

Dimension to suit

MDF base board

B

A

D

C

Dimension to suit

Dimension to suit

Cross section of board

Countersunk clearance hole through base

Softwood front molding

MDF packing strip

Cutting list

The size and shape of this project relies on the dimensions of the cork tiles you can find, though of course you could cut larger ones to size or build them up from smaller tiles. The thickness of the packing pieces (**C**) sandwiched between the molding (**B**) and base (**A**) must match the thickness of the tiles (**D**) and be ¼ inch (6 mm) narrower than the molding you choose. The packing piece can be made from MDF, plywood, or lumber. With so many potential variations, we are not publishing a full cutting list, though as a guide, our bulletin board is 28 x 40 inches (711 x 1016 mm), and the base is made from ⅜-inch (10-mm) plywood or MDF.

Shopping list

Extra tools for the job

Two hanging brackets
Contact adhesive

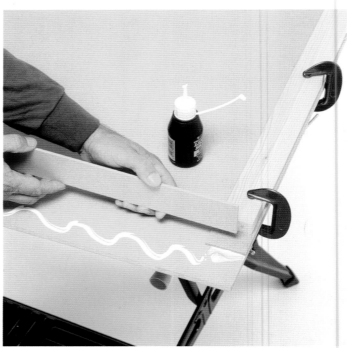

1 Start by laying out the cork tiles (**D**) on the base (**A**), with the base about 1 inch (25 mm) smaller so that you can trim the cork to size once the tiles have been laid. Fix the tiles in place with contact adhesive, following the manufacturer's instructions for both safety and application.

Overlap the molding (**B**) on the tiles by about ¼ inch (6 mm) and measure the size of the base. Cut accordingly with a handsaw or band saw if you have one. I tend not to use a jigsaw for this job, since I get a better finish cutting by hand.

2 Instead of using a packing piece between the molding and base, you could buy rabbeted molding to match the thickness of the cork tiles. Most picture framers will supply lengths of profile. It is actually a neater solution.

Glue the packing piece (**C**) around the outside of the cork tiles, ideally mitered at the corners for the neatest result, though with MDF or ply, a butt joint (shown in the illustration) will hardly be seen.

3 Plane the edge of the base and packing piece, and check the diagonals to ensure it is "square." Drill countersunk holes through the base and packing piece to attach the molding.

Cut the miters on the molding and glue in place on the packing pieces using carpenter's glue.

4 Clean up the joints, and paint or varnish the moldings; then screw hanging brackets to the base and hang in the kitchen, hallway, or a child's bedroom.

Lessons learned

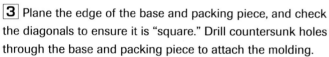

- Miters aren't as easy to cut and assemble as you might imagine. You need care to cut them well and a few little tricks to make accurate frames.

- The approach you take to the making of a project depends so much on the tools you own and the materials you can buy. By using rabbeted moldings to make the bulletin board, you can save a couple of stages and produce a better piece.

Lesson 8
Making Panels

Getting started

Making up panels from narrow boards can be one of the most rewarding of woodworking jobs. Not only do you produce more stable boards, but you are also able to produce wide panels from narrow stock—often an economic approach. Should I ever be employed in a furniture-making factory, it's the job I'd be happy doing all day. Having previously worked largely with softwoods or as a wood-turner, I remember thinking that I'd become a proper woodworker the day I made my first oak panel.

One of the surprises of this operation is that it can be very quick. The boards need only to be rough sawn, with the edges planed straight and square. Then you have to juggle the boards to arrange the grain in a stable and attractive manner. This seems a very suitable end to the first term of woodworking, and it opens up all sorts of horizons for anyone wanting to become a self-sufficient woodworker, unrestrained by the restrictions inadvertently imposed by the normal supply of lumber and tools.

In many ways the first steps into woodworking are a lesson in what you do and what you don't need to do to make some simple projects and some progress. So far, the investment has been extremely low by way of machinery and tools, and there's no reason why that shouldn't continue. I find that the more woodworking I do, the fewer tools I need, mainly because I find which tool is best for specific operations and I don't bother buying tools that only have a vague purpose. And as my skills have developed, I've been able to discard some equipment, though I've rarely thrown out a clamp of any sort, and it is clamping that we will discuss here.

Making panels

It's quite possible to cut very wide boards from a single log. In fact, my desktop is made from a single slab of cedar of Lebanon 48 inches (1219 mm) wide, and it hasn't moved a jot. Sadly it no longer has the delicious aroma of a fresh-cut plank. More often than not, such boards will crack and cup, and quite possibly twist and bow as well. As woodworkers, we have to tame that beast while working with wood's natural forces and beauties.

The simple solution is to use a series of thin boards to produce a broader one, just as you can buy softwood stripwood and just as many work surfaces are made from short lengths of beech, maple, cherry, or walnut. Even if you've bought boards surfaced, this will still be a necessity if you want to make solid wood doors or tabletops. The ability to construct thin panels to fit inside a frame, for instance, enables you to cut thick boards into thinner stock and then reassemble them as panels. This is economical, but you will need a band saw at least.

Arranging the boards into a panel is a skill in itself. The first lesson to learn is that panels generally look best when comprising an odd number of boards. However good your assembly, the join lines are likely to be visible, if only to the subconscious, and the same stern judge will automatically be drawn to the line that often bisects a panel comprising an even number of boards. Three, five, or seven are good options. If the strips you use are too narrow, the join lines will be obvious. If they are too wide and you use too few, the panel is likely to be unstable.

Once you have chosen the boards you need, study the end grain to alternate the growth rings for maximum

Lesson planner

Key techniques	Key tools and materials
• When to make panels	• Woodworking clamps
• How to make a panel	• Sanding options
• Planing bevels	• Marking out tools
• Working with short grain	• Fittings and fixtures
	• Wood stains

Note the unnatural strippy effect (left) and the attempt to match darker parts (right).

stability. Check the edges for knots and conspicuous grain patterns that will show up if they are on a join line. You are trying to achieve something natural, just as you'd expect in natural wood. In the photos (top left) of three strips of ash, you can see that in one permutation the darker band of grain narrows to an unusual point. I would not arrange the boards like this, since it looks wrong. The other way looks better. Once I'm satisfied with the order, I draw a large triangle across all three boards so that they can be reassembled with ease when it comes to gluing up.

Some woodworkers plane boards to be butt-jointed into a panel in pairs, planing the meeting edges at the same time. Then they flip them over to ensure any angle on the plane matches. Personally, I prefer to do one at a time and make sure the edge is straight and true. I like to build up a muscle memory and get all the edges right.

Assembling a panel

To produce a large panel, say for a tabletop, it is a good idea to insert biscuits, dowels, or a loose plywood tongue to strengthen the joints. More important, it helps to align the boards so that they all lie level, and you won't have to waste wood and time planing both sides flat. Dowel rod is probably the simplest with the tools we have so far, but the biscuit jointer is the ideal tool for the future. Use a marking gauge to show the center line on the edges of each board; then clamp the boards together and mark across pencil lines with a set square to show the positioning of the dowel holes. You need a hole every 18 inches (457 mm) or so.

One of my best decisions ever was to ask Santa Claus for bar-clamp stands one year. These support your bar clamps and can transform them into holding devices for all manner of routing operations. Do a dry run

Keep some wooden cauls for distributing clamp pressure along a board.

assembling the panel so that the clamp heads are positioned correctly and you are sure about the arrangement of the boards. By habit, I use a caul to protect the wood from the clamp heads and hopefully even out the pressure a little. I use an old chisel to clean glue off these cauls: In fact, I always keep a semiblunt chisel on the bench ready for doing the sort of tasks that normally ruin an edge. It happens to be an old, long paring chisel, so it also has good reach.

Make yourself an area for clamping up panels.

Use a wedge and alternating bar clamps to inhibit any bowing.

Spread glue along one edge of each butt joint and gently tighten the bar clamps. You should see small bubbles of glue appearing along the join lines; otherwise there might not be enough glue if there is a dip (which you should have already found when you did a trial run). You can use only a certain amount of pressure before the bar clamps start to bend and the boards start cupping. In fact, it is a good idea to alternate the clamps, and you can use wedges to stop the boards at the center from pushing upward. There may be some tendency for the boards to buckle if they are positioned above the center line of the clamp screw.

Once the glue has set, you can plane the panel flat. If you have a workbench, you'll find this easiest against a benchstop, or even quicker with a jointer and thickness planer. Final sanding can be done with a random orbit sander, though the portable belt sander is useful for cleaning up large panels or tabletops.

Planing bevels

The corner cabinet in this lesson requires a fair number of edges to be beveled. This is typical for any project that incorporates angles. The technique is relatively simple, as long as you are methodical. Mark up the bevel carefully, and be sensitive to the fact that the plane won't be flat on the edge, and you will need to get used to using it at an angle.

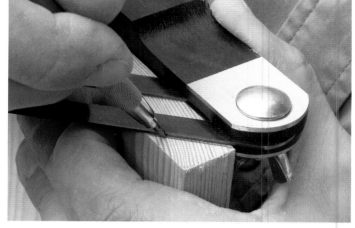

1 Once the board has been planed to thickness and width, score a line a fraction in from one edge using a marking gauge. It is tempting just to plane the point of the bevel to the existing edge, but the trouble with that technique is that you never quite know if you've planed any of the edge away. By planing down to a scored line, you know when you have reached the mark.

Use a protractor to set your adjustable square to the correct angle, in this case 45 degrees.

2 Mark the bevel across the end grain and then set the marking gauge to the bottom of the bevel. This is when it's useful to have a couple of marking gauges—one set for the top of the bevel and the other for the bottom.

Trade secret

Improving clamps

An important refinement for bar clamps is to make pads to protect any wood you are clamping. I've made them here from American whitewood, which is also known as yellow poplar and tulipwood, depending on where you come from, but I have also used plywood, which is less likely to break. These are a fraction wider than I'd normally make them, about 2 inches (51 mm) wide, and slightly more likely to break, but at least they spread the pressure even more widely. You can glue wood or cork pads to other C- and F-clamps as well, using "Super Glue" or hot glue.

3 Having marked the line, start planing the bevel, with the plane held roughly at the angle. Try to keep the planed edge even and straight to give the plane something to rest on. You will notice that you've reached the scored lines when the shaving suddenly becomes a fraction thinner on one or both sides.

Always be sure to mark the line to which you are working when planing a bevel.

Tools

Buying bar clamps

Bar clamps are made to a couple of designs, but the most common in the United States have a round bar, with the clamp foot held by the friction of a clasp of loose steel leaves. This makes it very easy to adjust. In the United Kingdom, the rectangular section bar is more common, with the clamp foot resting against a pin that fits in one of a series of holes. This design is lighter, and though the pins make for more certain pressure, they take time to adjust.

The round bars are sometimes painted, protecting them from moisture and glue, therefore reducing the risk of a reaction between oak and iron. When this happens, the wood can be tainted with a black mark, though it usually doesn't penetrate too deeply.

You can buy bar-clamp stands for both designs, and these are a superb addition to any workshop. Clamp-head protectors are also available.

Other clamps

There are various other styles of clamp you might consider buying. Ideally you need a good combination of all types of clamp, with some small light ones, some powerful C- clamps, and some good access, fast-setting clamps for holding jigs or workpieces to the bench.

The C-clamp. Known in the UK as the G-clamp, the C-clamp is powerful and can be long, but it doesn't have very good reach and tends to be heavy.

The F-clamp. Also using a screw for pressure, the F-clamp has one fixed end with the other sliding along a bar. These give good access and are very fast to adjust but don't always give as much pressure as the C-clamp. They are ideal for fixing machines and jigs in place.

The cam clamp. Based on the same principle as the F-clamp except that the pressure is exerted by the turning of a cam. Pressure is even less than the F-clamp, but they are very light and maneuverable, and superb for sensitive fixing.

The pump-action clamp. A refinement of the "guns" used for distributing silicone, these offer speed, power, and lightness, and are very useful to have around the workshop.

The random orbit sander

One of the most successful power tools to have surfaced in the last 20 years is the random orbit sander. An amalgamation of the disk sander and the orbital sander,

this provides the fine finish of the latter with the power of the former. Because the sanding disk spins in an oscillating pattern, it leaves few marks and yet can remove a significant quantity of waste.

The random orbit sander also produces clouds of dust. Not only must you wear a dust mask or respirator, but I suggest you start collecting old vacuum cleaners and hoses for fitting to power tools to remove the dust at source. They come supplied with a bag, but I find extraction is a far better option.

Marking angles

As your collection of tools and equipment grows, you will be tempted to buy all sorts of gadgets for marking out. Personally, I favor having very few and have grown to love the versatility of the combination square I've been using to make some of the projects for this book. Most of the time I use a simple protractor for marking out angles, but I do love the plastic angle templates that can be used for setting an adjustable square or perhaps a machine. I was given them as a going-away present when I moved on from editing one of the British woodworking magazines some years ago, and I think they are made by Richard Kell.

The sliding bevel is ideal for marking out angles.

All about wood—short grain

In the best of all best possible worlds, to paraphrase Voltaire, the grain in a board is straight and true. But often enough it curves away and in some cases becomes a line of weakness, especially when the piece is load-bearing for table or chair legs. In the case of a chair leg, you're looking out for lines of grain running at an angle across the workpiece. The wood is most likely to split where the grain line runs from one side to the other. Sometimes you can use this grain to your advantage, especially if the component is shaped, but watch out that you aren't creating a future fault.

Where the grain runs at an angle across a board, there may be short grain that can easily be split off (shown here by a chalk mark).

Materials

Foaming adhesives

Once you get into making panels of your own, you will discover the challenges of cleaning up dried adhesive. My solution is to use a foaming polyurethane glue for assembling panels, since it is very easy to clean off with a chisel and won't dent a plane cutter. Other dried adhesive is likely to chip a plane iron. These foaming adhesives react with the moisture in the wood, and you can buy them in slow (a couple of hours), fast (30 minutes), and superfast (5 minutes) types.

Buying hardware

Home centers usually have a good stock of hardware, including locks, doorknobs, and hinges. Poor hardware can really undermine the quality of your work, so it's worth paying a little extra and finding a specialty supplier of solid brass fixtures. Though coated hinges and handles will do for some projects, try to find quality hardware to complement your efforts when it matters. The best

furniture makers will also spend some time cleaning up hardware to remove rough edges and will check that the slots in their screws are all in line.

Water and pigment stains

Often suspended in water but also in solvent, pigment stains comprise relatively large particles that can fix themselves only into the open pores of coarse-textured woods like oak and ash. They give the wood a wash of color that is highlighted by variations in the grain. The water content also raises the grain of the wood, which can cause problems in finishing. You need to wet the surface first, sand it back, and only then apply the stain.

Stained varnishes and oils

You can easily buy varnishes that are ready-colored, particularly for antique pine or mahogany. The trouble with these is that the color sits on the surface rather than soaking deep into the fibers, and you can always tell that the wood has been stained. Also, when the varnish starts to degrade, the blisters will reveal unstained patches.

Dye stains

The best stains, though only available in a limited range of colors, are dye stains. These are made from much smaller particles of color and soak deep into the wood. You can almost see them biting into the surface. They are usually dissolved in spirit or alcohol, and don't raise the grain. Apply them with a brush or cloth.

Project **Wall cabinet**

For glasses or cups

Simpler to construct than you might imagine, this
wall cabinet needs good planing skills and introduces
the challenge of hanging a door on hinges.

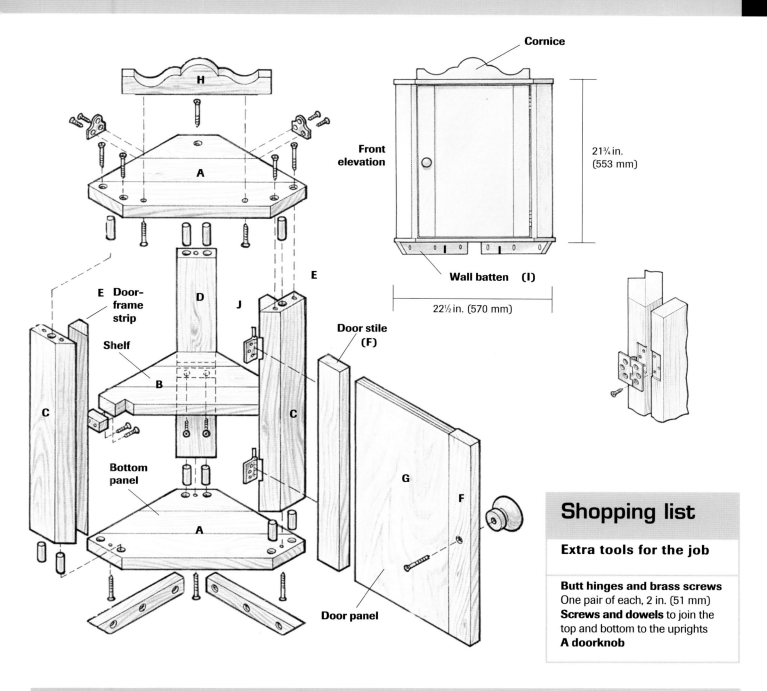

Cornice

Front elevation

21¾ in. (553 mm)

Wall batten (I)

22½ in. (570 mm)

E Door-frame strip

Shelf

Door stile (F)

Bottom panel

Door panel

B

C

C

A

A

D

J

E

G

F

Shopping list

Extra tools for the job

Butt hinges and brass screws
One pair of each, 2 in. (51 mm)
Screws and dowels to join the
top and bottom to the uprights
A doorknob

Cutting list

Part	Material	Quantity	Dimensions thickness, width, length
A Top and bottom	softwood	2	1¼ x 11½ x 22½ in. (32 x 292 x 571 mm)
B Shelf	softwood	1	1¼ x 9½ x 21¾ in. (32 x 241 x 552 mm)
C Front upright	softwood	2	1¼ x 7½ x 22 in. (32 x 190 x 559 mm)
D Rear upright	softwood	1	1¼ x 4½ x 22 in. (32 x 114 x 559 mm)
E Door-frame strip	softwood	2	1¼ x 2¾ x 22 in. (32 x 70 x 559 mm)

Part	Material	Quantity	Dimensions thickness, width, length
F Door stile	softwood	2	1 x 1¾ x 22 in. (25 x 44 x 559 mm)
G Door panel	plywood	1	¾ x 11 x 22 in. (19 x 279 x 559 mm)
H Cornice	softwood	1	1¼ x 3⅛ x 15¾ in. (32 x 79 x 400 mm)
I Wall battens	softwood	2	1¼ x 1½ x 9 in. (32 x 38 x 229 mm)
J Internal support	softwood	3	Softwood offcuts to fit

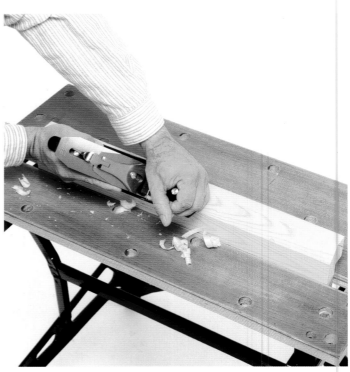

1 Glue up the boards for the top, bottom, and shelf (**A** and **B**), using bar clamps if you have them or foxed wedges otherwise.

While the glue sets, cut the front uprights (**C**) and rear upright (**D**) to length. Don't fall for the temptation to plane the bevels at this early stage: You'll find it easier to drill the dowel joint holes before the bevels are formed. Also cut the door frame strips (**E**) to length.

When the glue has set, plane and sand the panels; then cut them to shape. Make sure the top and bottom are identical and that the back edges of the shelf match those of the top and bottom. Notice how the front edge of the shelf is set back a little to accommodate the door. It is also notched for the door-frame strip.

Drill the dowel holes in the three uprights. Notice how there are two dowels at the bottom to stop the uprights from twisting. Using dowel-center markers, position each upright to the top and bottom to mark where to drill the corresponding dowel-rod holes. Drill and countersink the screw holes in the top and bottom. Drill the holes in the top to fit the cornice.

2 Plane the bevel of each front upright and glue the door-frame strip to the inside face of each upright. Tidy up that joint with a jack plane once the glue has set.

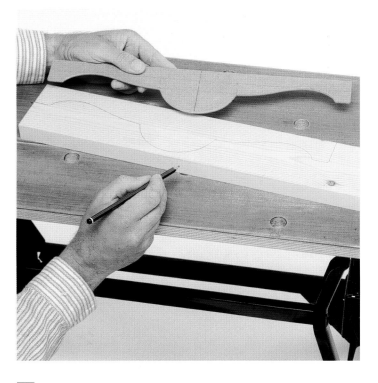

3 Attach the shelf supports to the front and back uprights, and then assemble the uprights and the top and bottom, remembering to insert the shelf at this stage, since it might not fit later. Add glue to the dowel rod, but use the screws to bring the joints together. This is a good solution for anyone who doesn't have many bar clamps and is perhaps using ready-prepared stripwood for the top, bottom, and shelf.

Glue the door stiles (**F**) to the plywood panel (**G**), measured carefully to fit the opening in the cabinet. You could use a solid piece of wood or even tongue-and-grooved boards. Then cut the hinge recesses in the door stiles and uprights.

4 Cut out the curved cornice (**H**) with a coping saw, scroll saw, or jigsaw and screw to the top. Then cut and drill the wall battens and fix them to the walls.

Sand and tidy up the cabinet, and apply the finish of choice. I don't much like the stained effect—which has, however, worked well in this case—as I think it can reduce the impact of the new wood. Use hanging brackets at the top to hold the cabinet to the wall, and add a knob and catch.

Lessons learned

- It doesn't take much to be able to make your own panels, and this corner cabinet would be greatly enhanced by a solid lumber door.

- If you mark up carefully first, it isn't difficult to plane beveled edges on boards.

Building
Your Skills

What you will find in this section

What to Expect

Tools

I am a great believer in building up a toolkit gradually, investing in tools when the need arises, rather than equipping an entire workshop on day one. Otherwise you may spend valuable timber vouchers on machines you rarely use, and you may wrongly that assume new tools compensate for lack of skill. However during this chapter we'll be looking at some essential power tools that will transform the way you work, in both speed and accuracy.

Materials

With improved skills and more equipment you can start working with a wider range of lumber types, notably hardwood. The results are often more pleasing, and hardwoods can sometimes be easier to use than softwoods, but they also put greater demands on your tools and skills, and also require a better understanding of timber technology.

The bandsaw is one of the most important machines you'll ever buy, and a small one will last for many years (see page 111).

Liming is just one of many effects you can achieve with open-grained hardwoods (see page 123).

A good workbench will transform your work, giving you a solid platform and a place to cut and plane (see page 130).

Use contrasting species for dramatic effects, as shown here, where a dark bung has been used to hide a screw head (see page 131).

With time you will develop the ability to find your own solutions, but always protect yourself from the noise and dust (see page 163).

Not all hardwoods are easy to use. Yew wood, in particular, has grain running in many directions and is very difficult to plane without tearing (see page 161).

Techniques

The woodworker has to learn to work with wood in the way it wants to be shaped. Though there are all sorts of new jointing systems available, learning how to cut interlocking joints from solid wood boards is an essential skill and will ultimately give you the greatest freedom. In this lesson we will look at some of the most important joints.

You will learn as much as most woodworkers ever need to know from marking up and cutting a series of mortise-and-tenon joints (see page 99).

Though it is valuable to learn how to plane boards by hand, power-sanding options can speed up stock removal and give dramatic finishes (see page 118).

The corner rabbet joint is just one of many variations of interlocking joints that rely on a good glue lines and shoulders for strength and stability (see page 147).

Projects

This chapter's projects introduce you to hardwoods and various types of lumber and how they can be worked and jointed. Learning the characteristics of lumber is a key skill in understanding what can be achieved.

Occasional table **p. 102**

Child-size table **p. 142**

Hardwood stool **p. 112**

Plate display **p. 152**

Garden bench **p. 124**

Picnic table **p. 162**

Workbench **p. 132**

Plate rack **p. 170**

Lesson 1
Square Hole, Square Peg

Getting started

Though plenty of projects can be made without an interlocking joint, most woodwork involves some mechanical connection between components. Glues, screws, and nails were enough for the Birdhouse project last lesson, but usually these will not provide long-term solidity. The basic and obvious principle of any joint is that a cavity, often known as a mortise, is formed in one or both components, into which fits the other part or a loose piece that joins the parts together. In this lesson we will be introducing the tools and techniques for simple jointing.

Mortises, to use a specific term in its most general sense, come in many different forms, but there are a few types that are more common than others. Learning when to use which particular joint and how to cut it are two of the most important skills a woodworker will ever learn.

The most frequently used joints are the round hole, which takes a loose dowel or round-section component, and the square-side hole, which is the most usual definition of a mortise. To produce this, woodworkers tend to use a chisel of some sort, and it is this operation we will examining here.

When to use a mortise-and-tenon

The best way to join narrow sections of lumber to produce a frame of sorts—as opposed to using wider boards to make a box or case—is with a mortise-and-tenon or a dowel joint. Many chairs are mass-produced

with the latter, using dowels drilled and glued into each component. There is a great simplicity to this joint, and it is very cost effective and relatively strong. However, it is surprisingly difficult to produce successfully for four reasons:

1 You need more than one dowel, or the components will twist. With very thin components it may be difficult to find space for more than one dowel.

2 Aligning the holes in both components is awkward unless you have a special jig.

3 Chances are you will need to drill into the end grain of one component. Doing so is far harder than drilling across the grain, and the drill bit is far more likely to wander unless the component is locked into some sort of jig.

4 Both ends of the dowel have to be glued into a hole. With modern adhesives this isn't a problem, but it does raise the risk of the joint breaking sometime in the future, since glues are more likely to deteriorate than wood.

With the mortise-and-tenon, on the other hand, you fashion a male tenon where you would need to be drilling a dowel into end grain. It has the integral strength of the wood and reduces the risk of breaking because only one part of the joint (the tenon into the mortise) is glued. Cutting a rectangular or square mortise in the other part is slightly more difficult than drilling, but there are simple marking tools and chisels for making the task easier.

Matching the mortise-and-tenon

To understand how a mortise-and-tenon is cut, the following terminology describes the components:

The width of the mortise = the thickness of the tenon
The length of the mortise = the width of the tenon
The depth of the mortise = the length of the tenon
Mortise sides = tenon cheeks
Mortise ends = tenon sides
Mortise bottom = tenon end

Types of mortise-and-tenon

The simplest style of tenon is nothing more than a male

Lesson planner

Key techniques	Key tools and materials
• Marking out a mortise • Using a chisel • Cutting the mortise: removing waste and improving the fit	• Mortise gauge • Wooden mallet • Rubber mallet • How to create a cutting list • Developing a bill of materials from a cutting list

component fitting into a similar hole. This is used in chair-making, often with round tenons in round holes. To give the joint more strength, you can cut shoulders to reduce the risk of pivoting. This doesn't increase the gluing area, but it improves the mechanical fit and hides the mortise from view. These shoulders can be cut on one, two, three, or four of the sides of the component. In this lesson we will be using barefaced tenons, with a haunch (see page 89).

Marking out the mortise

Once you have some machines and jigs, you will be able to cut mortises-and-tenons accurately without having to mark them up individually, but for the moment you will need to mark up each joint. An accurate fit depends on good marking. The mortise gauge is an essential tool for this.

The width of a mortise should be roughly one-third the width of the component to provide the greatest strength. But the actual width should be determined by the chisel with which you will remove the waste from the mortise. It is this width that you set the mortise gauge to mark. First, though, mark the length of the mortise on the component, using your square to mark the lines across the surface. These lines don't need to go around the piece unless you are cutting the mortise through the wood and want to cut from both sides.

Once you have marked the length of the mortise on one component, you can then use this to repeat the mark on other components. This not only speeds up the process but also guarantees that the joints are consistently positioned.

Mark up mortises, avoiding any knots that might weaken the joint.

Adjust the mortise gauge to suit the chisel you use to chop out the waste.

Marking up the mortise is easiest with the workpiece held in a vise.

Trade secret

Holding the mortise gauge

It's good perceived wisdom to plan the components so well that you hold the stock of the mortise gauge against the appropriate face for both the mortise and tenon. However, in my experience, this takes too much planning in the early stages of woodworking, and it's better to adjust the mortise gauge accurately so that you can use it against either face.

Cutting the mortise

Seeing that the width of the mortise and thickness of the tenon is governed by the width of the appropriate chisel, the best place to start cutting is with the mortise. The tenons can then be cut to fit them. The challenge when cutting the mortise is to remove the waste without damaging the sides and ends of the hole, which determine the strength and accuracy of the joint. There are various ways of removing the waste.

With the bevel downward, make feathering cuts along the mortise.

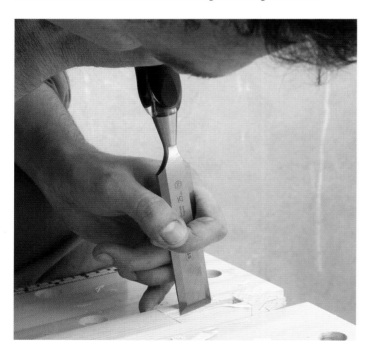

1 Using just a chisel, first cut the edges of the joint with the chisel vertical. You then knock down the ends deeper vertically, initially a fraction inside the marks, since you can trim the joint accurately at the end. To remove the waste this way, you work your way down the mortise, alternating between vertical cuts down the sides and ends, and feathering cuts to take out the wood. This is best done with the chisel bevel facing downward for better access. You'll usually find you have more control of the chisel by tapping gently with a mallet than by trying to force the chisel by hand.

2 A faster solution is to remove the waste with a drill first, but this can also lead to inaccuracy. Once you have the machines, this can be done simply enough, but for the moment you will need to use the electric drill you have around the house, ensuring that the holes are cut vertically or the joint will be angled. You are better off using a narrower drill bit and trimming later with a chisel (see pages 138, 178, and 270).

Trade secret

Keeping the horn

Often, but not always, a mortise will be positioned at the end of a component. It is important to leave some waste on the end of the component, since there is a danger that the wood will split during cutting or assembly of the mortise. This excess wood is sometimes referred to as the horn and can be cut off later, after the glue has dried and the joint is secure.

Tools

Mortise gauge

This device enables you to mark up mortises-and-tenons. It comprises two pins, one of which is adjustable, and an adjustable stock. The best mortise gauges have a threaded adjustable pin, and this is worth buying because they are the easiest to adjust and there should be no reason to buy another in the future. (Mine has lasted years.)

Other tools to buy

Rubber mallet Buy a heavy one that can be used to thump components together. It is equally useful for dismantling failures!

Wooden mallet This is usually made from beech and should last you for years. Check the comfort of the handle in your hand, since you may be using this for many hours, and you don't want to develop blisters.

Materials

The success or failure of a project relies not only on your skills and tools but also on the materials you acquire to make it. One of the most common mistakes is not buying enough or buying the wrong dimensions. Learning how to plan the materials you need is a vital part of woodworking, though the buildup of offcuts from mistakes has its benefits.

Making a cutting list

With every project it's important to make a list of all the components you need. This is known as the cutting list and shows exactly the length you need for each piece, not forgetting the joint. The cutting list relates closely to any drawings or plans you make for the project. In this book we don't normally show the bill of materials, because this very much depends on the available stock and on any adjustments you want to make.

On the cutting list, mark the number of components, the type of wood, and then its length, width, and thickness. This should be a simple extension of the drawings, and you should already have considered it if boards exist for the making of the parts.

The bill of materials

The cutting list is essential in the workshop for working out what you need to cut, but it isn't of much value in the lumberyard, where you need a clearer idea of what you want to buy. You need a bill of materials, which shows exactly which boards you need. However, the yard may not have what you planned, so it's always worth bringing the cutting list as well. It's just that some yards won't be willing to do the entire conversion then and there and will expèct you to have a reasonable idea of what you need.

To develop the bill of materials, you need to know roughly what boards are available and in which thicknesses, widths, and lengths. Length may be determined by what you can carry in the car! Look through your cutting list for parts that complement one another when it comes to board dimensions, though once you have a jointer and thicknesser, you'll have more freedom to mill lumber to the sizes you need. Remember that you can make boards wider or thicker by gluing them together, but it's very difficult to make them longer. Length is very often the determining factor when it comes to creating your bill of materials. Remember when you make the bill to leave a bit of excess on the end of each component for mistakes and natural wastage (see page 156).

Project **Occasional table**

A table of many uses

Though we have explored more complicated mortise and tenon joints in the lesson, this occasional table employs just about the most simple of them—the barefaced tenon. It has a shoulder on the top edge, known as a haunch, and the rails are connected by what's known as a cross-halving or center lap joint.

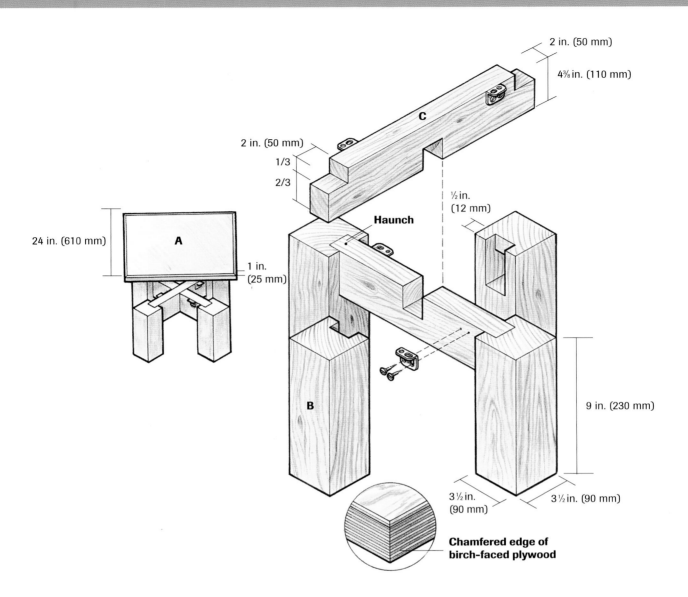

2 in. (50 mm)

4⅜ in. (110 mm)

C

2 in. (50 mm)

1/3

2/3

½ in. (12 mm)

Haunch

24 in. (610 mm)

A

1 in. (25 mm)

B

9 in. (230 mm)

3½ in. (90 mm)

3½ in. (90 mm)

Chamfered edge of birch-faced plywood

Cutting list

Part	Material	Quantity	Dimensions thickness, width, length
A Top	plywood	1	1 x 24 x 24 in. (25 x 610 x 610 mm)
B Leg	softwood	4	3½ x 3½ x 9 in. (90 x 90 x 230 mm)
C Rail	softwood	2	1½ x 5½ x 24⅜ in. (38 x 140 x 620 mm)

This project has been designed specifically with commonly available sizes of softwood, so the design and cutting lists were determined by what can be bought easily. Therefore, deciding what we need is relatively easy. Remember that the thicknesses quoted here are nominal and relate to how they are sold in the yard, rather than the thickness and width of the board you take home.

Shopping list

Bill of materials	Extra tools for the job
Top 1 in. (25 mm) plywood: one piece measuring 24 x 24 in. (610 x 610 mm) **Legs** 4 x 4 in. (102 x 102 mm) S4S softwood: One piece 40 in. (1016 mm) long, allowing about 1 in. (25 mm) on each leg for wastage **Rails** 2 x 6 in. (50 x 150 mm) S4S softwood: One piece at least 51 in. (1295 mm) long, allowing 1 in. (25 mm) or so on the end of each piece for wastage **Steel brackets** Four to fix top to the rails	**Steel brackets** Four to fix the rails to the top This table can easily be assembled with a rubber mallet and held in place by screwing the frame to the top while the glue sets. You should consider buying some 36-in. (1-m) sash clamps. Advanced clamping (see page 180).

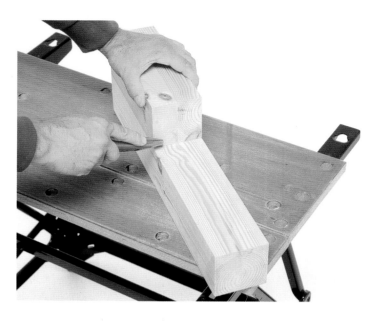

1 Cut the legs exactly to length. Mark out a mortise on one leg.

2 Lining the legs up together at the bottom, use the first mortise to mark up its position on the other legs; then use the mortise gauge on each to mark the mortise. Remember to mark the depth of the haunch on the top.

Use a drill with a 1-inch (25-mm) or 1¼-inch (32-mm) flat bit to remove as much waste as possible.

3 Notice that the tenons will be too wide to be determined by the width of your widest chisel. Instead they must match the exact width of the rails. In some ways this makes the joint more difficult, since the edge of the mortise won't be hidden by a tenon shoulder, but at least, joints will be right under the table and hard to see. Then trim the mortise sides and ends with a chisel. Cut the rails to length.

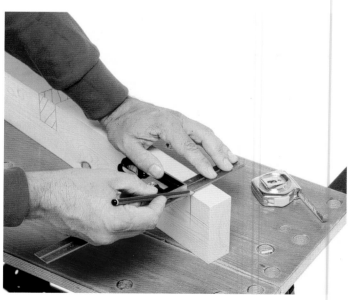

4 Mark up the tenons on the ends of the rails and use a tenon saw to cut the notch for the haunch.

Positioning the cross-halving joint is a bit tricky. The best way is to find the center of each rail along the length and then measure away from the point half the thickness of the rail—¾ inch (18 mm). Draw squared lines down each side at that point, then measure down half the width of the frame and mark across there. You can use a marking gauge for this (see page 44).

5 To remove the waste from the cross-halving joint, cut down each side, making sure you keep to the waste side. It is worth doing this accurately, since it is difficult cleaning up the end grain with a chisel.

Chop out the waste from the joint with your widest chisel, working from both sides so as not to split the wood as your chisel exits.

Use the cut joint to mark up the second rail, ensuring that you position this one on the opposite edge of the rail. If it's not in the right place, you'll have two joints cut in the lower or upper edge and they won't fit together.

Cut out the top, or just clean up the edges if you've bought it ready cut. You can bevel the edges with abrasive or a plane if you own one already (see page 64).

6 Dry assemble all the joints and screw a bracket to each rail. Take the components apart and apply wood glue to the tenons, spreading it across the joint. There's no point gluing the cross-halving joint, since the end grain won't adhere well enough for it to be worthwhile: This joint should be tight anyway and need no glue.

7 Knock the legs onto the rails, then screw the rails to the top to hold the assembly while the glue sets.

Lessons learned

- If the mortise sides aren't chopped out square, the leg will be forced into an angle. You may be able to get away with this on a heavy project like this, but on more refined work, pieces won't go in well and the fit will be poor.

- The tolerance between the cross-halving joint being too tight and too loose is very fine, and though it doesn't make much difference here, sometimes this will be critical both for looks and strength.

Lesson 2
The Ubiquitous Tenon

Getting started

Dovetails might be challenging to cut and a conspicuous example of woodworking skill, but no joint is as important as the tenon. In learning when and how to use the tenon, the woodworker develops techniques and abilities that can be used in so many situations.

There are so many ways to cut this joint, from the simple tenon saw and a chisel, to various jigs, templates, and guided cutters. It doesn't really matter which technique you end up choosing. Whether your choice is determined by the equipment you own, by speed and accuracy, or by the enjoyment of cutting joints by hand, nothing is sweeter than slotting home a neat-fitting tenon.

Though the joint itself is hidden, any defects or inaccuracy in the cutting of a tenon can have significant consequences in both the structural integrity and tidiness of the job. That's what makes the marking up or the setting of fences and guides so important. The tenon can be cut quickly and accurately, and is very easily reproduced in batches, but only if the preparation is done properly.

Marking out the tenon

Although it's not the case with this lesson's project, the key measurement for tenons is usually the distance between the shoulders, since you will often have a tenon at each end of the piece. Mark up the first shoulder, working your way round from the face and edge marks with a pencil and set square. Once you have the shoulders

marked up on one piece, you can copy them across onto the other components (see pages 75 and 180).

Then use the mortise gauge you set earlier for the mortise to mark up the tenon. I tend to do this with the component angled up and away from me, resting on the top of one leg or in my stomach, but you might want to start with it held in the vise. Ideally you will want to run the stock against the face mark you made earlier and be consistent with all components. That is certainly the safest way to position the joint accurately, but you will have to learn how to hold the mortise gauge in both hands, which is a skill worth developing anyway.

Cutting the tenon

The fit of the joint also relies upon the accurate cutting of the tenon.

- The tenon cheeks and ends must be parallel and at the right angle.
- The shoulders around the tenon must be level, or the joint will pivot as it is clamped up.

I prefer to cut the tenon cheeks and sides first and then the shoulders. If you cut the shoulders first, you lose the control the wood offers as you near the end of the cheek cut and the waste begins to break away.

1 Hold the wood in the vise at about 45 degrees, with the tenon facing away from you. Cut down the marked line, which I often make more conspicuous by running a pencil down the groove, keeping the tenon saw to the outside. Do the same for the other cheek.

Lesson planner

Key techniques	Key tools and materials
• Marking out the tenon • Cutting tenons • Types of tenon • Wedges, cutting etc.	• Band saw—Many people use nothing more than a band saw for cutting tenons. If you're searching for a mechanized version of the tenon saw, look no further.

2 Turn the piece around and repeat the cuts. Then position the piece vertically in the vise and cut down to join up the angled cut. Do the same for the sides if your tenons have them. Cut the shoulders with a tenon saw using the bench hook.

3 Clean up where the cheek and shoulder meet using a chisel on an angle, with gentle strokes toward you.

Test the fit in the appropriate mortise, trimming the tenon to fit. For softwoods the fit can be quite tight, as the wood has some give, but for hardwoods it must be more accurate. It can help to bevel the end of the tenon with the chisel to guide the tenon into the mortise.

Trade secret

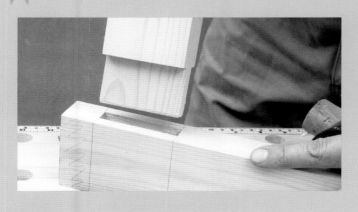

One tenon fits all mortises

One bit of early discipline to learn is to ensure any tenon can fit any mortise when you are assembling a frame. To do this, your mortises must be identical, which will certainly happen once you start mechanizing your processes. Then when you cut the tenons, test them in one mortise. If you don't feel confident about this, make sure you clearly mark which tenon fits well in which mortise, though this takes a lot of thought and can go wrong (see page 221).

Cutting tenons on a band saw

The band saw is ideal for cutting the tenon cheeks and ends because it cuts along the grain so well. This is also a good introduction to repetitive cutting and illustrates how machines can reduce the amount of marking out.

1 Mark out a tenon on the end of a board, possibly an extra piece that you can experiment with but which is exactly the dimensions of the others.

Use these markings to set the band-saw fence to cut the cheeks, making sure the cut is to the outside of the line.

You don't need to cut the full length of the tenon for the moment, just ½ inch (3 mm) or so on both cheeks. Cut away the waste and test the fit in a mortise you've cut already. Adjust the fence accordingly and keep testing until it's right.

2 You can now set a stop to ensure you cut exactly the right length, stopping just short of the shoulder. To do this, you will have had to cut all your components for tenoning exactly the right length. Cut a sample tenon to the shoulder mark on one piece, stop and band-saw and clamp a piece of scrap wood to the fence to act as a stop.

Now you can cut all your pieces; then cut the shoulders by hand. The band saw isn't ideal for cutting the shoulders, as they need to be even more accurate, though it can be done with the miter guide to push the piece and the fence to act as a stop.

Tools

The band saw

It's time to buy your first machine. You could carry on with a jigsaw, handsaw, and coping saw and make superb pieces, but woodworking will become a new experience once you own a band saw. A small one is inexpensive to buy and can be used for many jobs:

- Cutting boards thinner and narrower
- Cutting sheet materials
- Cutting curves
- Cutting tenons and some other joints

You will no longer be governed by the dimensions of stock sold in the local lumberyard or home centers, though you will still need your handsaw and sawhorses for cutting boards to length. Band saws are quiet, take up relatively little space, and cause very little dust, especially if they're hooked up to a shop vac, and should last for years. Shop vacs are relatively inexpensive and better than household vacs, since they can handle high levels of sawdust.

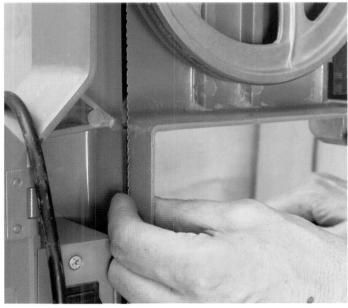

Self-lubricating guides are also available to direct the blade more tightly.

The blade teeth should protrude over the front of the rubber tire on the top wheel.

Get a feel for the blade tension. Most blades need about ½ inch (12 mm) travel.

Attach a shop vac to the band saw to achieve dust-free cutting.

Anatomy of a band saw

A band saw has two wheels, around which travels an endless blade, driven by a motor attached to the lower wheel. Most of the blade is guarded, but for a short section it is open, and it is here, above the lower wheel, that a metal table is positioned to support cutting.

• Band saws are defined by the diameter of the wheels and by the size of the motor. The smallest band saw is a 12-inch (300-mm) model, with a ½ hp motor.

• Guides above and below the table ensure the blade runs vertically so that you can make accurate cuts.

• A shop vac can be attached to the extraction port at the rear of the band saw to keep dust to a minimum.

• The top wheel can be adjusted in two dimensions, to tighten or loosen the blade and to ensure the blade runs on the wheel correctly and doesn't spring off the front.

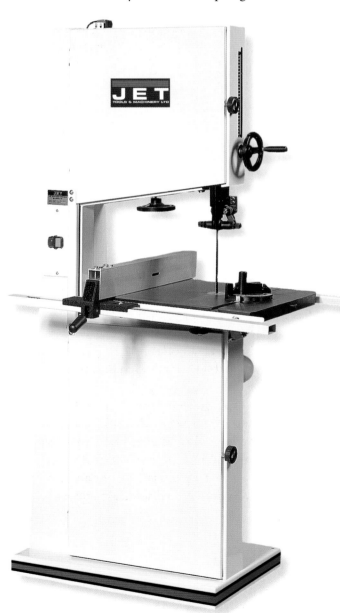

The ideal alignment is to have just the teeth protruding over the solid rubber tire that protects the wheel.

• The table usually tilts to 45 degrees, but only to one side for cutting on an angle with the grain. This can be very useful.

• There is usually a groove in the table for sliding a guide to make cuts across the grain at 90 degrees, an angle of your choice. But band saws aren't known for their accuracy for cuts across the grain, and there are better tools and machines for this job. A band saw will, however, do the job, especially if you take care setting it up (see page 75).

Choosing a band saw

In my opinion, you can't go wrong buying a band saw, even if you buy the smallest, cheapest model. That's what I did 10 years ago, and it remains my main cutting machine. Given my time again, I might just go for the next size up, a 14-inch (356-mm), 1 hp or 1.5 hp model, with a 15-inch (381-mm) table, but the most important thing is to set it up properly and keep the blade sharp.

Some of the features you'll be asked to consider are:

1 Table size (see point 4)

2 Motor size (see point 2)

3 Depth of cut, between the table and the upper guide. The depth of cut is more often than not limited more by the size of motor than by the available space.

4 Width of cut, determined by the distance between the open and closed sections of blade. Though you can cut sheet materials on a band saw, the table isn't big enough to cope with large, broad pieces, so a more significant issue is the distance you can achieve between the fence and the blade. Though the throat is about 7 inches (178 mm) on my band saw, I can only get 3½ inches (90 mm) between the blade and the fence, which limits what I can do.

5 Minimum and maximum blade width. I generally have a ¼-inch (6-mm)-wide blade in the band saw and find this ideal for most uses, but also sometimes fit a ½-inch (12-mm) blade. I wouldn't want a band saw that couldn't cope with either end of this range.

Setting up the band saw

The critical issue with a band saw is to have the blade running smoothly and vertically, without any tendency to twist. There are a few key tricks to achieve this:

1 Keep a stock of new blades. As they lose their edge, band-saw blades will tend to pull to one side and won't cut parallel to the fence. Make sure the join in the blade is smooth, if necessary filing it a little if it is catching the guides.

2 Set up the guides well. The blade should run vertically

without the guides, and it's then just a case of gently tapping the guides within a credit card's width of the blade to stop twisting.

3 Some people file the back of the blade to round it. Do this very carefully with the saw unplugged and then rotate the wheels by hand while using a metalworking file to remove the edge from the back of the blade. This also helps when it comes to cutting curves.

Trade secret

Band saws that don't run true

Often a band saw won't cut parallel to the fence, but you don't want to change the blade. Draw a line along a board and start cutting. You will automatically find the angle the blade wants to cut. Now place the fence at that angle, and the blade will cut parallel. It's not a long-term solution, but it will work for a while. By the way, when buying a band saw, make sure that you can position the fence at an angle like this on the table.

Materials

Band-saw blades

Joined with a soldered scarf joint, band-saw blades are defined by the width of the blade, the number of teeth per inch, and by the shape of the teeth. You also have to tell your supplier the length of blade you need, since all machines are slightly different. I tend to buy 10 tpi regular form ¼-inch (6-mm) blades for detail cutting, and 6 tpi skip-form ½-inch (12-mm) wide blades for ripping boards to width.

You can make your own blades by buying the blade stock on a large roll and beveling the ends with a file or grinder. You then join the ends with silver solder, heating the blade with flux and a blowtorch. When it's cool, you file back any excess solder. This is certainly an economical approach, once you have gained some experience in making the blades.

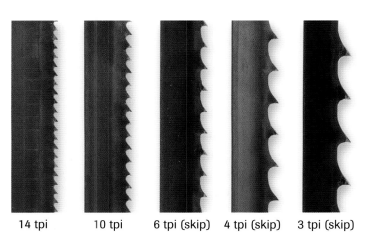

| 14 tpi | 10 tpi | 6 tpi (skip) | 4 tpi (skip) | 3 tpi (skip) |

For fine cutting with a band saw, you need as many teeth per inch as you can get, but a good compromise is the 6 tpi option.

Project **Hardwood stool**

For perching

This three-legged stool looks simple to construct. To make it well, you need accurate jointing and good planing skills, but the result should be a superb piece that will display what you've learned so far. Oak is used here, but other hardwoods, such as cherry or walnut, will work just as well.

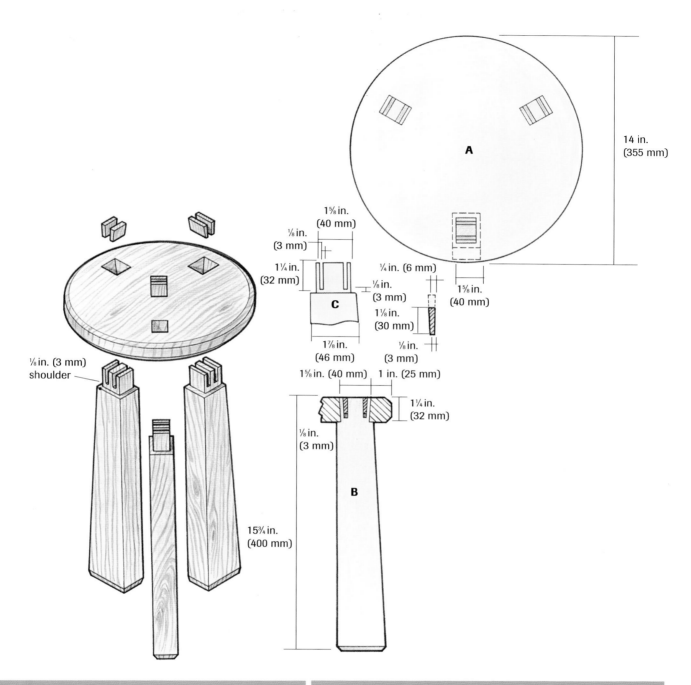

1⅝ in. (40 mm)

⅛ in. (3 mm)

1¼ in. (32 mm)

¼ in. (6 mm)

⅛ in. (3 mm)

1⅝ in. (40 mm)

1⅛ in. (30 mm)

1⅞ in. (46 mm)

⅛ in. (3 mm)

⅛ in. (3 mm) shoulder

1⅝ in. (40 mm)   1 in. (25 mm)

1¼ in. (32 mm)

⅛ in. (3 mm)

15¾ in. (400 mm)

14 in. (355 mm)

A

B

C

Cutting list

Part	Material	Quantity	Dimensions thickness, width, length
A Top	hardwood	3	1¼ x 5 x 15 in. (32 x 127 x 381 mm)
B Leg	hardwood	3	1½ x 3 x 17 in. (38 x 75 x 430 mm)
C Wedges	hardwood	3	¼ x 1⅜ x 1 in. (6 x 35 x 25 mm)

Shopping list

Extra tools for the job

Jigsaw If you haven't bought a band saw, you will need a jigsaw for cutting the top round. The tapers on the legs can also be cut on the band saw or by hand with a handsaw. Using a handsaw will take longer, but there will be less cleaning up than if you cut with a jigsaw.

A pair of sash or bar clamps will help you glue up the top, but this can be done with the dogs of a portable workbench if it's wide enough or with wedges.

Router Later you'll discover how a router can be used for shaping the top.

1 Cut three lengths of hardwood to glue up for the stool top. Check that the edges are straight and square, and align to check they mate well and to see how the grain matches. Once you are happy with the arrangement, draw a large triangle across all the boards so you can reposition them when it comes to assembly. Although you won't necessarily be able to notice where you've glued up boards like this to make a larger piece, always do so with an odd number of pieces since it looks better to have a board (rather than a joint) running down the center.

There will be no give when it comes to clamping up, so there must be no gaps. Plane the edges if you are in any doubt, making sure you don't remove more from the ends than the center.

Glue up the boards with bar clamps or the dogs on a portable workbench, or try using foxed wedges. Try to keep the boards level to reduce the amount of cleaning up later (see page 129).

2 Once the glue has set, plane the top smooth on both sides. It is easier to do this before you cut it round. Set the plane to cut very thin shavings, since there is a risk you will tear the grain, especially as you can't guarantee that the grain direction is consistent between the boards. For that reason you may need to work across the grain or at an angle if there is a lot of planing to do.

Find the center of the board and draw a 14-inch (356-mm)-diameter circle. Cut around this with a band saw or jigsaw, being careful to keep the cut as smooth as possible to reduce the amount of cleaning up later. The edges of hardwood disks can be very hard work to smooth using a block and abrasives. A router will speed up the process (see page 118).

Mark up the top for the mortises, dividing the circle into three. Use a set square to mark around the edges and then join up on the other side so you can mark up the mortises on both sides.

3 Chop out the mortise from both sides, with the top splayed for the wedged tenon. Take great care not to split or damage the top side, since this will be visible and difficult to clean up unless you have a portable belt sander, which you could rent for the job.

Lessons learned

- Do everything you can to reduce the amount of cleaning up you will need to do with a plane or abrasive. Thinking ahead and cutting carefully will save you time later.

- Planing a taper is much easier one way than the other!

- End grain is harder to clean up than long grain.

4 Cut the legs to length, not forgetting the tenon, which you should leave about ⅟₁₆ inch (1.5 mm) overlong, since it can easily be tidied up after assembly. Mark out the taper. Cut the taper and clean up, making sure the tenon isn't tapered. Bevel the bottom of each leg with a block plane.

5 Mark out the shoulders for the tenons. Because the shoulder is the same ⅛-inch (3-mm) width the whole way around the tenon, it is probably easier to use a marking gauge than a mortise gauge to mark up the cheeks. Work on a trial piece first to be sure the tenon will fit snugly in the mortise.

Cut the cheeks and then the shoulders, and then cut down into the tenon for the wedges, stopping short of the shoulders. Don't make the cut for the wedges as wide as it looks on the drawings: It should be one tenon saw-cut wide.

6 Do a dry run, testing the wedges but not tapping them home. The fit must be good because there is no going back once the wedges are tight.

7 Spread glue around the tenon on one leg and knock into place with a rubber mallet. Then glue in the wedges and tap them home so the tenon expands tightly. Do the same for the other legs, either immediately or once the glue has set on the first leg.

Clean up with fine abrasive and apply a finish—oil would be ideal.

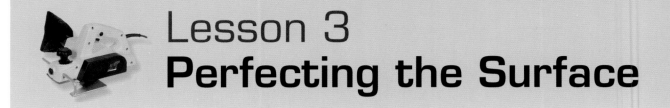

Lesson 3
Perfecting the Surface

Getting started

So far we have really only used the bench plane for truing edges and tidying up joints. Planing a board to thickness by hand is one of the most challenging skills for the woodworker, and for this reason many people prefer to buy a thicknessing machine and jointer for quick, accurate results. I can't say I'm a purist in these matters, personally favoring this approach more often than not, but to ignore the technique would be a dereliction of duty.

There used to be a maxim—and many tutors and craftspeople probably still follow this rule—that the only way to learn woodworking is to build up hand skills first and only then move on to machines. Though I can see why someone who had spent years learning skills would want future generations to follow his path, I consider it a myopic approach that must put off many potential converts. So I sympathize with those beginners who buy a few machines to get going and only later are engaged by the beauty and enjoyment of working by hand.

Whenever I've done woodworking demonstrations at a home-improvement show, the crowd is always most engaged when I'm planing. Planing with a sharp bench plane is certainly one of life's treats. There's no dust, just the hiss of shavings spilling off the bench and the revelation of a smooth surface with a luster that cannot be matched by any machine. Sycamore is a superb wood to practice planing, and with a well-tuned tool you can remove shavings less than 1/1000th of an inch. However, you'll soon want the challenge of taking on oak and other more awkward hardwoods.

Lesson planner

Key techniques	Key tools and materials
• Planing-the-board surface • Smoothing boards • Sharpening planes	• Bench planes • Cabinet scrapers • Using waterstones • Bench grinders

Surfacing the face of a board

Planing a board to the correct thickness by hand is a laborious procedure that requires a sharp cutter and plenty of patience, whether or not you are starting with rough-sawn lumber or a presurfaced board that is just too thick. There will be times when the lumberyard won't be able to supply the exact thickness you need.

To illlustrate the technique, I've chosen a piece of black cherry, which has a fine texture and a benign grain that is usually straight so that you won't suddenly tear the surface. Black walnut is similar, as is white oak, but ash will tear if you plane the wrong way and is hard to work. Just to show it's possible, the photographs show me planing on a folding bench, with the workpiece held against stops using foxed wedges (see page 129). To be honest, though, it is not an operation I'd recommend, since you have to put most of your weight on the bench to stop it jumping about. This sort of planing is best done on a proper bench, which we will be discussing in the next lesson (see page 128).

I prefer placing a cupped board concave side down first and then planing the convex surface. This contradicts the advice you'll be given for planing with a machine, which demands you machine the concave surface first. In planing a convex surface, there is a risk that the plane won't sit flat on the board and you'll end up with a tilted surface that wastes thickness. However, when working by hand, the rigidity of the board is the most important consideration and using wedges to chock up a convex surface can be time-consuming.

Whichever technique you choose, your first strokes will be to find the high ground. Gradually work your way down, watching as the planed surface grows. Keep an eye on how this is happening to ensure you don't remove too much in one spot and always try to keep the plane flat. Remember to press down on the front knob at the start of the stroke and on the rear handle at the end to keep the tool level.

Once the surface is near level, you can start angling the plane to surface in all directions. This will also reduce the risk of tearing—you can acually do some of the planing at right angles to the grain direction on hardwoods that are tearing whichever way you plane.

Once you have one face surfaced, you can use a marking gauge to mark the thickness you need along the edges and across the ends. Use the same procedure for planing to thickness, watching out for that moment when the cutter hits the scored line and the shaving narrows fractionally.

With the plane at an angle to the board, you can gradually remove the high points of a board.

Using a cabinet scraper

When grain is awkward and you can't get a perfectly planed surface without tearing, you may need to turn to a cabinet scraper for finishing. Some woodworkers don't like using abrasives because they believe the grit dulls the surface of the wood, whereas the cutting action of a scraper or plane leaves the fibers fresher. It is certainly true that a scraper can remove stock more quickly than sanding by hand (see page 58).

Generally you use a cabinet scraper once the project has been assembled for finishing, but it can be employed on components earlier, especially if you want to apply a finish before gluing. Hold the scraper in both hands, with the thumbs at the back and fingers around the front. By pressing with your thumbs, you bend the scraper slightly, so that only an inch or so of the edge is in contact with the surface. You can then push or pull to cut with the miniscule cutting hook that you form along the edge.

Take care not to scrape grooves in the wood as you work. You'll soon learn that you can scrape in almost any direction, but watch out for scratch marks in the surface caused by a poorly sharpened edge or a piece of dust caught in the scraper.

Though diagonal planing will normally do, you may sometimes need to plane at right angles to the grain on really awkward lumber.

By curving the cabinet scraper, you can adjust the depth of cut, but you are always aiming to produce shavings rather than dust.

Belt sanding a board

To get the feel of planing a board, you could use a portable belt sander. I've always rented these, usually when I have a tabletop to smooth, but they make quick work of awkward grain and are used in the same way as a bench plane. You have to be even more careful with a belt sander that you don't dip at the corners or ends and remove too much, and the addition of a skirt accessory helps with the leveling and stops the dust from escaping. I always attach the sander to an old vacuum cleaner, ever since the day I forgot to check the dust bag, which got clogged up and overheated the motor.

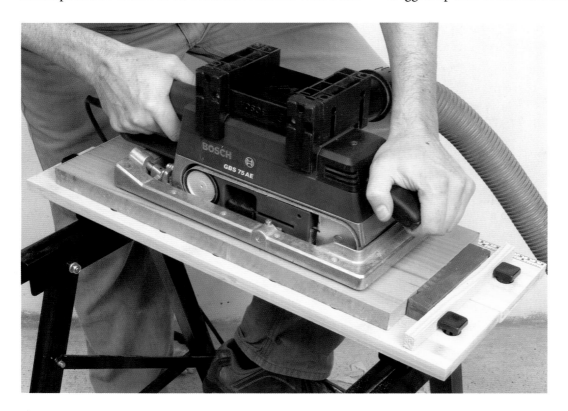

Belt sanders can be used to surface boards, but they are fairly difficult to control because they can remove stock very quickly and are often heavy and unmanageable. Make sure dust is extracted at the source. Notice how the board is held in a portable workbench with wedges.

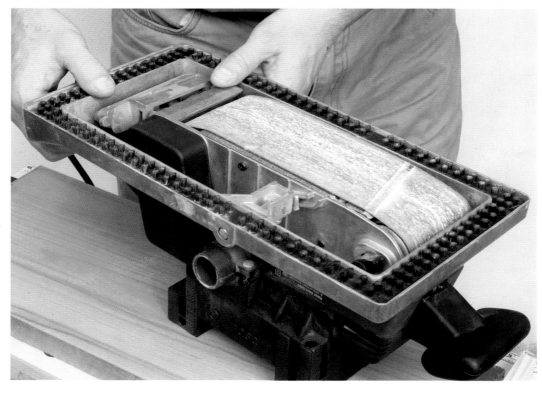

Frames can be fitted to some belt sanders for better control. Brushes give some flexibility but also a firm base.

Tools

Buying cabinet scrapers

Along with rectangular cabinet scrapers, you can buy versions incorporating one convex end and one concave end. There is even a French curve version with an ever decreasing radius. The quality of scrapers does vary, though as a general rule, the thicker ones are probably better. The only way to test, then, is to see how well they hold their edge and how easy they are to sharpen.

Sharpening a cabinet scraper

So much has been written about the sharpening of cabinet scrapers that some woodworkers are frightened off, believing it to be a dark art they dare not try. Actually, it is very simple. The scraper cuts with a hook that is turned over during the sharpening process by filing and by friction.

2 Use a burnishing tool (or the shaft of a screwdriver) to turn the hook over, initially at right angles to the scraper and then at an angle of about 20 degrees, but you should experiment to find an angle that suits you.

1 Start by using a metalworking file to clean up the edge, to remove any vestige of the previous "hook," and to straighten the edge. Filing along the edge also helps get the new hook going.

3 Feel for the hook along the edge: I find the tip of my middle finger is the most sensitive.

Trade secret

Scrapers

You can make your own scrapers from a hacksaw blade, and Rolf Harris, the Australian performer/artist, once introduced me to the idea of using broken glass for scraping. (Remember to use tape on 3 sides to protect your hands.) Using a cabinet scraper is hard on the hands, and the metal can become very hot, so there are various jigs and devices for holding the scraper.

Buying waterstones

Long ago I gave up on oilstones and turned instead to Japanese waterstones. These are relatively soft but can produce the most superb edge. You can also dress them with ease so that any dipping can be flattened. I have two stones: a 3000 grade for reshaping an edge and a 10,000 grade for honing.

This works well, and you can store them and use them in a pond with special holders that invert the stones in water when they are not in use. The pond top is made of glass, to which you can fix wet and dry abrasive sheets for dressing the stones or fettling the sole of a plane.

Slipstones

For smaller jobs, like touching up router cutters, you need slipstones, which are available for all types of stone. Using them is a good way to experiment with different types to see which one gives you the best edge. I often use a diamond slip because they fold away neatly and you can buy them in coarse, medium, and fine grades. I rarely use waterstone slips but have a teardrop ceramic slipstone. These were all the rage a few years ago, and they are lubricated with a little water or saliva. You either love them or hate them.

Using a grinder

To sharpen bench planes, you will need a grinder. Pretty much any one will do, but there are a couple of refinements to make. In time you will want to buy quality stones from a specialist woodworking supplier, but initially it is a good idea to fit a custom-made tool rest. These are wider and much more flexible and easier to adjust to the angle you need. Touch is so important when it comes to sharpening,

and with a good rest you don't need so much pressure and can feel how the edge is sharpening against the stone.

It takes time to build confidence with a grinder, but once you've mastered the skill, you'll be amazed by the neatness of the bevels. Some tool rests come with jigs to hold plane cutters when you are starting, but you'll soon find doing it by hand quicker. Be particularly careful not

The corners of plane irons are particularly vulnerable to overheating when the steel blues and the temper is lost.

It's a very good idea to replace the manufacturer's tool rest on most bench grinders with one that gives you a better platform and wider range of angles.

Redress the wheels on a bench grinder when the grit fills with debris.

to overheat the corners, which will go blue if they are too hot. They will become too brittle to hold an edge and therefore will be impossible  to sharpen. Keep a jam jar of water beside the grinder for cooling the edge. Don't remove the guards from the grinder, and always wear safety goggles or glasses. When the stone has a glossy look and doesn't cut well, you can use a dressing stone to flatten the surface.

Sharpening a plane iron

The process of sharpening a plane cutter with waterstones is pretty much identical to the technique used on an oilstone. With a bench plane, as opposed to a block plane or chisel, most people round the corners after grinding the angle using a small file to stop sharp corners from digging into the wood. You should also work a very shallow curve along the edge of the cutter so that it cuts a fraction more at the center than at the edges, but only a tiny amount. Aim to have a mirror finish on the honing bevel and on the back of the cutter along the edge.

A pond for waterstones is a tidy solution to a messy but effective method of sharpening.

Japanese waterstones need to be flattened regularly on wet-and-dry abrasive, stuck to glass.

Watch for the way the water cascades over the edge as a sign of a well-sharpened blade.

Hone the back of the cutter until it shines like a mirror.

Flatten the sole of a new plane on wet and dry abrasive that is glued to a sheet of plate glass.

Fettling a plane

While you are learning, you won't know which of the frustrations you encounter using a bench plane are because of your lack of skill or because the plane is poorly set up. If tools were sold perfectly set up, the first stages of woodworking would be much easier. The approach you take depends on your character, so don't be concerned if you want to get going quickly and only later level the sole of your plane and make sure the cutter is held flat and tight on the frog. Once you feel confident, take the plane apart completely, tidy up all the parts, and check that the ground surfaces are all flat. Then reassemble it in a better fashion.

Specialized planing tools

There are a few specialized tools and gadgets that will make planing boards by hand easier.
- **Winding sticks.** You can make these yourself, using them to check boards for twist (see page 66).
- **A long steel rule.** Use this for marking up and for testing the trueness of an edge or face.
- **Try planes.** These longer bench planes help in the leveling of a board, as their length keeps the plane flatter, the wider cutter removes more stock, and the substantial weight gives you more power. All of which adds up to greater expense.
- **Power planer.** An alternative to both the belt sander and bench plane. This is very useful for cleaning off old finishes and for very rough boards, since the blades are disposable and easily replaced. But they are quite difficult to use accurately.

Materials

All about wood—sap and gum

Black cherry (*Prunus serotina*) has become one of the most popular species for woodworkers. It has an interesting grain pattern, color that can be used naturally or stained to match mahogany, and an even texture and high luster. And you can buy it from certified sustainable sources. Not surprisingly, it's becoming more expensive. But it's not without its faults. It usually contains some sapwood and can have black gum streaks or pockets that are difficult to avoid and give a dirty appearance, though many woodworkers like that natural feel. Unlike knots, the dark streaks are often difficult to see on rough-sawn boards and can suddenly appear. If it is a concern, make sure you buy more lumber than you need to build wastage into your estimates.

Watch out for sapwood along the edge and dark gum lines on woods like black cherry.

Sanding grades

Abrasives for belt sanders are supplied in varying widths and lengths. The lower the grit number, the coarser the abrasive. The grade you use with a belt sander is usually much lower than you would use by hand. You won't find many sanding belts finer than 180, but you will certainly want to use 320 or finer for final hand-sanding.

Limed finishes

Woods with an open grain pattern, like oak or ash, look superb when they are limed. This process involves the rubbing of a wax/chalk paste into the grain to emphasize the pattern. For an added touch you can stain the surface with a colored water-based stain (see page 49).

1 Roughen the surface of the board with a brass wire brush to open the pores. You don't want to use a steel brush with oak, because any loose metal fibers could get contaminated and stain the wood.

2 Rub liming paste into the grain using a woven plastic scouring pad. These are available in coarse, medium, and fine grades, and are much easier to use for applying wax than steel wool, since they tend not to shed their fibers so readily and are cleaner to use. They are never, however, as hard-wearing as the coarsest steel wool.

A soft brush is ideal for burnishing a wax finish.

3 Before the paste dries, rub off as much excess as you can with a cloth. The harder you work, the more subtle the effect will be.

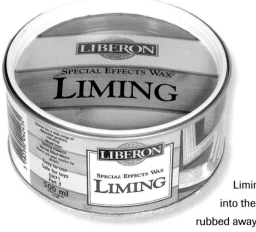

Liming wax is rubbed into the grain and then rubbed away—a subtle effect.

Project **Garden bench**

For the patio or garden

As an introduction to working with hardwoods, this garden bench is both dramatic and easier than you might expect. We used beech, which has a very subtle grain so that the design details aren't lost, but you could use oak or one of the more rot-resistant softwoods, like western red cedar. The dimensions of this bench are very flexible and will almost certainly be determined by the boards you can find. We used beech for all the components, but this is a matter of choice, though for outdoor furniture we recommend wood that is naturally rot resistant.

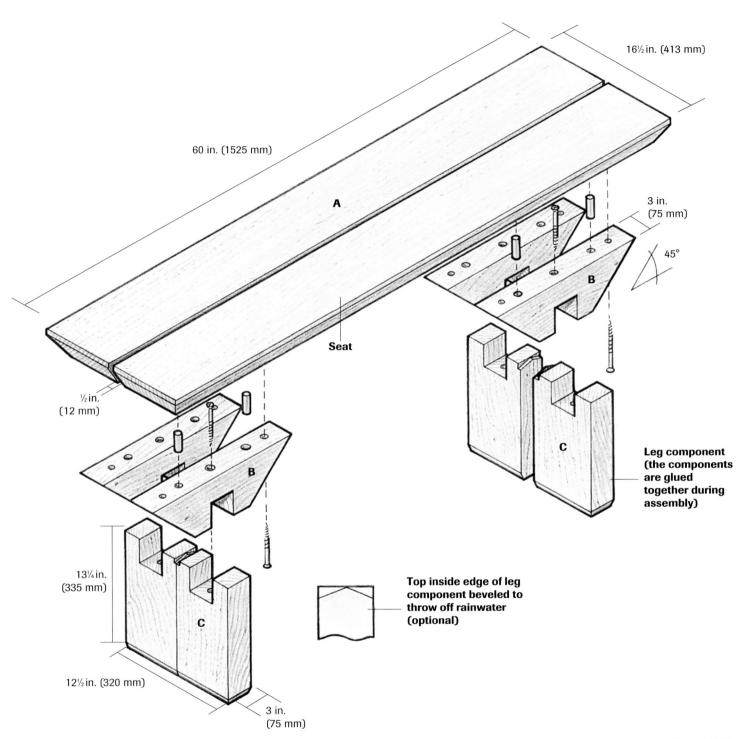

16½ in. (413 mm)

60 in. (1525 mm)

A

3 in. (75 mm)

45°

B

Seat

B

½ in. (12 mm)

C

Leg component (the components are glued together during assembly)

13¼ in. (335 mm)

B

C

Top inside edge of leg component beveled to throw off rainwater (optional)

C

12½ in. (320 mm)

3 in. (75 mm)

Cutting list

Part	Material	Quantity	Dimensions thickness, width, length
A Seat	beech	2	3 x 8 x 60 in. (76 x 203 x 1524 mm)
B Support block	beech	4	3 x 4¼ x 16½ in. (76 x 108 x 419 mm)
C Leg	beech	2	3 x 12½ x 13¼ in. (76 x 317 x 337 mm)

Shopping list

Bill of materials	Extra tools for the job
Dowel rod ⅜ in. (10 mm) diameter for fixing the seat to the support blocks. The dowels are about 1 in. (25 mm) long **Flathead screws** Twelve 10 gauge, 3 in. (75 mm)	If you don't feel happy about planing with the bench plane we've been using to this point, you will need a power planer, belt sander, or a jointer and thicknesser planer.

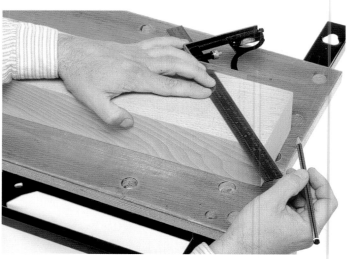

1 We have assembled the legs (**C**) from two boards, glued together with a butt joint. Plane up a length of wood about 28 inches (711 mm) long, and 6¼ inches (159 mm) by 3 inches (76 mm) in section. This is a good length for planing by hand, since you won't need to move much as you work from the beginning to the end of the stroke. You will need to prepare two of these lengths, then cut each one in half.

2 Plane and thickness the board for the support blocks (**B**). This needs to be about 64 inches (1626 mm) long, though you can save wood by alternating the diagonals when you come to cut them up.

Cut the support blocks to length, then tidy up the angled cuts with a block plane and a sanding block.

Once the glued leg components are set, you will need to clean up the joint and level the surfaces, since the butt joint is rarely perfect.

TIP: One way to resolve any inaccuracies in joint lines is to make a feature of the joint line by beveling the edges before you glue up the components.

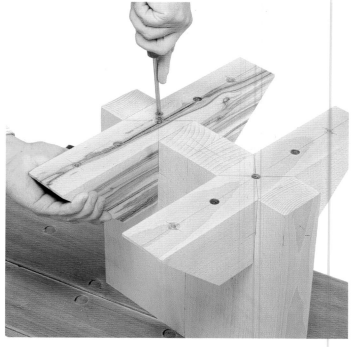

3 Mark up the lap joint between the support blocks and legs, leaving the top of the legs flush with the top edge of the support blocks. Cut down the shoulders with a tenon saw, remove the bulk of the waste with a coping saw, and then tidy up the end grain with a chisel (see page 45).

4 Cut the little beveled notch from the center top of the legs so that rainwater runs off this exposed area of end grain.

Drill the support blocks for screw-and-dowel rod holes.

5 Plane up the seat boards. These are quite long for hand planing, and you will need to shuffle along as you stroke the plane along the board.

A band saw or table saw (see pages 109 and 218) is the ideal tool for cutting the waste off the beveled sides of the seat. Otherwise you will have to do this with a bench plane. Bevel the ends first, by cutting with a handsaw and then tidy up with a block plane. Then you can bevel the sides, as we did for the uprights in the corner cabinet project a couple of lessons ago (see pages 86 and 92).

6 Use dowel center markers to transfer the dowel holes in the support blocks onto the underside of the seat. Drill these holes (see page 57).

7 Assemble the legs and support blocks, then screw them to the seat. Clean away any excess glue (which should be water-proof) with a damp cloth and clean up once set. Finish with oil.

Lessons learned

- Planing and thicknessing a board really does rely on a well-set-up and sharpened plane.

- Hardwoods can be easier to use than softwoods because they bruise less easily and their texture and grain pattern are often more uniform.

- Planing needs a solid platform, so the sooner a woodworker has a good bench, the sooner he can do more ambitious work.

Lesson 4
The Workshop

Getting started

There is a common maxim among woodworkers that you can never have enough clamps. In contrast, you need only one workbench, but the irony is that to make your own bench, you might be expected to need a selection of long bar clamps to assemble the underframe. Fortunately, there are various techniques and fitting to help you build that most important part of any successful workshop.

I have to admit that I bought my own bench from a company exporting bubinga benches from Africa. It's far from the biggest bench in the world, and for a while I covered the tool well to give myself more space for woodworking. I often considered the tool well as nothing more than a dust-catcher. Nowadays, though, I have a good assembly area that provides a flat space for constructing projects, and the workbench has the dedicated task of holding lumber for planing, shaping, and cutting.

For that purpose the best benches are heavy (or held down firmly) and flat. If you can't hold the workpiece without wobble, you've little hope of planing it accurately, and I've found myself perpetually improving and renovating the vices and holding devices as my woodworking skills and expectations have developed.

Drawboring

If you look at old oak furniture and wood-framed buildings, you may notice the ends of pegs holding mortise-and-tenon joints in place. While certainly performing this function, the pegs are also used to tighten

Lesson planner

Key techniques	Key tools and materials
• Drilling into end grain • Drawboring • Pulling joints tight—foxed wedges?	• Anatomy of a bench • Vices • Fittings

1 Drill holes through the mortise with a false tenon in place to reduce splitting.

2 Matching holes are drilled in the tenon, nearer the shoulder to pull the joint tight.

3 Cut lengths of dowel longer than you need. They will be cut flush later.

4 Sand off the dowel edges to make it easier to insert through the mortise-and-tenon.

5 Cut off the ends of the dowel rod with a flush-cutting saw and then sand smooth.

the joint in the absence of long clamps to do the job or, in the case of buildings, the impossibility of doing so. This is called drawboring and is a particularly neat trick.

You cut the mortise-and-tenon joint just as you would normally. Once it has been cut, you drill a hole at right angles to the mortise, usually placing a piece of scrap wood in the mortise as a fake tenon to stop the inside face of the mortise from splitting. With the hole drilled, you remove the scrap and insert the real tenon. With a sharpened dowel the diameter of the hole, you mark the hole center on the tenon. You pull the rail out and then drill a similar hole through the tenon, positioning it a fraction nearer the shoulder than the mark you made.

When you reassemble the joint using glue, you can push a dowel through the holes and it will pull the tenon into the mortise. There are a few golden rules for this to work.

Drilling end grain

Drilling into the end of a board is surprisingly difficult. The wood fibers are designed for the job, and you'll find

the bit wanders, creating a sloppy hole that won't hold a dowel or direct a bolt. For this job you might try using a drilling jig, which is held against the board and helps to guide the drill bit. I'm not too keen on this, because I don't like dowel joints. They are difficult to position, and I don't like drilling into end grain, but they are useful for this particular job. Don't buy an expensive jig, but if you are having problems drilling end grain, it is worth a try.

It's very important to make an indentation when drilling into end grain, or the bit will wander.

With time you will be able to drill vertically just by muscle memory.

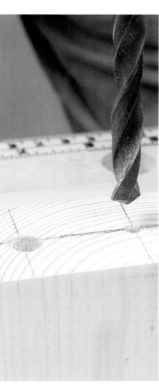

Drilling a narrow hole first can help keep the drill bit straight as you drill into end grain.

Trade secret

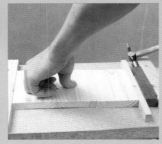

Using wedges for clamping

If you don't have sash or bar clamps for assembling the stool top, you can make your own with what are known as foxed wedges. To a ¾-inch (18-mm)-thick piece of chipboard or similar, screw and glue two lengths of 2-inch (51-mm) nominal softwood about 16 inches (406 mm) apart. Now cut four 4-inch (100-mm)-long wedges, tapered along one edge from 1 inch (25 mm) thick down to ¼ inch (6 mm), from offcuts the same thickness as the stool top. The wedges work in pairs, overlapping to push the boards for the stool top together tightly.

Tools

Anatomy of a workbench

The workbench performs differing tasks in all workshops depending on what woodworking is being attempted, though there are a few basic principles that apply. Many workshops will have at least two benches—one for planing and forming joints, and the other for assembling components. Then there are the many work surfaces used to support machinery and equipment.

The basic bench is built on a frame with legs and shelves, sometimes open and sometimes enclosed with doors. All that matters is that it is heavy and won't move as you plane. The bench top is usually made from thick hardwood, a dense variety like maple, and must be flat as a reference for anything you are working on. Other features include:

1 A vise at the right-hand end. This is used more commonly to clamp lumber against dogs that fit into holes along the front edge of the bench.

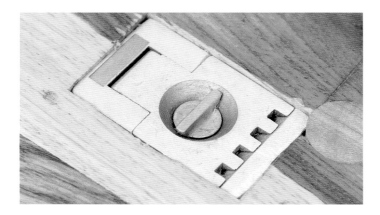

2 A second vise to the left-hand end of the front, used to hold boards on edge for planing and for many other holding jobs.

3 Some benches have a trough at the back called the tool well, into which you can put tools and bits below the surface.

Using a tape to measure

Spring-loaded, flexible steel tapes are useful in the workshop, especially because they can measure internal and external measurements. The hook on the end slides in and out by the thickness of the hook for that purpose. However, no two tapes are usually the same, so once you start using one, stick to it.

The hook of a retracting tape can be used over, and against, the workpiece. These measures may not be as accurate as a steel rule.

Add-ons for a workbench

There is an industry of manufacturers producing sophisticated gadgets for the bench. You don't need them all, but some are very useful.

The hold-down. An L-shaped device that fits into a hole in the bench top and clamps down boards to further reduce the risk of movement.

The bench stop. A hinged metal plate with teeth along the front edge, against which you hold a board for planing.

Homemade panel stop. Designed as a stop against which you can plane wider boards or panels without them pivoting.

Bench vise. Many woodworkers favor adding an engineer's vise when needed for holding odd-shaped components. These can also give you better access around the workpiece.
Board support. I have a hole drilled into the front edge of the bench for a peg to support long boards in the vise for planing the edge or cutting mortises.

Positioning the workbench

It's worth taking some time working out how to lay out your woodworking space. The direction of cut on some machines will regulate how the space is used, but a key criterion is the siting of the bench. You must leave plenty of space around the bench, especially at the right-hand end, which you will be using for holding boards in the dogs. But you also need to be able to plane beyond the vise on the front at the left. If that's a problem, you could position the vise toward the middle of the front edge, but this isn't ideal.

Assembly table

If you have the space, a table for assembling projects is a good idea, with overlapping edges so that you can use clamps around the edges. This lesson's project is ideal for this purpose and for storing tools or lumber. The table doesn't need to be as sturdy as the workbench.

Materials

Making plugs to hide screws

A good way to hide the use of screws as fasteners is to drill a wider hole for the screw head to sit in (known as counterboring) and then fill the hole with a plug. Using a special cutter in a drill, you can cut your own plugs and then glue them in place. You cut the plug back with a flush-cutting saw, and then pare it with a chisel. One of the key skills is to pare across the grain of the plug so that you don't tear the grain. Finally, sand smooth.

The best plug-cutting bits produce tapered plugs for the tightest fit.

If at all possible, keep the grain of the plugs in line for a neater finish.

Tap the plugs home with a smear of adhesive.

Take care paring back the plug, as the fibers can easily tear.

Project **Workbench**

For the workshop

A portable workbench is ideal for many jobs, and
I still use mine around the workshop and whenever
I work on-site. But a permanent, solid bench not only
gives you a better, bigger base for working, it also
allows you to add various holding devices and gives
you a space to store tools. Don't be put off, though—
just because it's large doesn't mean it's difficult to
make. This bench is made entirely from surfaced
softwood, direct from the lumberyard or home center.

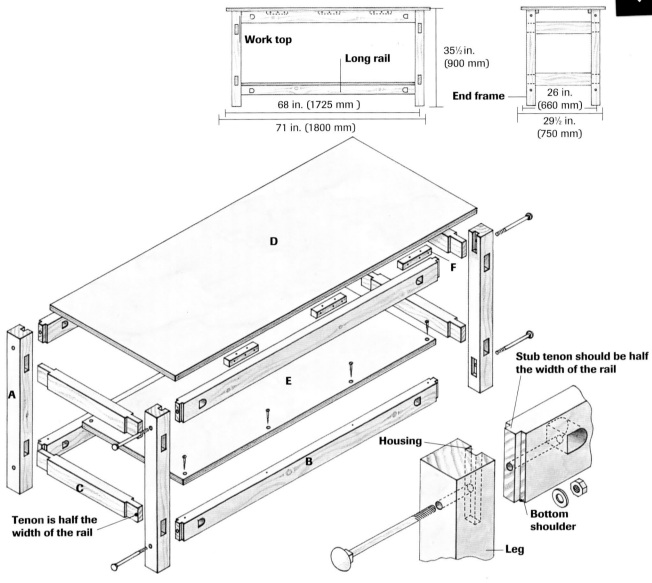

Work top

Long rail

35½ in. (900 mm)

End frame

26 in. (660 mm)

68 in. (1725 mm)

29½ in. (750 mm)

71 in. (1800 mm)

D

F

Stub tenon should be half the width of the rail

A

E

Housing

B

Bottom shoulder

Tenon is half the width of the rail

Leg

C

Cutting list

Part	Material	Quantity	Dimensions thickness, width, length
A Leg	softwood	4	3½ x 3½ x 34½ in. (89 x 89 x 876 mm)
B Long rail	softwood	4	1½ x 3½ x 62¾ in. (38 x 89 x 1594 mm)
C End rail	softwood	4	1½ x 3½ x 26 in. (38 x 89 x 660 mm)
D Work top	birch ply	1	1 x 29½ x 71 in. (25 x 749 x 1803 mm)
E Shelf	birch ply	1	1 x 25½ x 63½ in. (25 x 648 x 1613 mm)
F Fixing block	softwood	6	¾ x ¾ x 5 in. (19 x 19 x 127 mm)

Shopping list

Bill of materials	Extra tools for the job
Carriage bolts eight 7 in. (178 mm) with nuts and washers **Countersunk screws** a box of 1½-in. (38-mm) no. 8 for fastening the blocks and the shelf	**Wrench** for tightening the carriage bolt nut

Softwood parts listed here are dressed dimensions, not nominal. To find the nominal width and thickness to ask for, see page 17. Measurements show inches, with millimeters in parentheses.

1 Mark up the positions for the mortises on one of the legs (**A**). Square the whole way around the legs for the through tenons on the end rail (**C**) and just across the inside face for the long rail (**B**) stub tenons. This will help remind you which is which. Once you have marked up the positions on one, use that to copy across to the other legs.

Normally the mortise should be one-third the thickness of the rail, but in this case, for extra substance, I've gone for tenons half the thickness of the rail (¾ inch or 19 mm). You should be able to set the mortise gauge to mark up all the mortises and all the tenons, so make sure it is accurate. Mark up all the mortises.

Glue the legs using bar clamps and leave to set.

2 Drill and chop away the waste from the mortises, working from both sides for the through ones.

Cut the end rails (**C**) a fraction overlong so that the tenons will protrude through the legs by ⅛ inch (3 mm). Mark up the shoulders at each end on one rail, and then use that to copy across to the others; square the lines the whole way around. It doesn't matter if the length isn't exactly as we've shown as long as the shoulder-to-shoulder distance is the same for all the rails.

3 Use the mortise gauge to mark up the tenons.

You can use a band saw to cut the tenons, as explained in Lesson 7, but these rails are quite deep, and balancing larger components like this on the small band-saw table can be tricky. It is difficult to tell if you are cutting the workpiece accurately. I'd probably cut these by hand—first the cheeks and then the shoulders. Always cut one tenon first and check the fit in the mortise.

4 Repeat the marking-and-cutting process with the long rails (**B**), but this time don't leave the rails overlong, since the stub tenons must fit exactly. The important thing, again, is to ensure the shoulder-to-shoulder distance is identical on all these rails.

Dry-assemble one set of end rails and two legs to check the fit. If you don't have bar or sash clamps, the best technique to use is the most traditional, called drawboring (see this lesson's techniques), which uses pegs to pull the tenon into the mortise. You could also use wedges to tighten the joint.

5 With both end frames glued, mark the position for the carriage bolt in the top of each leg and drill, making sure the hole is true by lining up with a square or by asking a friend to eye it for you. There is a trick you can do with a pair of mirrors, but I've never tried it, because a square and a bit of luck seems to have worked for me. Use a drill bit a fraction larger than the carriage bolt so that there is no scope for wow and flutter when it comes to locating the nut in the rail.

6 Drill out the recess in the long rails for the nut using a flat bit, measuring it carefully so that the bolt protrudes the nut by about ¼ inch (6 mm) once the joint is tight.

Dry-assemble the bench frame, and mark the positions for the holes in the end of each long rail by tapping the drill bit you've just used into the end grain. You can do this joint by joint without assembling the whole frame.

Drill into the end of the long rails, aiming to hit the nut opening dead center. One day, when you're a professional, you'll have a horizontal borer for this job, but for now you'll have to do it by eye. Do this for all the long rails.

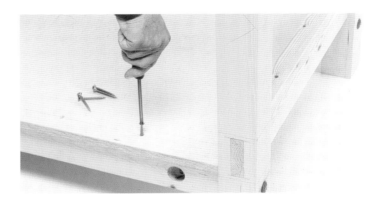

7 Assemble the end frames and long rails, and secure with the bolts. You might need a friend again to help support the ends. Screw the attachment blocks along the top edge of the long rails, with clearance holes drilled for screws into the top.

8 Cut the shelf to size and screw to the bottom rails; then cut out the top and screw that up from below. You are ready to discard the portable workbench.

Lessons learned

- The recesses for captive nuts in the end rails are easier to work with if they aren't just drilled, but a flat side is chiseled so that the nut has better grounding and there is more space for the wrench.

- Check exactly what overlap you want on the top to suit any vises you plan to add. Check also that the height of the bench suits you.

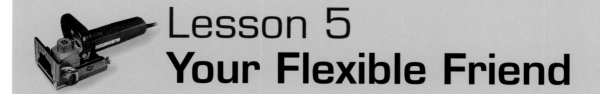

Lesson 5
Your Flexible Friend

Getting started

If there is one tool that sets the woodworker apart from the home improver it must be the router. With an ability to cut joints and add decoration, the router is versatile and flexible but requires dedicated cutters, fences, and jigs to maximize the opportunities it offers. Perhaps that's why there are so many unopened routers in the garages of aspiring woodworkers who've yet to make the leap from DIY.

Perhaps there is also a fear of the router. I've never quite understood this, as the router cutter is normally protected by the "cage" of tool's body. I've done myself far more damage with a powered jigsaw, accidentally turning it on with flesh too close to the blade. In fact, I once demonstrated the inherent safety and brilliance of the router by operating one blindfold at a woodworking show. While not a procedure I'd recommend at home alone (I had a helper at hand in case of emergencies or slips), it proved that a router can be set up accurately and then used safely as long as you are disciplined in your approach.

Discipline is of course a critical component of successful woodworking, not to mention safe work. Any number of safety devices can't save the fool from injury; indeed, there is an argument that too many safety controls make the woodworker dangerously complacent. The router is certainly a tool to respect, but use it properly, and you'll discover the most flexible of friends.

Holding for routing

One of the most significant challenges for routing is how to hold the workpiece without the holding mechanism

To rout across the grain, simply cramp a straightedge across the workpiece.

interfering with the router travel. On a proper workbench this can often be achieved between the end vise and a dog, though more sophisticated products use either the suck of a vacuum cleaner or just friction. Whichever you choose, the lumber must be held firmly, since any movement is likely to lead to slips and mistakes.

Routing safely

Some people consider the router a dangerous tool. In theory it certainly is, but with the plunge router, the cutter can be disengaged and retracted faster than on any other power tool. By using guides and jigs, you control the router, and you should obviously change cutters only with the plug pulled from the socket. For safe cutting, you should always work in the opposite direction to the cutter rotation, just as pedestrians walk against the flow of traffic on country roads. Never use the router handheld with any cutter that is designed for use in a router table, as will be stated in the catalog, and keep the depth of each pass to a minimum.

The router is one power tool that I don't necessarily recommend sucking away the shavings at the source, since any hose can inhibit maneuverability and potentially make the router more dangerous. That said, I would always use extraction at the source if I have to rout MDF or any of the lumbers that irritate the skin or affect breathing. I have

Lesson planner

Key techniques	Key tools and materials
• Routing safely • Routing with fences • Using a biscuit jointer	• Buying a router • Router cutters • Biscuit jointers

added clear plastic to the base of my routers to improve the visibility and keep the base level. You must use a dust mask or respirator, goggles or safety glasses, and ear defenders.

Routing in steps

It is tempting, but invariably counterproductive, to make every routed cut in one pass. Not only are you likely to burn the wood, but there is a risk that the cutter will loosen in the collet and drop into the wood. So take it in small steps. This is one of the real advantages of the plunge router (as opposed to the fixed-base router), because you can usually set three depths that you can return to time and time again if you have more than one cut or workpiece to rout.

Routing with the side fence

The side fence, which comes with almost all routers, is a useful accessory for routing along the length of a board, whether that's to rout a rabbet or profile on the edge or to cut a groove farther in. You can also use a side fence to rout across the grain, but this isn't the best way of doing the job, since the fence will be running against end grain, which tends not to be as smooth as long grain.

An important early step is to add a wooden lining to the side fence, ideally using something fairly hard so that it runs easily. Without the lining, there is often a gap around the cutter, which can lead to awkward jumps at the beginning or end of a cut. You can cut into the wooden lining with the router cutter and reduce the risk of tear-out.

When routing, always be ready to raise the cutter, with your hand on the locking lever.

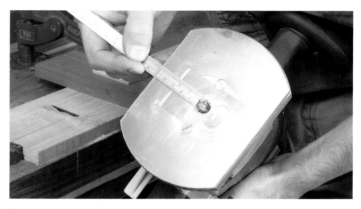

An acrylic sub-base provides a firmer platform. Measure the offset between cutter and side of the base for routing against a straightedge.

The simplest way to use a hand-held router hand is with the side fence.

When taking a series of cuts in steps, do so by adjusting the depth rather than the side fence, which should remain fixed once you've found the right setting with some practice cuts.

Trade secret

Too much of a good thing

It is always a good idea to have some extra lumber for a project, surfaced to the appropriate dimensions to set up tools and machines, and in case of mistakes. One saves so much time by having extra lumber for such eventualities, since it won't necessarily be easy to set up a thicknesser or marking gauge again to achieve the same result.

Routing across the grain

Today's routers, especially the fixed-base models, bear a surprising resemblance to the traditional hand tools of the same name. These are still available, though little used, with a cutter fixed centrally to a metal base to which is attached a handle on each side.

Using bearing-guided cutters

Bearing-guided cutters, whether for cutting rabbets, profiles, or grooves, are relatively easy to use, and little can go wrong by way of a catch except at the beginning of the cut. At this point, the cutter can slip the wrong way around the corner, so if possible, do a very light cut to start, or make sure there is excess on the end of the board. Try to keep the stroke steady so there are no hesitations because you could make an indendation if you stop.

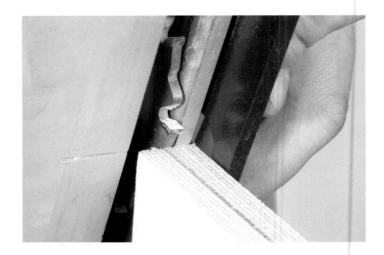

With a bearing-guided cutter you don't need to use a fence to rout a profile or rabbet.

Using a biscuit jointer

Though biscuit jointers can be used for various grooving tasks, their prime purpose is to make slots for compressed hardwood biscuits. This can be done just as you might cut a groove with a router, either against a guide bar or by using the fence that is built into the biscuit jointer. It is one of the easiest of power tools to use, but it is best designed for forming casework joints at corners where the side fence can be employed for both cuts and doesn't have to be moved. A routed dado is probably an easier joint to cut for dividers or for shelves that aren't at the corners of the casework. Joining two pieces of ply is simple with a biscuit jointer, and great results can be achieved in a few steps.

1 Line up the two pieces and mark the positions of the biscuits.

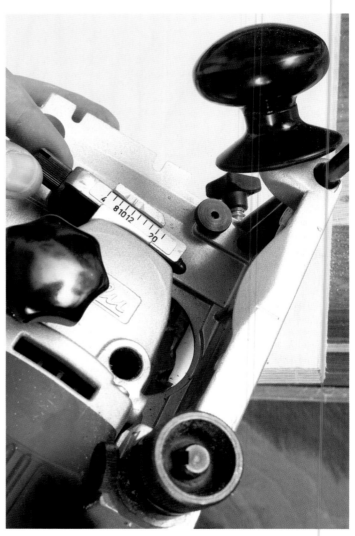

2 Adjust the biscuit jointer to cut roughly at the center of the workpiece. This is done by moving the side fence, then fine-adjusting the blade itself with the knurled knob that moves the blade within the body.

Set the depth of cut. Good biscuit jointers have settings that relate to the standard sizes of biscuit.

3 Cut the groove in the edge of one piece. Notice how much dust shoots out without extraction being fitted.

Now make the corresponding cuts in the face, with the marks lined up through the hole in the fence. Fitting extraction is a good idea.

Insert the biscuits and do a trial run. Once you've applied glue to the biscuit, they expand and you will never get the joint apart.

Tools

Buying a router
There are two types of router. The newest designs are what's known as plunge routers, with the motor sliding up and down two steel columns, inside which are heavy springs. Push down on the handles, and the rotating cutter plunges into the wood for simple cutting of stopped dados and mortises. Release the locking lever at the end of the cut, and the router springs back up again. An advantage of the plunge router is that you can pre-set depth stops on a rotating column so that you can make a series of deeper cuts that can be repeated from one piece to the next.

Fixed-base routers do not plunge so easily, and the depth is set by screwing the body down into the base. This works well for edge routing when you need only one pass rather than a series of deeper cuts, but generally the plunge router is easier for the beginner to use. It is also safer because the cutter springs back up above the base the moment you release the lock.

Routers are sold in different sizes, defined by their motor power and the size of the collet that holds the cutter. The best router to start with has a ¼-inch collet and is of medium size, with variable speed, so you can adjust the speed according to the diameter of cutter. Even the most economical router will make a good introduction, but it is worth checking what accessories can be fitted to the router you buy, since its versatility derives from the ability to use a system of templates, guides, and jigs.

Router features to look out for
• Routers with a spindle lock only need one collet wrench or spanner for fitting cutters.
• Check the position of the locking lever and switch. You need to be able to use these quickly and with the least movement of your hands or fingers.
• Ask how far the collet plunges below the router base. This becomes an issue when fixing the router in a router table because the depth of cut is restricted by the thickness of the table (see page 146).
• Some medium-sized routers have collets for both ¼ inch (6 mm) and ½ inch (3 mm). This makes them more versatile because larger cutters are supplied with a ½-inch (3-mm) shank.
• Base shape. Plunge routers will usually have a base with curved ends and two straight sides. This is ideal for running against a guide. Other routers may have a round base, with the cutter accurately centered.

Router accessories

Most routers will be supplied with a side fence—which is used most frequently for cutting rabbets and profiles along an edge—and some will have other accessories. Even if they are not supplied with the router, check what accessories are available for your model.

- Fine depth adjuster. This effectively converts the plunge router into a fixed-base router, with a very simple mechanism for adjusting the depth of cut. You'll want this feature if you expect to use a plunge router in a router table.
- Some side fences can be fitted with a fine adjuster, which is incredibly useful because fences can be tricky to set accurately otherwise.
- Bushings are screwed to the router base and follow a shaped template that is fixed to the top of your workpiece. You can use the template for cutting out apertures or making shaped pieces.
- Jigs for cutting joints. These can be bought to cut specific joints, like dovetails and mortises, or made in the workshop for specific jobs.

Buying a biscuit jointer

Unless you intend to make a lot of casework from sheet materials or joint up large panels for tabletops, you probably won't need to use a biscuit jointer very often. More expensive models will be a bit more accurate, but the most basic one will do for most home woodworkers. Do check, however, that the blade is tungsten tipped and that you can fit on an extractor.

Biscuit jointers produce an accurate joint quickly and simply, and the compressed beech biscuits expand when in contact with the glue to form a very strong bond. You can also buy various hinges and plastic biscuits so you can dismantle the joint if needed. In addition, there are gluing accessories to assist in applying adhesive to the groove.

The combination plane

One of my favorite hand tools is the combination plane. Along with a set of cutters, you can trench grooves and

Even though routers are quick and accurate, there is a certain joy to beading with a combination plane.

rabbets along the edge of a board, as well as profile with beading and other shaped cutters. I love the way little knives in the nose stop the grain from tearing, and I'm always satisfied when I get it to work well.

Materials

Router cutters

The true flexibility of the router is determined by the amazing range of cutters available. The best way to learn what your router can do is to flick through the pages of a routing catalog and explore the multitude of shapes and purposes. Here, though, are some of the key types of cutter for using the router by hand, rather than in a table (see page 146).

Straight cutters

The simplest of cutters, straight cutters are the most frequently used. These are produced with one or two cutting edges (or flutes), or with a spiraling edge for a finer finish. Only the very narrowest cutters have one flute; otherwise the finish is too rough. A wide range of diameters is available, plus long cutters for working with a router table and for cutting deep mortises.

Bearing-guided profile cutters

One of the simplest ways of applying decoration to the edge of a board is to use a bearing-guided cutter, with the bearing following the edge. The advantage of this is that the bearing doesn't spin with the router and so doesn't burn the edge. Many shapes of cutter are available.

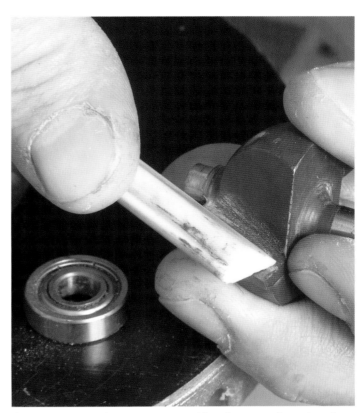

Clean up the face of the router cutter with a slipstone to hone the edge, but take care you don't alter the profile.

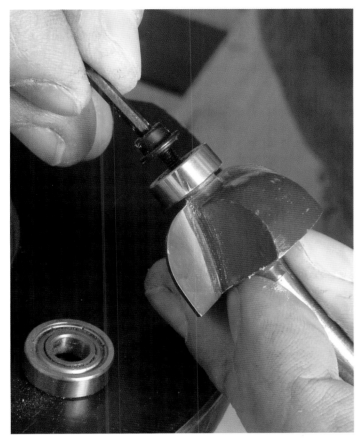

You can change the diameter of the bearing to adjust the depth of cut.

Bearing-guided rabbet cutters

With a bearing attached either above or below the flutes, these cutters can be set to cut a rabbet along an edge. By using different diameters of bearing, the dimensions of the rabbet can be altered.

Trimming cutters

Similar to the rabbet cutters, these trimming cutters feature a bearing exactly the diameter of the cutter. Fix a shaped template above or below the workpiece for the trimming cutter to follow and reproduce.

Sharpening cutters

Because most cutters these days are tungsten tipped, they aren't very easy to sharpen, and there is always a risk that you will change the profile or diameter of the cutter.

However, you can tidy up the back with a slipstone, and soaking them in a cleaning agent can remove any buildup of resin and prolong their life.

All about wood—MDF

Medium-density fiberboard is my least favorite woodworking material, but it has its uses. It is ideal for building simple chairs and tables, as in this lesson's project, but I'd always choose quality plywood first. The advantage of MDF is that you can shape the edges with a router, though this can also be done with the best ply.

Always use extraction and a dust mask or respirator when working with MDF, and watch out for the chips because they can be very sharp and are horrible if they get in your eyes. I would even use extraction for routing MDF because the dust is unpleasant and potentially carcinogenic. Work outside if you can. Expect your tool edges to dull more quickly working with MDF than with probably any other material.

Project **Child-size table**

For the nursery

Biscuit jointed and routed, this child-size table and chair is a good trial for making projects entirely with power tools. The process is so simple that we only need explain how to make a chair. These projects are made entirely from MDF or plywood, with small offcut blocks needed to support the seat and top, though this job could also be done with biscuits. Both the chair and table are made from ¾-inch (18-mm) thick material, which is why the cutting list can be so simple.

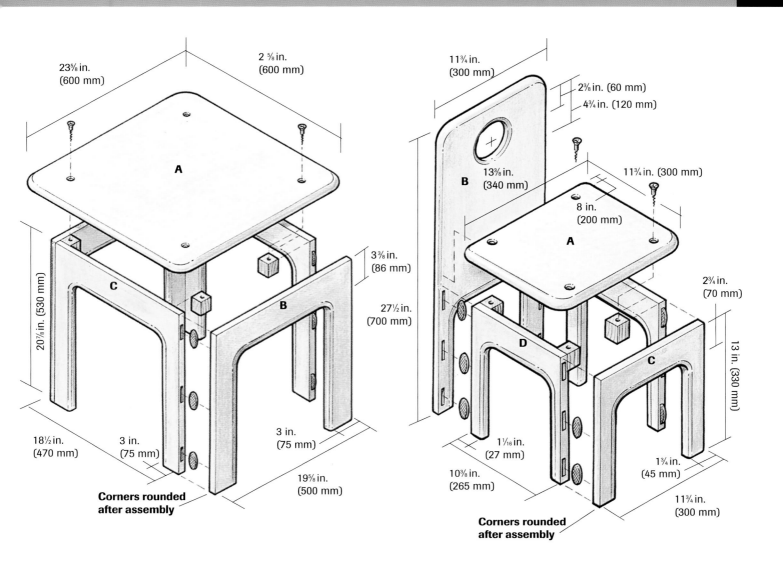

23⅝ in. (600 mm)
2 ⅝ in. (600 mm)
11¾ in. (300 mm)
2⅜ in. (60 mm)
4¾ in. (120 mm)
13⅜ in. (340 mm)
11¾ in. (300 mm)
8 in. (200 mm)
3⅜ in. (86 mm)
27½ in. (700 mm)
2¾ in. (70 mm)
13 in. (330 mm)
20⅞ in. (530 mm)
18½ in. (470 mm)
3 in. (75 mm)
3 in. (75 mm)
19⅝ in. (500 mm)
1⅟₁₆ in. (27 mm)
10⅜ in. (265 mm)
1¾ in. (45 mm)
11¾ in. (300 mm)

Corners rounded after assembly

Corners rounded after assembly

Cutting list

Part	Material	Quantity	Dimensions
Table			thickness, width, length
A Top	MDF or plywood	1	¾ x 23⅝ x 23⅝ in. (18 x 600 x 600 mm)
B Front and back leg	MDF or plywood	2	¾ x 19⅝ x 20⅞ in. (18 x 498 x 530 mm)
C Side leg	MDF or plywood	2	¾ x 18½ x 20⅞ in. (18 x 530 x 470 mm)
Part			
Chair			
A Seat	MDF or plywood	1	¾ x 11¾ x 13⅜ in. (18 x 298 x 340 mm)
B Back	MDF or plywood	1	¾ x 11¾ x 27½ in. (18 x 298 x 700 mm)
C Front leg	MDF or plywood	1	¾ x 11¾ x 13 in. (18 x 298 x 330 mm)
D Side leg	MDF or plywood	2	¾ x 10⅜ x 13 in. (18 x 264 x 330 mm)

Shopping list

Bill of materials

Biscuits 1¼ in. (32 mm) 8-gauge wood screws to fix seat

1 Draw a 4 x 8-foot (1219 x 2438-mm) sheet and work out exactly how you are going to cut the components. Some of the leg parts may be able to interlock to save material.

2 Cut out all the parts, ideally on a table saw (perhaps at the lumberyard) so that the edges are smooth and clean. If you go down this route, you probably won't be able interlock the components, and it comes down to whether you either want to save time or waste material).

3 Mark up the cutouts, using the 2-inch (51-mm)-radius template for the curved corners.

TIP: Designing with sheet materials in mind. Often, how you design a project will have a significant impact on how efficiently you can cut parts from sheet material. For instance, if you build casework, sides anything over 24 inches (610 mm) wide, you are likely to drastically reduce the number of pieces you can extract from one sheet. And don't forget to account for the kerf of the saw, which is likely to be at least ⅛ inch (3 mm).

4 Use a jigsaw to cut away the cutouts. Always wear goggles (and, of course, a mask) when cutting with a jigsaw because it can very easily kick small particles up into your eyes as you watch the cut. In fact, I've had more problems with jigsaws than almost any tool. Cut out the circle in the back of the chair.

Use a belt sander to smooth the internal edges and the curved corners.

5 **TIP:** If you are making a series of these chairs and tables, it is worth making jigs to shape the legs with
a router, template, and trimming cutter. I would make the side, front, and back legs the same size so that one template fits all, at least for the chairs.

Line up the components, marking which one matches which, and mark where the biscuits are to be positioned. Cut the grooves for the biscuits.

Use a bearing-guided rounding over the cutter to round the edges, where appropriate.

Dry-assemble each piece, and then assemble with glue, using bar clamps. You can often get away without clamps for a biscuit joint, since the biscuit expands quickly and the joint is so strong.

Glue blocks to the leg assemblies; then drill the seat and tabletop and screw them in place. Alternatively, you could screw a batten along the top edge of the legs and screw up through that into the underside of the seat or tabletop so that the screws are hidden.

Lessons learned

- The router is incredibly versatile. You don't need an expensive one to get going, and you need only a few cutters. Much can be learned from a routing catalog.

- Routers create a huge amount of dust, particularly when you are working with MDF. You will probably discover that it isn't the nicest of materials to work with, and many woodworkers avoid it completely. Don't assume it is strong because it is heavy: The fibers are actually pretty short, and MDF shelves tend to sag.

- Biscuit jointers are good but not used as frequently as many woodworkers imagine.

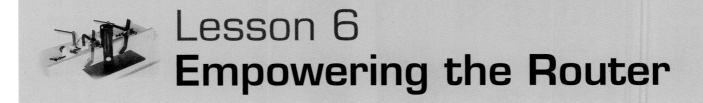

Lesson 6
Empowering the Router

Getting started

If buying a router is the seminal moment that elevates the woodworker from home improver to potential craftsman, making or acquiring a router table is the step that truly maximizes the power of the router. My first router table was no more than a piece of MDF, with the router screwed to the underside. I clamped a straightedge to the table as a fence. It did me very nicely for years, and I've seen professional woodworkers using models of similar standard.

You soon discover, though, that the router table can easily be enhanced by improving the fence and routing grooves for a miter guide. If there is an imperative, it is that the table must be flat; otherwise all the benefits of being able to control the cut will be lost in a sea of inaccuracy.

Though any router can be inserted in a router table, some are better suited than others, particularly when you consider the need to change the cutters and raise the router by grappling underneath the table. Fortunately, a few new accessories have improved both cutter changing and router raising, to make the router table yet more useful and even easier to use.

Using a router table
You work with a router table just as you might a hand-held router, it's just that the lumber moves instead of the tool. There comes a time when boards are large and unmanageable, and then it is better to move the router and hold the wood. However, for most small- and medium-sized components, it is safer and more accurate using a router table except that stopped cuts are often easier using a hand-held plunge router.

As a rough guide, you use the main fence for routing along the grain, just as you would use the side fence on a hand-held router. The miter guide on a router table is

It's worth having a selection of wooden facings for the fence, each with an opening cut to suit particular cutters.

the equivalent of running a hand-held router against a straight edge to cut a dado or similar. You can also use bearing-guided cutters on a router table, though this can be an awkward operation and it is a good idea to use some form of fence to guide the wood onto the cutter. Otherwise it is very easy for the cutting to catch the end grain and send the lumber flying. Some router tables have a pin for this purpose, raised above the surface of the router table.

When you fix a new wooden lining to the fence, you will need to cut a cavity for the cutter. This cavity is ideally wider at the back than the front to give space for the shavings to be sucked away.

The housed rabbet joint
Like one song, sung to the tune of another, the housed rabbet is effectively two joints in one. It combines the

Lesson planner

Key techniques	Key tools and materials
• Using a router table • Cutting the housed rabbet joint • The miter lock joint	• Making a router table • Power tool centers • Router table accessories

The housed rabbet joint is a favorite for drawers and boxes, being simple to cut and offering a large glue area.

through dado or housing (or the stopped dado for that matter) with the rabbet. The shoulder on the rabbet gives the joint more rigidity, and there is plenty of gluing area. It is ideal for corner joints in the making of utility furniture where you'd choose the dovetail for drawer, casework, and box construction (see page 206).

This is a simple joint to cut, especially using a router table—though also with hand tools—and once you get the hang of the technique, you'll be cutting them in your sleep. It is particularly easy to produce repetitively and to set up stops and jigs to repeatedly reproduce it accurately.

Marking out the housed rabbet joint

The simplest way to try this joint is by using material of the same thickness for all the components. By dividing the thickness in two, you can mark up the joint easily, using a marking gauge and a mortise gauge. Of course, once you start using a router table to produce joints like this, you won't need to worry so much about marking up, because it's a case of just setting the cutter and fences.

There are a couple of ways to mark up this joint, and it doesn't matter that much if you start with the dado or rabbet, though generally you want to cut the dado first and fit the "tenon" to that. If you're not that confident with a marking gauge, you can simply measure off the positioning of the dado and square around the workpiece. Or you can set up a mortise gauge and use that to mark out the waste to be removed. You need only a marking gauge to mark up the rabbet on the other piece.

Mark out the first joint carefully, and use that to position cutters for making the rest of the joint.

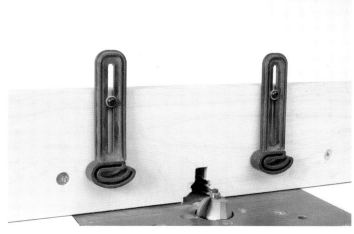

Using hold-downs, means you don't need to have fingers close to the cutter as you push the workpiece across the router table.

Cutting the joint

However you mark up the joint, it's a good idea to do a trial first to get used to the technique because it can be a bit confusing. Cutting a housing or dado with a saw and chisel was one of the first techniques I was taught at school, but the saw is very difficult to control across the width of the board.

1 With the joint marked up, saw down the shoulders of the dado, stopping a fraction short of the bottom. It's safer to do this than to risk cutting too deep. The wood you leave between the dado and the end of the workpiece is likely to be very short and hence is vulnerable. Take care of it.

3 Cut down the shoulder of the rabbet, and chisel away the waste, first with the grain using a mallet and then across the grain for a smooth finish just with hand pressure. Test the fit.

2 Chisel out the waste, making sure you work from both ends so as not to tear the grain. An alternative technique is to hold the workpiece against the fence of a bench hook and chisel toward the fence to reduce the risk of tear-out.

Cutting the housed rabbet on a router table

You can look at the cutting of the dado in two ways. In one approach, you cut the component exactly to length and work off the ends. This is the easy way and works well enough. You simply use the fence on the router table as a stop and push the component across the cutter with the miter guide.

The alternative approach, perhaps for making a box or drawer, is to consider the distance between the dados as the critical issue. In this case, you can leave the component about ½ inch (13 mm) overlong. You cut the first dado roughly in the right position, but for the second dado you set up a jig, with the first dado dropping over a tongue that is fixed to the miter guide at the appropriate point. You rout the first dado on all your components and then rout the second one using the jig. This is perfect if you have a series of identical boxes or drawers to make, as is the case for this lesson's project.

Once the dado is cut, you can rout the rabbets on the ends of the other part. You cut this workpiece exactly to length because it has to fit perfectly into the housing. All these parts must be cut neatly to exactly the same length. Then you use the miter guide to push the lumber over the cutter. You can cut the rabbet with the end against the fence or by using a bearing-guide rabbeting cutter. Do all the housed pieces first (with some extras in case of mistakes) and then do all the rabbets to fit.

When it comes to assembling the joint, there will be extra on the ends of the housed pieces. These are known as the horns. Leave them on at this stage, and then plane or sand them off once the joint has been assembled and the glue has set.

Cutting a miter-lock joint

A neat alternative to the housed rabbet joint is the miter-lock joint. Just as the housed rabbet combines two joints, the miter lock is part miter, part rabbet. It is produced by using a 45-degree cutter and a straight cutter, and the advantage, once you have set up the router table, is that it

is very easy to glue up because the miter doesn't slide about (see page 74).

1 Cut the parts to length and rout a 45-degree miter across the ends of one part. You could do this with a miter saw (see page 77).

2 Insert a straight cutter into the router table and cut a rabbet from the miter.

3 Put the 45-degree cutter back in the router and gradually raise the cutter and move the fence until it is cutting a stepped shape that is a perfect fit in the other piece.

Tools

Making machines of power tools

The router table is one of the few occasions when I'd advocate the conversion of power tools into machines by fixing them into some kind of stand or table. If you are woodworking on a limited budget or have very

Use a 45-degree cutter to rout the miters.

The joint combines rabbet and miter.

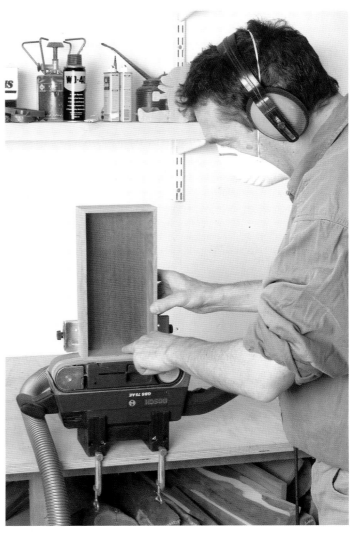

Some belt sanders have a frame and fence for working as a pad sander.

limited space but have plenty of time, there is an argument for buying a work center into which you fit your power tools so that they can either be used hand-held or as machines.

Though some of these work centers are actually very well made—and plenty of woodworkers have startling results with them—I have always found the situation to be a compromise, and I don't like having to waste time changing tools around. I'd rather have fewer dedicated machines and adapt my techniques to suit what I own.

The router table, however, does make a superb substitute for the shaper; indeed, for many home woodworkers it is more than enough. I also use a drill in a drill stand, but only for drum sanding and because I've come to own so many drills. I have a portable belt sander that was supplied with a stand for using it upside down. This has proved very useful for cleaning up joints when a bench disk-sander would mark the wood with telltale curved scratches.

Making a router table

You can buy superb router tables, but they are very simple to make and in the early stages you are well able to experiment with one of your own. Cheap router tables are not hugely accurate, and you may find them more frustrating than the one you make yourself. Only by learning what makes a good or bad router table will you come to realize what you need to buy and understand what an invaluable piece it is.

1 The table must be flat. Probably the best material for this is a dense plastic, known commonly as Tufnol. The ½-inch (13-mm) or ⅝-inch (16-mm) thickness should be enough, though you can reinforce the underside with ribs. Drill the table to suit the holes in the router base and screw in place.

2 For a fence, you can simply clamp a straightedge to the table. This will at least do for a while. As your skills grow, you will want a proper fence, which you can adjust easily and finely. These can be bought on their own. The fence must be able to take a changeable wooden lining, which will have to be replaced from time to time.

3 You must be able to fix some sort of extraction behind the fence, using hose or plastic pipe. Otherwise the cutter will get clogged with shavings and won't perform very well.

4 By routing a groove along the table, you can make a miter guide with which you can push lumber across the cutter. This makes for steadier progress.

5 To cope with router cutters of varying diameters, you can cut an access hole where the cutter protrudes. The trick is to have a rabbet on the top face of this circular aperture and then make rabbeted rings that fit inside this hole, level with the table surface.

6 Featherboards work as springs to hold the workpiece against the fence and also as a ratchet to stop the lumber from kicking back toward the operator. You can buy these to fit in the miter-guide groove or to clamp or screw to the table. You can make one yourself by creating a series of angled cuts in a piece of hardwood that has some flexibility.

The featherboard pushes the workpiece against the fence and reduces any risk of kickback.

The miter guide is useful for making routed cuts across a board, but first the main fence must be at right angles to the miter fence.

Accessories for the router table

Remote switch It is a good idea to buy a remote switch for the router table so you don't have to search for the router switch when you need to turn off in a hurry. The router is plugged into the back of the switch instead of directly to the power supply.

Collet extension Whatever material you use for the router table, you will lose some depth of cut, even if the router's collet protrudes through its base. A solution to this is to buy a collet extension, which fits into the existing collet. Some of these have the added benefit of needing only a single hex key to tighten and loosen the cutter, which makes access under the table far easier.

Router lifter There are now various gadgets that help you raise the router in the table from above. This makes fine adjustment easier and improves the whole experience.

Miniature brass bar clamps Few miniature tools are particularly useful, but small brass bar clamps are well worth their low cost. They are ideal for assembling small boxes and drawers.

A collet extension improves the depth of cut by raising the cutter.

With a device for raising the router, you no longer need to fiddle underneath the table to set the depth of cut.

Trade secret

A router for the router table

Though it is a good idea to buy a small- or medium-sized router for hand-held operations, a table-mounted router has other qualities to look out for. Fixed-base routers, for a start, are good for router tables because they incorporate fine height adjustment. Choose a larger router, and one that can take ½-in. (13-mm) cutters because the router table enables you to use far bigger cutters than for hand-held operations (see page 137).

Do consider, however, the method of changing the cutter. Under the router table you will have much more limited access, and fiddling around with two wrenches can be very awkward.

Project **Plate display**

For the kitchen or dining room

This introduction to making drawers uses housed rabbet joints rather than dovetails. The sides and shelves of the plate-display unit are held together with wedged tenons. The length of the shelves and drawer dividers does not include any excess beyond the through tenons. The excess can be pared and sanded back flush after assembly.

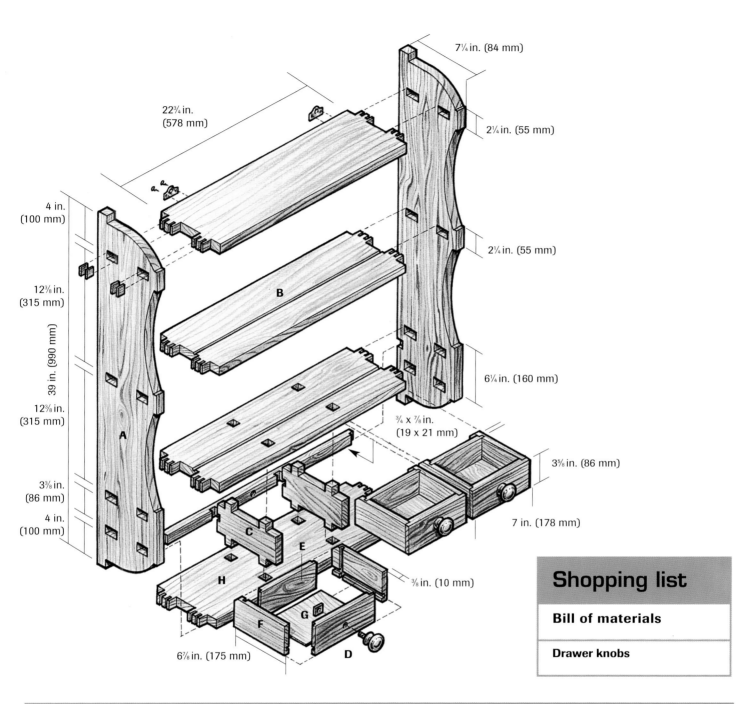

22¾ in.
(578 mm)

7¼ in. (84 mm)

2¼ in. (55 mm)

2¼ in. (55 mm)

4 in.
(100 mm)

12⅜ in.
(315 mm)

39 in. (990 mm)

12⅜ in.
(315 mm)

6¼ in. (160 mm)

¾ x ⅞ in.
(19 x 21 mm)

3⅜ in. (86 mm)

3⅜ in.
(86 mm)

4 in.
(100 mm)

7 in. (178 mm)

⅜ in. (10 mm)

6⅞ in. (175 mm)

A **B** **C** **D** **E** **F** **G** **H**

Shopping list

| **Bill of materials** |
| **Drawer knobs** |

Cutting list

Part	Material	Quantity	Dimensions thickness, width, length	Part	Material	Quantity	Dimensions thickness, width, length
A Side	stained softwood	2	¾ x 7¼ x 39 in. (19 x 184 x 991 mm)	**E** Drawer back	stained softwood	3	½ x 3 x 6½ in. (13 x 76 x 165 mm)
B Shelf	stained softwood	4	¾ x 7¼ x 24¼ in. (19 x 184 x 616 mm)	**F** Drawer side	stained softwood	6	½ x 3⅜ x 6⅞ in. (13 x 86 x 175 mm)
C Drawer divider	stained softwood	2	¾ x 3⅜ x 7¼ in. (19 x 86 x 184 mm)	**G** Drawer bottom	plywood	3	¼ x 6½ x 6⅞ in. (6 x 165 x 175 mm)
D Drawer front	stained softwood	3	½ x 3⅜ x 7 in. (13 x 86 x 178 mm)	**H** Support bearer	stained softwood	1	¾ x ⅞ x 24⅛ in. (19 x 22 x 616 mm)

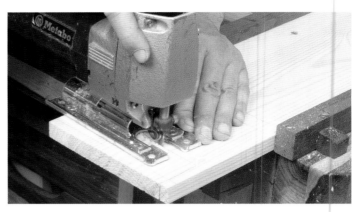

1 Assuming all the components have been surfaced to thickness, start by marking up the mortises on the sides (**A**) and tenons on the shelves (**B**). Make sure the mortises are marked up accurately, the whole way around each part, so that they can be cut from both sides to reduce tear-out.

2 Cut out the mortises first from one side and then from the other. Position the piece over the leg of the bench for maximum stability, and place a piece of scrap beneath the mortise to protect the surface. The mortises should be slightly splayed toward the outside so that the wedges can expand the tenons (see page 113).

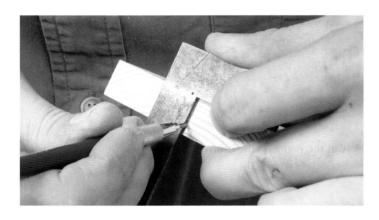

3 Cut the tenons, with grooves cut for the wedges. Make sure the tenons protrude the mortises by at least ⅛ inch (3 mm) each.

4 Stop the grooves short of the end of the tenon so that it can't be seen once the unit is assembled.

Do a dry run of the shelves (**B**) and sides (**A**), and mark up the position of the drawer dividers (**C**). This is a bit tricky and has to be carefully measured. You can go for even gaps for drawers or have the outer drawers narrower or wider than the central one.

Lessons learned

- A router table is really useful and can transform a woodworker's life, but it must be set up accurately to work well. Any ridges or bumps will be amplified when they knock the lumber off its course.

- Practice makes perfect when it comes to setting up and cutting the housed rabbet joint, and there is a great advantage in developing a system that works on the same thickness of lumber each time.

- Wedged joints are particularly attractive when done well.

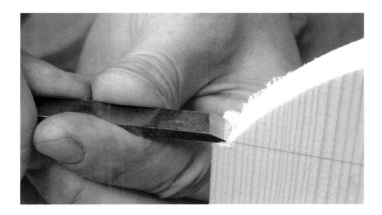

5 Cut the mortises in the shelves for the drawer dividers and then cut the corresponding tenons. Cut the notches in the back of the sides for the bearer (**H**). There are similar notches in the drawer dividers for the bearer.

Rout the groove along the middle shelves for the plates to rest and then cut the curves on the front edge of the sides. It's best to leave this as late as possible, since you will have found it easier to mark up the mortises before the curves are cut. Make a template of the curves for quicker and more accurate marking.

Clean up the sides, shelves, and drawer dividers. You might want to finish the shelves and inside faces of the sides at this point.

Cut out the top, or just clean up the edges if you've bought it ready cut. You can bevel the edges with abrasive, or a plane if you own one already (see page 64).

6 Foaming polyurethane adhesives work well for prefinishing because the hardened glue just snaps off, but make sure you experiment with it first.
TIP: Finishing before assembly. By cleaning up and applying a finish before assembly, you can save yourself a huge amount of time trying to clean up awkward spots. However, there are risks. If you go down this route, you must be able to remove any signs of adhesive without it smudging the surface. And it is difficult to use this technique when the piece is being stained, because the stain will be vulnerable and tricky to match if you make a mistake.

7 Cut yourself a number of small wedges to fit tightly in the tenon grooves. Do a dry run of the assembly, and then assemble using adhesive, holding the unit in place with bar clamps. Make sure you remember to check the diagonals. Before the glue goes off, tap the wedges home, using some glue on each.

When the glue has set, pare back the tenons with a chisel and block plane; then clean up with abrasive. A flush-cutting saw speeds up the paring back of the tenons.

Measure the gaps for the drawers and start cutting out the components to suit. I've heard of woodworkers who make the drawers first and would then make the shelves or surround to fit them.

Cut the dados in the drawer sides (**F**) and then the rabbet in the drawer front (**D**) and the rabbet on the drawer back (**E**), which has to fit in the dado. Groove the sides for the plywood base, with the groove the same depth as the dado. This way the ply base is the same width as the drawer back.

Clean up, sand, and finish the insides of the drawers; then glue up and tidy up the outside.

Finish the whole piece, and attach the knobs.

Lesson 7
Lumber Control

Getting started

Milling lumber is my favorite part of woodworking. I love taking rough boards, finding the best cuts, and then planing them up to reveal the beauty of the grain, figure, and color. With a wood-burning stove in my workshop I even get to enjoy warmth from the shavings! Of course, it's all made possible by owning a jointer and thicknesser.

So much depends on this stage of preparation. Unless the edges and faces are planed straight and square, you will face interminable challenges in attempting to join boards and accurately mark and cut joints.

I started with the smallest combination of planer thicknessers. In fact, the first machine I owned was a device to hold a portable power planer and convert it into a thicknesser. Then I owned a small planer thicknesser, which was ideal for my transition from home improver to hobbyist woodworker. Now I own a jointer and a site thicknesser, so I can leave them set however I want and don't have to move the tables on a planer thicknesser.

Using both the jointer and thicknesser is fairly simple. The important technique when jointing is to feel for the face, keeping the board flat on the tables. Make sure it moves steadily and you aren't fighting against the grain. The rest should be simple.

Cleaning rough-sawn wood

It's a good idea to clean the surface of rough-sawn boards before surfacing, since there is bound to be some dirt embedded in the grain. Such particles, however small, are abrasive and will dull the edges of your jointer and

Brush rough boards with a steel or brass brush to remove any dirt that might blunt tool edges.

thickness planer. Using a wire brush also helps to reveal the grain pattern for deciding how to cut up the board to avoid defects. This is a good opportunity to study the board for any nails, screws, or stones that will wreck your tools, though this is very rarely a problem with lumber bought from a commercial source.

Converting square section into a panel

The advantage of owning a band saw, power jointer, and power planer is that you have the control to convert boards however you like. For instance, this piece of 2½-inch (64-mm) square section ash can be made into a panel more than 6 inches (150 mm) wide (see page 85).
• Study the grain to see which way you want to cut the piece into thinner boards.
• Set the fence on the band saw to cut the board equally.

A square section board can be divided into three to produce a narrow panel.

Lesson planner

Key techniques	Key tools and materials
• Cleaning up boards • Converting boards for panels • Setting up a jointer	• Fitting extraction • Selecting lumber • Jointers and thicknessers

A quick way to check the setting is to make a trial cut with each side against the fence and then measure or just survey by eye the width of the cuts. It is a useful check because band-saw fences aren't always that accurate, and it can be tricky to adjust them just with a rule.

• Make the cuts using the band saw, using a push stick at the end of the cut and keeping the workpiece held against the fence with your spare hand. Make sure the blade guard is set only just above the workpiece.

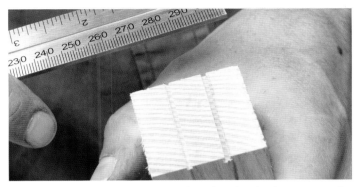

Set up the band saw to produce even boards to be glued up as a panel.

Use a push stick to keep the board moving through the band saw, but notice how the forward hand is holding the workpiece against the fence.

Once you've cut the pieces for a panel, mark them with a triangle to show how they fit together.

• Reassemble the boards as they were originally, which was defined by the triangular mark. Then open up and see how the grain runs before assembling into a panel, as we will in Lesson 8 (see page 166).

Using a jointer safely

Set up the jointer accurately and then you can surface first one face, then one edge easily. Once you have a satisfactory face and edge, you can thickness the board with a planer, sometimes known as a thicknesser. Because you pass the wood over the cutter with your hands using a jointer, there are some important rules for working safely.

1 Always make sure the guard is positioned correctly. For planing the face, this means the guard covers the whole table, above the workpiece. When you are working on an edge, use the guard to cover the exposed cutter block, and butt it against the workpiece. Some guards have give in them, so that they work like feather-boards, holding the lumber against the fence (see page 150).

2 If you are not very confident about having your hands so close to the cutter block, use a push block. Use one of these if there is any chance of your fingers slipping, perhaps because they are cold or if the lumber isn't running smoothly along the table. Wear earplugs, and possibly safety glasses and a dust mask, though I favor fitting effective dust extraction, which removes any dust and shavings.

Setting up the jointer

To work properly, the jointer must be set up accurately, but before you do anything, make sure it is disconnected from the power supply.

1 Check that the outfeed table is flat and level. There should be a ⅛-inch (3-mm) gap between the cutter block and the edge of the outfeed table, which you can test with feeler gauges. Use a straightedge to check that the outfeed table is parallel to the infeed table.

2 Most cutter blocks have simple mechanisms for fitting new blades. You can check if the blade is correctly aligned by placing a piece of lumber over the cutter block. As you turn the block by hand toward you, the board should move back by ⅛ inch (3 mm). Do this across the board to check that the travel is the same.

3 Routinely check that the fence is square every time you start a planing operation.

4 Spray the tables with a dry lubricant to make planing easier.

Jointing the first face

Check the board for defects and metal intrusions, and then decide which face to surface on the jointer. Traditionally, this should be the best face, since it is the one from which everything else works. However, power planers are so good these days that by the end of the surfacing operation, both faces could be used. You are better off starting with the board that is concave along its length or across its width. If the board is bowed badly along its length, you may need to cut it into shorter pieces, since you may be limited in how much usable lumber can be processed from the board. Bowing along the length is more difficult to deal with than cupping across the width.

1 Keeping your feet still, push the board forward with your front hand, feeling for the contact between the board and the jointer table. Once a flat area has been planed from the board it is important to keep this in contact with the table. If the board starts to wobble, you will find it very difficult to flatten the surface.

2 As your front arm is extended, start pushing more with your rear hand, or with a push block so that you can bring your front hand back again. It is vital to keep the lumber moving or you'll end up with marks, but keep the progress steady. If you push too fast there is a risk of the cutterblock making ripple marks across the face of the board.

3 Keep going, taking great care to keep your rear hand away from the end of the board as you complete the cut.

4 Check what areas have been surfaced and continue until the face is entirely flat. After the first pass, check for evidence of chipping, which might indicate that you are feeding the board the wrong way. If you find chips, raise the infeed table for a finer cut and try planing the other way.

Jointing an edge

With one face surfaced, you can use this against the fence to plane an edge square and true. It is very important to start with the edge that has high points at the ends, though you have to be a bit careful that the first cut of the corner of heavily bowed boards doesn't drop into the gap behind the cutter. Press the board firmly against the fence, checking along the rear edge of the fence that the lumber is flat on the fence. Shuffle long boards along with your hands, just as you did for the face.

Thicknessing with a planer

A power planer is easier to use than a jointer in that you feed the work in one side and it comes out the other. There aren't many things that can go wrong, and problems are usually associated with trying to remove too much stock in one pass. A common fault is that the lumber is torn or chipped, and you may notice pale tear marks, a bit like snakeskin. Adjust the planer to make a finer cut, and these will likely disappear.

It is important to machine components of the same desired thickness at the same time and to the same setting—you may not be able to replicate the setting again. Lay out the parts to be planed, and start with the thickest, gradually working your way down until you are able to thickness all the components on the same setting. Ideally, the final pass should be as shallow as possible for the best finish. A dial gauge is very useful for testing the thickness of the boards you are working.

Trade secret

Planing thin boards

Whether you choose to use the power planer to plane the second edge to width depends on the dimensions of the board. If the board is very thin and quite wide, there is a good chance it will topple over inside the planer. You can rectify this a little by inserting more than one piece at the same time, side by side.

Tools

Buying a jointer

You can buy power jointers to suit any budget and need. The largest have power feeds and can machine wide boards. For general woodworking, a 12-inch (305-mm) wide table and cutter block should be plenty. Check that the fence is sturdy and that the guard is easy to move into position and effective. Also study the position of the switch and see how quickly you can turn it on and off.

Most jointers have aluminum tables, either cast and ground or extruded. As a rule, the cast tables are the best, since they tend to be heavier and more robust, and the cast-iron tables are even better. If you can imagine woodworking for years to come, then it's worth investing wisely in a jointer because it will become your friend and ally for many years and there is no reason to change it. The small band saw you buy initially will always be useful for detailed work if you ever buy a larger one, but you will never need a standby jointer, so choose one carefully.

Buying a power planer

I use a portable planer (which I refer to as a thicknesser); it has a permanent home but can easily be used on-site. When you are using straight, clean boards, you can often get away with only a planer and not need a jointer, however suspiciously you'll be viewed by purists.

The planer has a shorter bed or table than the jointer, with rollers pressing the lumber down while the cutters surface the board. It relies purely upon the integrity of the other face for flatness, though you can hold a warped or bowed board onto a flat board with wedges for surfacing if you have only a power planer and no jointer.

These portable planers are ideal for home woodworkers, though they do tend to be very noisy. They can thickness boards up to 10 to 12 inches (254 to 305 mm) wide. The depth of cut isn't much of an issue. As with the jointer, look out for the switch and how easy it is to raise and lower the height. Also check the visibility of the depth measure, though I hardly ever use mine, relying instead on a Vernier or dial gauge for testing thickness.

What value the combination planer?

If you have only a small workshop or a limited budget, there is an advantage in buying a combination planer, once known as the over-under machine. They are cheaper than buying separate machines, and take up less space, but can be time-consuming to use if you have to move one of jointer tables to access the thicknessing component. I prefer having dedicated machines.

Fitting extraction

Both jointers and planers produce huge quantities of chippings and dust, which are extremely useful if you have a wood-burning stove designed to burn shavings. They must be collected by some form of extraction. Ask your supplier for an extractor designed to cope with your machines, with the important criteria being the capacity of the collector, the volume of shavings it can collect, and the dust-filtration capability. Some systems are designed for storing outside the shop because the fine filtration isn't low enough.

There are many ducting products on the market to attach all machines to some form of extraction. I have my jointer and planer attached to a chip extractor that collects the shavings in a bag. On each machine I have

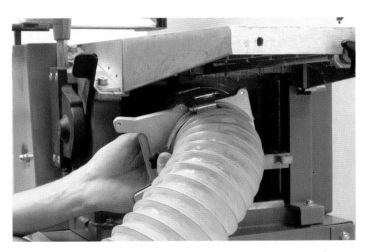

It is vital that you fit extraction to a thicknesser or jointer, since both produce mountains of shavings and dust.

a blast gate that can be closed, so the suction is always concentrated on the machine you happen to be using. For saws and other tools that produce more dust than shavings, I use a portable dust collector, which has a finer filter by a smaller collection bucket and only a 2-inch (51-mm) hose.

You can extend the use of such a small machine by connecting the hose to a plastic garbage can along the route, with another hose leading from the can to your machines. The garbage can can be made into a cyclone so that the heaviest dust or chippings fall to the bottom and only the finer particles make it to the small, but powerful vacuum extractor.

Materials

All about wood—studying end grain

You can tell a lot about wood from the end grain; in fact, botanists often rely upon it to identify species. Take the two boards pictured right as an example. The one on the left is ash, with clearly defined growth rings. The contrast is significant between the pale earlywood that helps nourish a tree in spring and early summer, and the much darker, far denser latewood that is designed to support the tree and grows later in the summer.

The cherry, on the right, has a much more even series of growth rings, and it's no surprise that it is much easier to use because the texture is so much more uniform through the lumber.

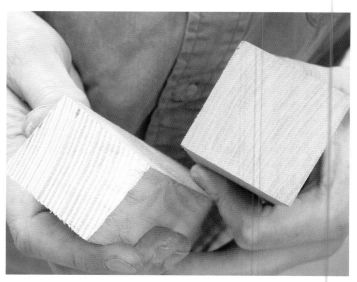

Look at the end grains. Ash (on the left) has a coarse texture, with open pores and distinct lines of grain. Cherry is much more uniform.

Selecting lumber

Though many boards are supplied with perfectly straight grain and no defects, others need more careful study to establish exactly what can be used to avoid any sapwood or defects.

1 There is a band of sapwood running down the edge of this sapwood offcut, with the shaded area showing what cannot be used.

2 The sapwood on oak often contrasts dramatically with the heartwood, and though it can be used for effect, it is much softer than the heartwood, so is vulnerable to worm attack.

3 On this brown oak board, the grain is gently curving across the face diagonally. You will probably want to follow the line of the grain rather than the existing edges when you come to select this board for use. This will raise the wastage rate, and ideally, I should have rejected this board in the first place.

Curved grain, however, can be useful for making curved components, like the legs of chairs and tables. The speckles and pale lines on the board are likely to be counted as a defect by one woodworker and as a feature by the next!

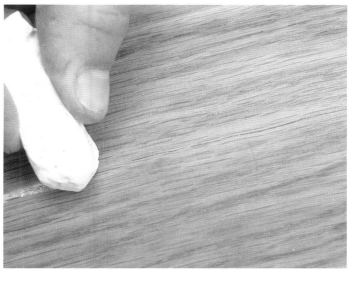

4 Look out for any splits or cracks when working out what to use. Mark and then cut along the line of a check or crack, remembering that there are likely to be more defects in the area, some of which might be hidden.

5 There's nothing much you can do about this major knot in a yew board. Smaller knots, like the one in the top-right corner, can be accommodated, but large defects will weaken the piece and make finishing very difficult. Notice the lovely flowing lines of grain in this piece, which make yew one of the most beautiful species but also one of the most difficult to use. Surprisingly, it is a softwood that is in fact extremely hard and has a contrasting (but soft) sapwood that you can see along the bottom. Wastage can be very high with yew, and it is not a lumber for beginners, though it is superb to turn.

Project **Picnic table**

For eating outside

This unusual project tests the woodworker's ability to cut angles and combines the miter with the tenon joints. You can use either a durable hardwood or treated softwood to make this project. We are assuming you make all the components from the same material, though that is not essential.

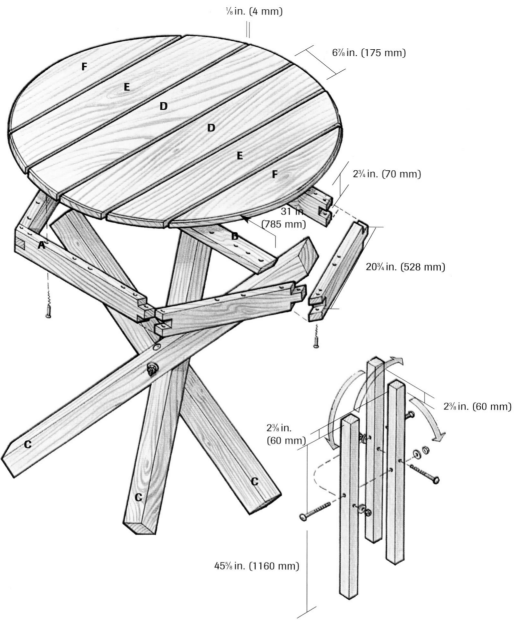

⅛ in. (4 mm)

6⅞ in. (175 mm)

2¾ in. (70 mm)

31 in. (785 mm)

20¾ in. (528 mm)

2⅜ in. (60 mm)

2⅜ in. (60 mm)

45⅝ in. (1160 mm)

Cutting list

	Part	Material	Quantity	Dimensions thickness, width, length
A	Underframe rail	hardwood or softwood	6	1 x 2¾ x 20¾ in. (25 x 70 x 527 mm)
B	Bearer	hardwood or softwood	1	¾ x 2¼ x 31 in. (19 x 57 x 787 mm)
C	Leg	hardwood or softwood	3	2⅜ x 2⅜ x 45⅝ in. (60 x 60 x 1159 mm)
D	Top	hardwood or softwood	2	¾ x 6⅞ x 42 in. (19 x 175 x 1067 mm)
E	Top	hardwood or softwood	2	¾ x 6⅞ x 39½ in. (19 x 175 x 1003 mm)
F	Top	hardwood or softwood	2	¾ x 6⅞ x 31 in. (19 x 175 x 787 mm)

Shopping list

Bill of materials	Extra tools for the job
Lag bolts 3½ in. (90 mm) with washers and nuts **Zinc flathead screws** Thirty 2⅜-in. (60-mm) 8-gauge to fix the underframe to the top **Zinc flathead screws** Ten 1⅜-in. (35-mm) 8-gauge to fix the bearer to the top	Band clamp

1 Surface all the components to the correct sections, leaving a few inches of excess on the ends of them all. And make sure you make a couple of extras in case of mistakes.

2 Cut the six underframe rails (**A**), cutting the 30-degree angles on the ends. Mark up the depth of the finger joint around each workpiece, with a finger on one end and socket on the other. You can set the marking gauge to the same setting for them all (see page 44).

3 Cut the shoulders with a tenon saw and remove the waste with a coping saw. Then tidy up the seat of the joint with a chisel.

Dry-assemble each joint, and then, when you are ready, the whole frame. I'd number each joint so that you can reproduce the layout with glue. The band clamp is ideal for this construction. Glue the frame and leave to set.

4 Cut the tabletop parts (**D**, **E**, and **F**) roughly to length and arrange. Drill the bearer, and screw it to the underside of the top, with ⅛-inch (3-mm) spaces between the top boards.

With the tabletop upside down, fix a routing trammel bar to the center of the bearer and set the radius for 21 inches (533 mm). Using a straight cutter in the router, work counterclockwise to cut smooth the edge of the top into a circle, taking great care where you jump from one board to the next.

5 Clean up and drill the underframe; then fix it to the top.

6 Turn the top the right way up and clean the edge of the boards with a sanding block (though it should be pretty smooth if your routing was successful). Now fit a bearing-guided beveling cutter in the router, and run the bearing against the existing edge to chamfer the top.

Lessons learned

- Unless the jointer is well set up, you won't be able to plane boards effectively and subsequent operations will be undermined by inaccuracy.

- Dust and chippings from machines must be extracted.

- The router is amazingly versatile. The trammel bar, which you can make yourself, is very useful for shaping circles. In this case the trammel will have to be offset from the router because the center point on the bearer will be higher than the router base.

7 With the top finished you can cut the legs to length and drill them for the fixing bolts, as shown in the picture. Sand and finish; then assemble with the bolts and drop the top over the leg assembly.

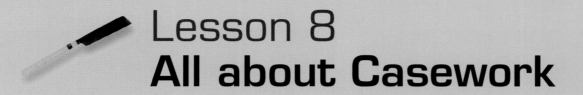

Lesson 8
All about Casework

Getting started

Around the home you'll find a plethora of casework projects, from kitchen cabinets, to bookshelves, wardrobes, and storage solutions. Sheet materials are ideally suited to casework, and are easy to work, but great casework projects can be made from solid lumber, just as our Plate Rack is this lesson.

Though modern flat-pack furniture relies on fittings to hold the components together, the dado is the traditional joint for joining wide boards together. It inhibits racking movements, especially with shoulders, and also increases the gluing area.

Once again the router is the ideal tool for cutting both male and female components of the dado, though the tenon is normally best cut on a router table.

Designing casework projects

This lesson's project is a typical construction for a book-shelf or rack of some form, as was the crockery shelf a couple of lessons ago. With the sides protruding above the shelves, both at top and bottom, it is easy to hide any joints and choose joints that have shoulders to give the piece more rigidity (see page 42).

A simple way to make casework with inherent strength is to insert a plywood panel into either grooves or a rabbet in the back. This may reduce the depth of the casework, but the plywood reinforces the construction. A solid wood back does a similar job, but you have to allow for wood movement and won't be able to pin and glue the panel in place as securely.

Traditionally, solid wood back panels of casework would be a series of vertical boards, probably joined by tongue-and-groove joints without using glue. Each board would be pinned into a rabbet top and bottom with a single nail, and the tongues would be able to expand and contract within the grooves to allow for changes in the moisture levels. Ironically, these days furniture often dries out more during the winter when the central heating is on (see page 238).

For this reason anyone making casework from solid wood must know the moisture content of the lumber he is using, especially when it is being used for panels. You can buy a moisture meter to measure this, and for a centrally heated home you need the moisture content to be right down to about 9 percent for it to be stable. If the wood expands or contracts too much, it can easily crack or break joints.

People often want adjustable shelves or dividers within casework, and fortunately, there are many shelving systems you can find to make this a simple task. But rigid shelves, jointed into the sides, make a casework more secure, so it is important to find a balance.

When the joints between sides and shelves are at corners, you will have to consider other joints. The rabbet is a simple choice but not very strong. Butt joints can be reinforced with biscuits or dowels, or even more simply with screws. The latter option isn't very attractive, since screws don't hold well in end grain, though you can use pocket screws in the long grain. The dovetail, which some people might consider a furniture maker's joint, is the strongest of all, and can either be left visible or hidden by some form of cornice or molding.

Cutting a stopped dado

The dado or housing is a great joint to cut for making casework, especially when the joints aren't right on the corners so that you can incorporate shoulders to stop movement. The best tool to cut stopped dados is the plunge router because you can easily raise and lower the cutter at the start or end of the cut.

1 Start by marking up the joint, but instead of marking it out in detail, all you need to do is mark a line, or even

Lesson planner

Key techniques	Key tools and materials
• Designing casework • Cutting stopped dados • Using a drum sander	• Japanese saws • Buying sustainable lumber • Choosing lumber

Run the router against a straightedge to cut the dado.

If you use a side fence for cutting the dado, check the offset between the cutter and the fence.

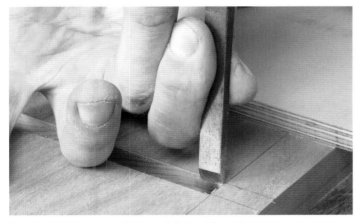

Square up the corners of a routed dado with a chisel.

To hide the joint at the front, cut away a notch from the tenon.

only two points, where the guide will be clamped, taking into account the offset between the cutter and the side of the router base (see page 137).

2 Clamp a guide to the workpiece, and make a mark where you want the cut to end. To ensure the gap between the dados is exactly the same on both pieces (assuming you are making a two-sided case), you can make a template that clamps to the workpiece. The template is as long as the distance between the dados, minus the offset between the cutter and router base, twice. Rather than the baseplate, you could use a bushing against the template, but there would still be an offset to consider.

3 Doing it this way means you have to rout from the back to front of the side for one dado, and from the front to the back on the other, because you always want to rout from right to left, against the cutter's rotation. This is why the plunge router is so useful. On the first cut you can start with the cutter extended, but at the end of the cut, when you reach the stop mark, you have to raise the cutter. This is particularly easy using a plunge router,

without having to stop the motor. For the other dado you have to plunge the spinning cutter into the lumber at the beginning of the cut.

4 Set the depth of the cutter either by using a depth gauge you make yourself or with a bought version. There are plenty on the market. A simple way to set the depth is to have a few pieces of plywood of set thickness and use them to judge the depth of cut.

5 Having cut the dado, you need to tidy up the rounded end with a chisel, though of course this will be hidden within the joint.

6 For a wide dado, I would use either a hand-held router with the side fence or the router table with the workpiece running against the fence. When the pieces are heavy, you are probably better off holding the lumber and moving the router.

7 Set the cutter to cut both sides of the tenon, testing it first on a suitable piece of scrap. Rout the tenon.

8 Mark off the notch for the front of the stopped dado, cut down the tenon, and chisel away the waste. Clean up with a chisel.

Tools

Making your own drum sander

The best way to clean up curved cuts is with a drum sander. You can buy these as machines, and some of the more sophisticated bobbin sanders (as they are often known) oscillate up and down to prevent scratching. Alternatively, you can make your own by buying a drum-sanding device for a drill.

One design of drum sander is pneumatic, with an abrasive sleeve held in place by the pressure of a blow-up inner tube. These work well, especially if you aim to sand carvings and actually want the drum to have some give. There are similar devices that have a foam core and likewise have some give, which wood-turners like. However, my favorite for furniture making are the solid drums, around which you wrap a length of sandpaper, held in place by a cam. That you can use your own abrasive and don't have to buy expensive sleeves is a bonus, but I prefer them for their more substantial feel.

The challenge of making a drum-sanding machine is dealing with the dust. The solution is to build a cowl around the drum, which catches the dust to the left (sucked away by a vacuum extractor) but is open to the

The drum sander is ideal for shaping curves.

right for access. You will need to raise the workpiece a little at the front of the drum so that you don't run against the bottom edge of the drum. This is a very simple device to make, and it will be useful time and again.

Japanese saws

Some of the finest woodworking tools are made in Japan, and probably the most popular elsewhere are their saws. The saw cuts on the push and pull strokes and has no kerf. They cut superbly, but my only concern is that they aren't always as rigid as a tenon saw, and I've found they can have a tendency to wander. However, I love the feel of them, especially the long handle.

Japanese saws cut on both the push and pull strokes.

Even if you make a suction hood to remove the dust from a drum sander, make sure you wear a mask and earplugs.

Materials

All about wood—sustainability

As woodworkers, we have an important role in promoting the future of the world's forests and trees. We know the value of lumber and understand the remarkable nature of wood as a beautiful building material that is strong, tactile, and attractive, and is renewable. Unless trees are given a value, they will be felled to convert the land to other uses, many of which are unsuitable and which will not give us the long-term benefits of forests.

In the temperate parts of the world, where many of us live, there are few problems with the sustainability of our trees, though some old-growth forests are still being destroyed at a faster rate than they can recover. In tropical forests, however, the balance is far more fragile—without the trees, any fertility is soon washed away and regeneration becomes increasingly difficult. We want to encourage the use of lumber from these parts of the world but without risking the extinction of some of the rarer or more overexploited species. That is why the Forest Stewardship Council and other organizations have introduced certification schemes to label lumber that is managed and harvested sustainably.

The FSC scheme has been very successful, raising awareness and enabling craftspeople to market their products as having only a beneficial impact on the environment. The only frustration is that the owners of temperate forests have the money to invest in management plans and the certification is a more complicated process in tropical forests. So you can buy all the most famous temperate species with an FSC logo, but very few tropical species. So to make the system really work, we need to experiment with some of the lesser-known tropical species that are plentiful and can be certified as coming from a sustainable source. The *peroba rosa*, which I used to make this lesson's project, is just such a species. Search the Internet for FSC suppliers and you will soon discover sources of such lumber.

Choosing which lumber to use

Up to now we have only looked at a limited range of hardwoods; most of the projects are made from softwood, which is easy to source and, for a beginner, easy to work. Ironically, as one's skills develop, so the softness becomes less of an issue and more experienced woodworkers find hardwoods with a consistent, even texture (like cherry, walnut, and birch) easier to use because the results are more exact and you can work more accurately.

Some softwoods are always going to be useful. Redwood, for instance, is naturally durable, so it can be used for outdoor furniture, while most softwoods can be treated with preservatives more efficiently than hardwoods, which tend not to be porous enough. Softwoods are usually cheaper than hardwoods, so white pine is attractive for interior trim and workshop fittings, while aromatic cedar is favored for the linings of chests and drawers because its smell and oils repel insects.

The most common hardwoods are red and white oak (of which the latter has a more intriguing grain pattern), cherry, hard maple, elm, and walnut, all of which are grown in North America. These are all counted as quality hardwoods for the making of good furniture or casework. For more utilitarian purposes, you might consider birch, hickory, aspen, or poplar, which are all pale in color,

relatively inexpensive, and easy to use. These can also be used inside frameworks where they won't be seen.

For a more exotic project there are imported hardwoods from the tropics and other temperate regions. From Europe you might look out for their version of oak, walnut, elm, and yew—all of which tend to have wilder grain and more defects. Tropical hardwoods that are available from specialist importers of exotic lumber include wenge, padauk, zebrawood, purpleheart, various rosewood species, ebony, and mahogany. However, some caution has to be paid to these species, and we recommend you study the lists of threatened species produced by Cites and the IUCN to check their status.

Exotics can be bought by mail order if you don't have a nearby supplier. Test the services with small orders first, but there's no reason why you shouldn't use such a method if it works for you. Personally, I prefer to visit a local lumberyard to have a good look through their stock, searching for gems.

Lumber grades

Both softwood and hardwood are graded to give the purchaser an indication of what they should expect by way of defects as a percentage of a board. The best hardwood boards are Firsts & Seconds (FAS) and Select, although there is some variation in nomenclature from one species to another. Anyway, the best approach is to check the boards yourself, especially if you think you can make do with a lesser grade that won't cost as much and that perhaps you won't mind the defects. The best softwood is called B Select and BTR (better). C Select is also counted as having only a few defects or blemishes, and D Select will have one face free of defects.

Trade secret

Buying softwoods

Softwoods are sold by the foot or inch, with a simple price given for each type or dimension of board. Hardwood, in contrast, tends to be sold by volume, with a price given for $\frac{1}{12}$ of a cubic foot, which gives you 144 cubic inches. This is known as a board foot. When you choose a board, the yard will calculate its volume first and then work out the price. The price is determined by the market, of course, but also by the rarity of the species and sometimes by the width and thickness of the boards.

Project **Plate rack**

For the dishes

Made to take a set of small and large plates, this plate rack isn't designed for wet dishes, but it is flexible enough to suit any chinaware. It was originally made from a lesser-known species of lumber, *peroba rosa*, that had been certified by FSC as being from a sustainable source.

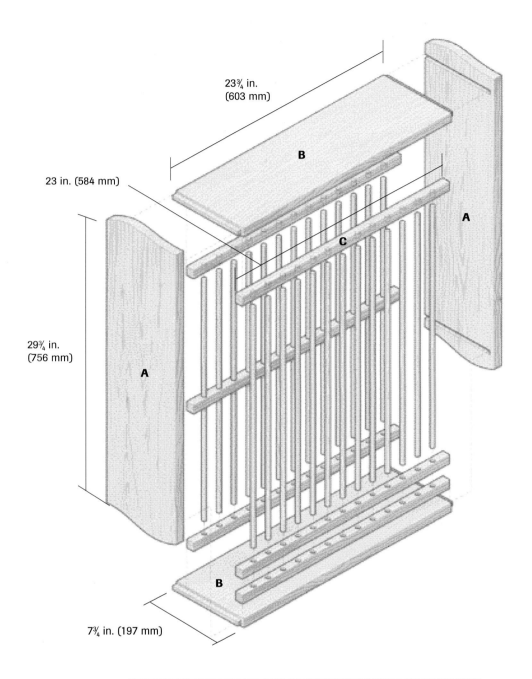

23¾ in.
(603 mm)

23 in. (584 mm)

29¾ in.
(756 mm)

7¾ in. (197 mm)

Cutting list

Part	Material	Quantity	Dimensions thickness, width, length
A Side	peroba rose	2	⅞ x 7⅞ x 29¾ in. (22 x 200 x 756 mm)
B Shelf	peroba rose	2	⅞ x 7¾ x 23¾ in. (22 x 197 x 603 mm)
C Bar	peroba rose	6	¾ x ⅞ x 23 in. (19 x 22 x 584 mm)
D Dowel	softwood	26	½ x ½ x 23⅛ in. (13 x 13 x 587 mm)

1 Surface all the components. Mark up the stopped dados in the sides (**A**) for the two shelves. The width of the dado depends on what router cutters you have, but ⅜ inch (10 mm) should be about right.

Rout the dados through at the back of the sides, but stop about ½ inch (12 mm) short of the front edge. Square the front of the dado with a chisel.

Cut the shelves (**B**) exactly to length; then rout the tenon on each end. This can be done on a router table against the fence, though each workpiece is quite heavy for this. The shelf is wide enough for you to use the side fence on a router to cut the tenons.

Cut away the notch at the front of the shelves; then tidy up with a chisel.

Make a drawing of the curves for the top and bottom of the sides. The curves are identical, just reversed. I drew them freehand on a piece of plywood and then cut that out and cleaned it up with a sanding block.

2 To cut the curves on the sides, use the template to draw the curves and then cut with a jigsaw or on a band saw. The finish from the saw is likely to be fairly rough, so smooth the curve with a drum sander in a drill, held upright in a drill stand (see page 185).

It's a good idea to mark the curve again with the template after cutting so as to have something to follow with the drum sander; otherwise you won't know how the shape should be. What you can do is draw a second line ¹⁄₁₆ inch (1.6 mm) behind the first line and make sure you keep your finished line a consistent distance from that.

Test-fit the sides and shelf. If it's all fine, sand the inside faces, plus the top and bottom of the shelves, and apply a finish. Glue using bar clamps, and check the diagonals.

Lessons learned

- Dado joints can be difficult to fit. The margin between it being too tight, just right, and loose is very fine. Make sure you test the fit on an offcut first.

- Drum sanders create a huge amount of dust that must be removed at the source by extraction.

- Casework depends on accuracy, both for strength and beauty, so make sure all the parts are cut to length correctly.

3 Drill the holes in the bars at 1⅝-inch (41-mm) intervals. This can be done with a special jig for repetition to save time if you have a bench drill (see **TIP**, right).

4 Drill the first hole in the bar and then position-drop that over the dowel stop on your jig. Clamp the jig to the bench drill and you can drill hole after hole without having to do any measuring and marking. You can even turn the bar over to drill from both sides to reduce the risk of tear-out, especially for the middle bar.

TIP: Drilling jig With a bench drill (see page 185) you can drill the holes in the bars without having to do any marking out. Simply fix a fence to a piece of scrap plywood that can be clamped to the bench-drill table. Then drill a ½-inch (13-mm) hole ⁷⁄₁₆ inch (11mm) from the fence, into which you tap a short length of ½-inch (13-mm) dowel rod.

5 Cut the dowel rod for the racking to length—the miter saw is probably as good as anything for this, being accurate and neat.

Dry assemble and test the fit of the sides and shelf. If it's all fine, sand the inside faces, plus the top and bottom of the shelves, and apply a finish. Glue up using bar clamps, and check the diagonals.

6 Drill through the bars a few times along the inside faces so that you can screw the bars to the dowel rod. I screwed the bars to the shelves for ease, but to avoid unsightly screw holes or bungs, you could glue them in place.

Fix the rear set of bars and dowels in place. Use the bars as bearers to fix the plate rack to the wall. Fix the front set in place.

Becoming Self-Sufficient

What you will find in this section

What to Expect

Tools

Balancing reliance upon jigs or workshop devices and developing one's own ability to create aids to improve efficiency are tricks of effective woodworking. During the final chapter we will look at how machines can improve your work and how jigs can help you repeat operations accurately, but we will also discuss how to make your own systems.

Materials

Learning how to machine your own lumber is a key skill that frees you from the confines of the lumberyard and means you can plane and thickness boards to whatever dimensions you require. Learning which finishes suit your work best is also essential, plus the ability to use special veneers and other skills to decorate your work.

Laying out the workshop effectively is essential if you want to be able to find tools with ease and keep them in good condition (see page 196).

Oil finishes are simple to apply and give a professional result (see page 187).

Here are some useful jigs for helping you lay out projects (see page 237).

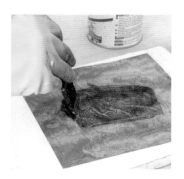

A quick option for veneering is to use contact adhesive (see page 239).

Some of the latest jigs enable you to cut strong and accurate joints quickly (see page 273).

With a wider knowledge of adhesives woodworkers can make their joints stronger and longer lasting (see page 261).

Techniques

So far we have looked at the jointing of wood, largely for strength. During this chapter we will study how to ensure those joints are accurate and the projects are assembled tidily. This is what distinguishes a well-made piece from a exceptional item. It is perhaps this part of woodworking that takes the longest to master as we try to find better ways to improve our skills.

Always make a test fit of any project before using glue (see page 182).

The mortiser speeds up jointing and guarantees accuracy once you've learned how to make the most of your kit (see page 194).

Neat touches, like the lining of a box, can make all the difference (see page 211).

Projects

During this term you will learn how to make paneled doors, a chair, two tables, drawers and much more. Here the vital techniques are put into practice.

Wine rack **p. 188**

Cherry bookcase 2 **p. 240**

Sideboard 1 **p. 202**

Kitchen chair **p. 252**

Sideboard 2 **p. 214**

Dining table **p. 262**

Cherry bookcase 1 **p. 226**

Shaker cabinet **p. 276**

Lesson 1
Quicker Mortising

Getting started

For many years I made do without a mortiser, relying instead on hand tools, a bench drill, and my router. Then a friend bought an industrial mortising machine and passed his hollow chisel mortiser down to me. It changed my life, and I'm beginning to see why he then upgraded, for mortising is all about accuracy, speed, and power. With a good mortiser you can cut beautiful mortises to a hair's breadth of accuracy and without the dust and whine of a router.

A mortiser takes some skill and time to set up, but it's easy for anyone who has reached this level. This is a quiet, businesslike, and accurate tool, and when it comes to assembling a project, nothing matters quite as much as the success of the joint-cutting. Any discrepancies in the joints will be amplified the moment glue is applied and you start clamping up. Which is why a test fit with clamps is so important.

When you have as many components as those used in this lesson's project (Wine rack on pages 188–193), you will discover the value of having tested the assembly first.

Designing projects

Creating a design is something of a jigsaw puzzle, with so many pieces coming together to form the complete picture. The woodworker has to consider function, space, shape, color, and ornamentation, not to mention what materials, techniques, and tools are available. Normally, though, one or two factors dominate, whether it's the inspiration of a detail you've noticed and want to reproduce or a specific function that has to be satisfied.

To take this lesson's project as an example, the design of a wine rack is likely to be influenced by the shape of the bottles. Unless you devise a particularly ingenious design, the basic construction will probably replicate the many wine racks that have gone before. So you have to look for other details to add your mark. In this case, it's both the use of metal for the vertical dividers and the shaping of the uprights that go some distance in diminishing the standard geometry of a wine rack. The choice of wood is relatively unimportant in this case, though the straightness of the grain in the uprights works well with the curved shape.

Space and style

Obviously you have to consider the space into which a piece fits and take into account the colors, style, and size of other fittings and furniture. It's pointless making a table too big for a room, and equally, the table must be able to accommodate the number of chairs you intend to use.

Everyone has his or her own style. Consider the pieces you really like, and look for influences in them that will determine how you might go about designing projects. Look for the shapes, the details, the curves, and the proportions. Don't be overwhelmed by dimensions—let your eye determine the proportions of the pieces you design. Some people need to draw them out in detail on graph paper, while others prefer a quick sketch to give them an overall feel, and then they add some detail to confirm the construction of the joints.

There are any number of ways to add ornamentation to a project. The router has become the ubiquitous tool for shaping edges with profiles, but beware the use of predetermined moldings that will make your projects look like everyone else's. There is a great temptation to pull out a router to add decoration to an edge when it would be more interesting to shape the components, though this usually requires more planning and thought. It all comes with experience and practice. Make a note of what works and what fails, and try to learn from your mistakes as well as from the mistakes and successes of other woodworkers.

Lesson planner

Key techniques	Key tools and materials
• Using a mortiser • Making a marking rod • Advanced clamping • Routing end grain	• The bench drill • Buying a mortiser • Reclaimed wood • Using oil finishes

Consult high-quality books on designing furniture and go out and visit exhibitions. Another approach is to restore old pieces. Through my family's furniture-repair business I've seen many failed joints and others that just won't come apart. And you will pick up lines and shapes that look superb and others that are clumsy.

Using a mortiser

The router may be a great leap forward when it comes to shaping wood, but the mortiser is perhaps one of the most useful tools for quickly producing accurate joints. It is also one of the easiest of woodworking machines to set up and use, and takes away all the pain of cutting mortises by hand. Unlike some machines, the mortiser derives its efficiency through brute force rather than the ability to repeat an operation time after time. In other situations, you can set up a device or jig to produce the same joint or shape with very little input from the woodworker. The mortiser offers a nice balance of user skill and machine power.

The accuracy of the mortiser comes from the setting up of the fence. You do this by marking up a joint with a mortise gauge. Gently lower the hollow chisel down onto the marks and set the fence from that. Then all you have to do is check that the chisel is parallel to the fence, set the depth stop, and lower the fingers to act as a lever to pull the chisel from the mortise. I generally find it safest and simplest to mark lines to show the length of the mortise and copy those to each workpiece for consistency.

One drawback of the mortiser is dealing with the shavings. These tumble from the mortise over the table and against the fence, affecting the accuracy of the machine. You end up having to blow the shavings away from the fence; otherwise the register is poor, and you lose accuracy. A solution is to attach a vacuum extractor hose beside the chisel and remove the chippings at the source.

When you fit a wooden face to the mortiser's fence, make sure there is a gap for shavings.

Set your mortise gauge to the width of the hollow chisel for marking up tenons and for your first mortise.

Access to the mortiser's chuck is through a gap in the side.

The mortiser slides up and down a rack-and-pinion-mechanism.

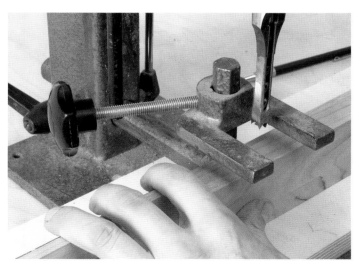

The U-shaped hold-down stops the workpiece from pulling up as you retract the mortise chisel.

Marking up with a rod

To mark up multiple joints, it's a good idea to draw up a full-size rod on a piece of plywood. This simply records the position of every important mark along the length of a component and is used, typically, for the manufacture of doors with all the mortises and profiles to consider. A full-size plan is useful for projects, like chairs, that incorporate angles. For this lesson's Wine rack, a rod can be used for positioning the mortises along the uprights.

Advanced clamping

Almost all clamps are designed for clamping square-edged lumber, with the force exerted at 90 degrees to the joint line. When the outside faces are at an angle to the joint, you may need to temporarily clamp "ears" to the workpieces to get the clamp to stay in position.

To assemble a wide miter, glue an ear to the workpiece temporarily.

Once you have marked up the critical dimensions on a marking rod, you can use them for all your joint cutting.

Trade secret

Working to order

A key lesson in woodworking is to devise a clear order for making a project. You will often need to start by surfacing all the components, leaving them overlong, ensuring you have more than enough lumber in case of mistakes, and setting up machines or gauges. Don't always follow the obvious course. One might, for example, jump into cutting the curves on the uprights of this lesson's project, since they are such a dominant feature. In reality, cutting the mortises will be far easier without the curves.

Cyanoacrylate glues are ideal because they dry quickly, but knock off any excess after use.

With the ear glued in place, the clamp can exert pressure across the joint.

Another solution is to stick cork or abrasive pads to your clamp heads to stop them from sliding. When clamping curved work, keep the offcut from the curved cut and use it as a packing piece.

Keep offcuts for curved pieces, as they can be used during assembly.

Another important lesson is to only assemble a project bit by bit. Do so one frame at a time, two-dimensionally, so to speak. Only when you are satisfied with each frame, should you consider joining them together. Beds, for instance, are always constructed in three stages. First make the headboard, then the footboard, and only when they are done, do you connect the two with rails.

Routing around a board

Whenever routing around all four edges of a board, start with the ends and then rout the long grain. This way any breakout at the end of the end-grain cuts can be tidied up when you rout the long-grain edges.

When routing around a panel, rout across the end grain first, as the end of the cut may tear.

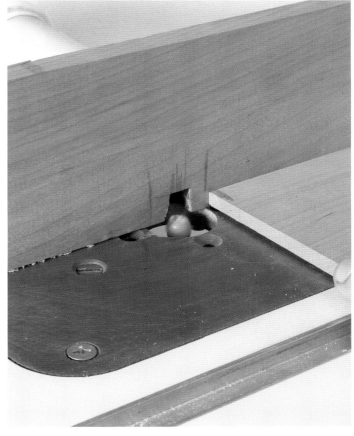

Rout the long grain after the end grain so that any tear on the end-grain cut is hidden.

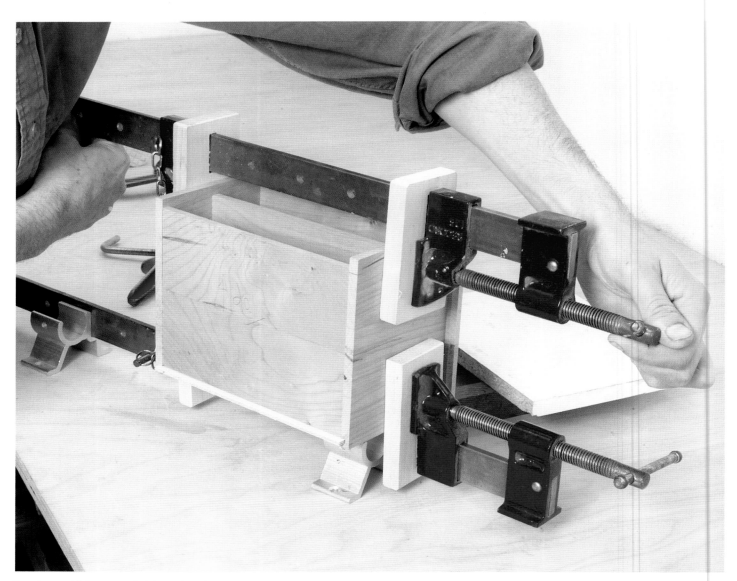

Stands on which you can hold your bar clamps are incredibly useful in keeping everything steady as you assemble.

Doing a test fit

Just as there's a maxim to measure twice, cut once only, there is also a sensible rule that you should always do a test fit—without glue—of any assembly that involves glue. It gets the clamps set up properly and also checks the quality of the fit. In addition, check the diagonals and fit before applying glue. Inaccuracies are usually caused by an inherent problem that will only be exacerbated in the presence of adhesive. And take your phone off the hook when you start gluing up. One of the best lessons I've learned is to buy a box of latex disposable gloves, which will keep the adhesive off your hands. Make sure your assembly area is clear of any dried adhesive, or your clamps will start rocking. Never use too much pressure with your clamps, as it's bound to knock something out of true. Solve the problem completely during the dry run, and then try it again.

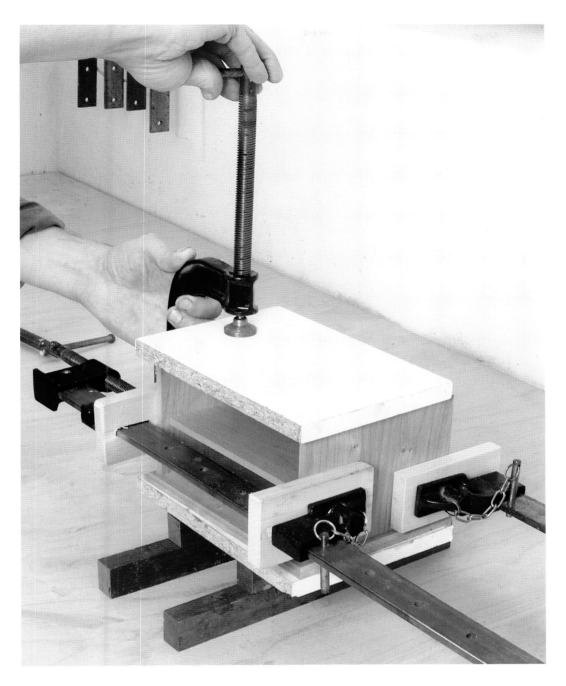

Melamine-faced chipboard is good for assemblies because glue can easily be chipped away afterward, but make sure it is flat.

Check with a small square and also across the diagonals during a test fit. Do a test fit exactly as you would if you were applying adhesive.

When attaching a tabletop to a rail, you can use an expanded hole that allows for seasonal wood movement.

Attaching tabletops in place

Attaching a tabletop to the underframe should be simple enough, but it is complicated by the fact that a solid lumber top is likely to expand and contract with the seasons. These days, a top will often do so against the tide of the seasons, expanding when the central heating is off and the doors and windows are open, and then contracting during winter when the house becomes a blast furnace. It does, of course, depend on the latitude of your home, since the opposite is the case for houses cooled by air-conditioning in the summer.

If the top is fixed to the underframe too rigidly, something will have to give as it expands or contracts. Even if you ensure the lumber is conditioned to the 9 or 10 percent that is appropriate for central heating, the wood is still bound to move a bit. There are a few options:

1 Expansion brackets. These right-angled steel brackets have slots cut in them so that the screw can move as the top moves.

2 If you are drilling through a rail into the top, you can either elongate the hole to make a slot, or you can expand the hole into a cone shape. This way you have pressure where the screw head meets the rail, but the hole is much wider where the rail meets the top to allow for movement.

3 Fit turn buttons to the top, and groove the inside face of the rails. The turn buttons are screwed into the top and are tightly fitted into the groove, but the top is still able to expand and contract.

Turn buttons are screwed to the tabletop. Because they are just a tight fit in a groove in the rail, the top can move.

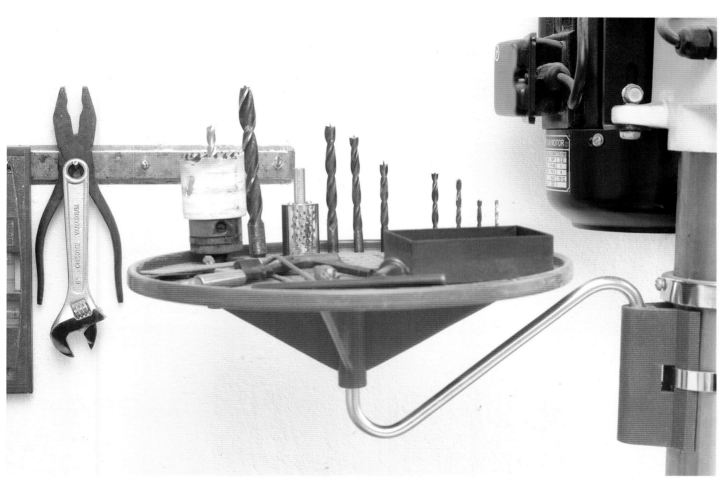

A drill tray is essential for a drill press and attaches to the main column.

Tools

You don't need to ask much of a drill press, but it is one of the most valuable pieces of equipment in the woodworking shop. Mine has countless speeds, but I've changed the belts and pulleys only once, and that was when I set it up the first time. It seems to work well enough. Actually, you can't go far wrong in buying a drill press except that it is worth selecting one with a simple chuck you can tighten and loosen by hand. Almost any deficiency can be overcome with a little tinkering, and drill presses are so cheap that they should be right up there as one of the first machines to buy.

The benefit of owning a drill press is that you can guarantee the accuracy of the holes you drill—you just have to hit the mark. They also give you more control when drilling with larger bits, especially Forstner drills and bung cutters. It is, however, worth fitting a wooden table to the drill, and buying an engineer's vise to fit to the bench drill can help if you need to drill awkward shapes or small pieces. Investing in a drill tray that fits to the drill press is also a good idea.

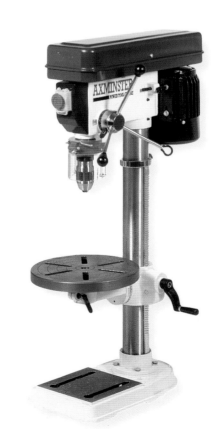

Buying a mortiser

Like drill presses, most mortisers are very similar, probably produced in the same factory and just badged with a different brand. You should, however, test the handles for adjustment, since some are very crude, while you may need a hex wrench on other types.

Set the U-shaped hold-down to keep the workpiece flat and level.

One of the first things to do when setting up a mortiser is to set the depth of cut.

Don't let the auger fall out of the hollow chisel when you undo the chuck.

When the mortiser is sharp, it will produce clean shavings instead of dust.

Materials

All about wood—reclaimed wood

The sideboard that we'll be making in Lesson 2 has a lovely old feel to it and could easily be made from reclaimed wood. Even when covered in old varnish or paint, lumber is still worth salvaging. I keep a battered old portable power planer for just such a job and very rarely change the blades. This way I can quickly remove old finishes without damaging the cutters in my jointer. I have rescued plenty of antique Cuban mahogany, which bears no resemblance to the stuff we have to use these days, though this material now should probably be avoided for environmental reasons.

Mixed media

We woodworkers often assume that all parts of a project have to be made from lumber. Actually, the contrast between wood and metal, for instance, can be amazingly effective, and other materials like glass, stone, and plastic set off lumber superbly. I once went through a phase of filling knot holes with epoxy resin and brightly colored pigment. For another project, I stuck veneer to a sheet of mild steel and then used powerful magnets to produce an alternative type of bulletin board.

Oil finishes

This lesson's project, the Wine rack, might well be finished with some kind of oil. These finishes are easy to apply and relatively hard-wearing, while providing a softer, less artificial barrier than some of the modern lacquers and varnishes. They vary in hardness—from linseed, which is very soft, to tung oil, which is strong enough to be used for tabletops.

Often oils are mixed with lacquers and waxes to produce faster-drying, harder-wearing applications. When, before the mixed oils, it was a case of using pure linseed oil, there was a maxim that you needed to apply a coat once a day for a week, once a week for a month, and once a month for a year. A common theme, still, is that oil finishes are applied with a brush or rag, and any excess is wiped off after a few minutes. In drying slowly, there's plenty of time to dab away any marks and to remove any dust or particles, but it does take a few days to build up an effective coat, which you can leave as it is or go on to wax.

Oil will form a skin in a jar very quickly.

Apply oil with a brush liberally, working with the grain.

After a short while, wipe off any excess oil with a cloth.

Project **Wine rack**

For bottles of wine

A simple design that takes a simple idea and gives it shape and contrast by adding curves to the geometric layout of racking and distinctive vertical dividers made from steel rod.

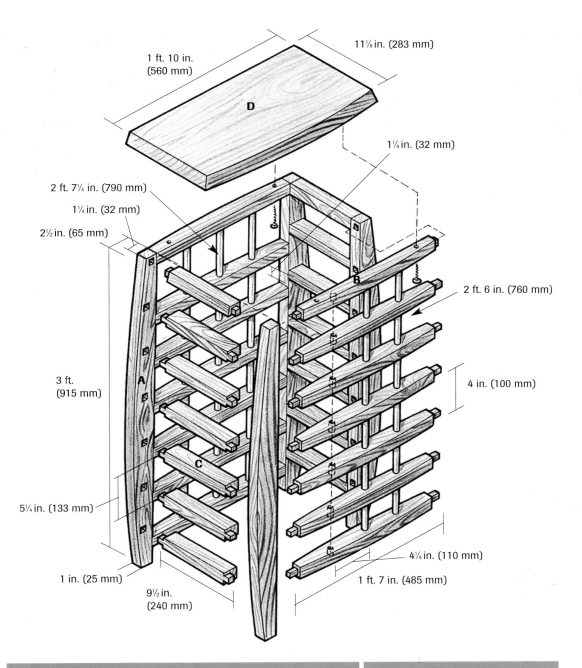

11⅛ in. (283 mm)

1 ft. 10 in. (560 mm)

1¼ in. (32 mm)

2 ft. 7¼ in. (790 mm)

1¼ in. (32 mm)

2½ in. (65 mm)

2 ft. 6 in. (760 mm)

4 in. (100 mm)

3 ft. (915 mm)

5¼ in. (133 mm)

4¼ in. (110 mm)

1 in. (25 mm)

1 ft. 7 in. (485 mm)

9½ in. (240 mm)

Cutting list

Part	Material	Quantity	Dimensions thickness, width, length
A Upright	cherry	4	1 x 2½ x 36 in. (25 x 64 x 914 mm)
B Rail	cherry	14	1 x 1¼ x 19 in. (25 x 32 x 483 mm)
C Side rail	cherry	14	1 x 1⅜ x 9½ in. (25 x 35 x 241 mm)
D Top	cherry	1	1 x 11⅛ x 22 in. (25 x 283 x 559 mm)

Shopping list

Extra tools for the job

Steel rod 6 lengths of 5⅛ in. (130 mm) diameter, each 30 in. (762 mm) long
Flathead wood screws to attach top (**D**)

1 Plane and thickness all the parts. Note that many of the pieces are 1 inch (25 mm) thick, so you ought to surface boards for those components at the same time. Make sure you have some extra lumber dimensioned to the appropriate section for setting up the mortiser and bench drill.

2 Cut the uprights (**A**) to length, though there's no harm leaving the parts a few inches too long at this stage. But don't think about cutting the curves yet: It will be far easier to do this after the mortises have been chopped out. Whether you use a mortiser or cut the mortises by hand, it is worth marking up the joints using a template or the more traditional rod (see page 180). Cut the mortises in a length of ¼-inch (6-mm) plywood, and then clamp this to the workpiece to mark the positions of the mortises.

3 Chop out the mortises by hand or with a mortiser. The mortiser not only removes the chopping, but it also means you don't need to mark up each joint with a mortise gauge, once you have set up the fence and depth stop.

4 There are any number of ways to cut the 56 tenons. Well set up, the band saw works best for cutting the cheeks and the table saw for cutting the shoulders (see page 218). But you could also use a router table, using the miter guide to slide the workpiece across a straight cutter.

5 Drill the holes in the rails (**B**) for the vertical rods. If you have a bench drill, set up a fence to repeat the operation. Otherwise use a marking gauge to position the holes along the center line of each rail. Use a rod to mark the position of each hole along the rails, and square the line around the component so that you can drill from both sides to reduce the risk of tear-out.

TIP: A test fit without glue: Always undertake at least one assembly of a project without glue, but clamped up exactly as you would for real. This will get all the clamps set to the right position and ensures that the joints will actually tighten comfortably. Glue, especially the prospect of it drying before the assembly is ready, complicates everything, and a test fit at least eliminates some of the potential complications.

6 Do a test fit (see page 182) of the joints before cutting the curved sides of the uprights. Make a template of the curve from plywood and use it to mark up each component; then cut them with a band saw or jigsaw. Make sure you keep the offcut, since this can be used as a packing piece when clamping up the rack (see page 129).

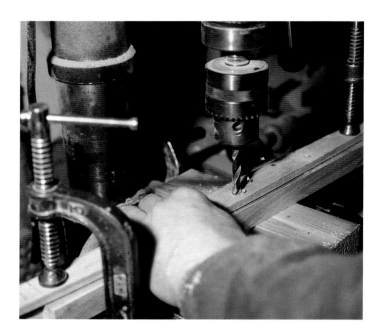

7 An alternative technique for cutting the curves is to make a plywood template, which is stuck to the face of the upright. Work the curve on the upright on the router table, using a trimming cutter running against the template (see page 138). Clean up the curves with a sanding block.

8 Assemble the front or back uprights and rails first. Once these two frames have been assembled and cleaned up, bring them together with the side rails. With so many parts involved, this can be a tricky operation, so be prepared. Test the diagonals at every stage of the assembly, but at the final clamp-up, check that the legs sit evenly on a flat surface.

9 You may be able to find a board wide enough for the top (**D**), but you will probably need to clamp up a panel from three narrower boards (see page 85). This will also make it more stable.

10 Having surfaced the top (though you may want to do this at the start with the other parts), cut it to shape, with gentle curves on the front and back. You can either bevel the edges with a bearing-guided bevel cutter in a router table, or do so by hand with a bench plane, working away from the center of each curve toward the ends to stop tearing. Always bevel the ends first, since the grain is likely to break at the end of the cut (see page 24), and this tear can be removed when you bevel the long-grain edges.

TIP: The holes in the bottom front and back rails for the metal rods must be stopped, or the rods will fall out. However, the holes in the top rails can be drilled right through so that the metal rods can be dropped down into position after assembly.

11 Screw the top to the top rails (see page 184). Clean up and apply a finish.

Lessons learned

- When you are dealing with curved components, you have to think carefully about the order in which you work. It is often best to cut the curves after all the jointing has been completed.

- It's worth finding a technique for repetitive cutting of tenons.

- Make sure any mortises are cut vertically. If the mortise is at an angle, it will be very difficult to assemble the project accurately.

Lesson 2
Cutting Tenons

Getting started

A woodworker without a workshop is like a bird without a nest. Once we've found our space to work, we have to piece it together in an endless process that involves perpetual evolution and development. The initial plan is bound to be inadequate within a few years, as the range of equipment grows and ambitions change. But you have to start somewhere, and there is no better place than at the bench.

Siting the workbench is one of the most important tasks for a woodworker. It must be level and ideally in good light. There must be plenty of space around it, especially around the end vise, which is usually positioned at the right-hand end. You'll probably want a shelf and some hanging space behind the bench for nearby tools, but the most critical thing is that the bench top be flat.

Fortunately, flat is a relative term, and what you could describe as level initially will only dissatisfy once you've acquired the skills to demand greater accuracy. The moment you become frustrated by a workpiece wobbling, you know that a) the bench top isn't as flat as you'd like and b) you're making progress.

Marking and cutting the mitered tenon

Common in chair construction, the mitered tenon is an essential mechanism when two rails or stretchers meet a leg or stile at the same point. To maximize the gluing area and length of the joints, the tenons are mitered at the ends and ideally should meet perfectly to improve the bond.

The cutting of the tenons is simple, carried out just as you would any similar joint, only the ends are mitered. However, chopping out the mortise is a little tougher than normal, since there is a risk of the wood breaking on the inside corner where the two mortises meet. The simple solution is to cut the first mortise and then insert a false tenon before you cut the second mortise.

When cutting the second mortise for mitered tenons, insert a false tenon to stop any breakout where the mortises meet.

Knowing how to make mitered tenons is an important skill that you will need to master in order to construct chairs and tables.

Lesson planner

Key techniques	Key tools and materials
• Cutting a mitered tenon • Identifying tenons • Laying out the workshop	• Workshop machines • Dealing with defects • Adhesives

Identifying tenons

While the mortise is, for all intents and purposes, just a hole in the wood, there are any number of different types of tenon. Each one serves a different purpose, though there are elements that are interchangeable. It is important to know the subtle difference between these different cuts, as each has properties making it suitable for a certain kind of join. Here are some examples of the different kinds of tenon you may come across as you gain experience.

Tenon for molded frame and panel. How the frame is rabbeted and how the profile juts out. This will be mitered to match the profile on the post.

A tenon cut from a rabbeted rail. Notice here that the haunch is angled. None of it is seen, but there is less tendency for the tenon to twist.

The basic haunched tenon. This helps retain some substance at the top of the stile while keeping some of the tenon full width to stop twist.

A simple full-width tenon. You use this when the tenon is entering a post at the middle rather than the ends.

This is sometimes known as a stub tenon, with shoulders on all four sides. It is the most common tenon and hides the mortise well.

The double tenon is used to increase the gluing area and strength of a tenon when you are using quite small-dimension stock.

This tenon is often used on the middle rail of paneled doors. The tenon is split so as not to weaken the post. It is wide to stop twist.

A more basic version of a tenon for doors has no shoulders at the ends. This makes the mortises more visible but stronger.

A haunched stub tenon is an example of how various techniques can be combined for a special situation.

I've found that a shelf just behind and above the bench is a great place to store the planes I use most often.

Tools

Laying out a workshop

I love reorganizing my workshop. At least once a year I'll have a purge and rearrange my machines, work surfaces, and tools, finding new places to store offcuts and equipment I rarely use. Some people happily work in chaos, but I prefer to have a reasonable platform from which to build, without being obsessive about tidiness and order. Though I hate not being able to put my hands on a particular tool when it's needed, that doesn't mean it has to be filed alphabetically: It just needs a logical home.

Here are some of the key features of a well-organized workshop.

The bench

This needs plenty of space so that you can work at both ends, with no obstructions for when you are planing with the bench vise or working around the end vise. Some woodworkers have large shops to position the bench in the center of the room, allowing 360-degree access.

The bench arrangement and tool storage are matters of taste bend need. Not everyone likes tool wells, which can fill with dust and shavings. I've devised a system of shelves behind my bench, with one above the bench level and one below the level. The one above the bench is ideal for placing planes away from the action but keeping them easy to pick up. The other shelf has holes for chisels and stores less frequently used tools. Behind the bench, I have a sheet of plywood attached to the wall, into which I fix screws to hold tools, the advantage being that I can move the additional screws around as my needs change. My bench has drawers and a cupboard, the former being particularly useful for storing abrasives, marking tools, and other small items.

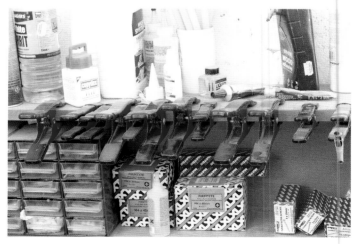

Most frequently used screws and glues are also near the bench.

Assembly table

If you have the space, I recommend you create a work surface dedicated to assembling projects, though it can also be used for temporary bench-top machines. Near this area you will need to store bar clamps, which are ideally hung from racks on the wall and within easy reach. A metal tube or thick piece of dowel rod can accommodate your small clamps, probably positioned near the bench.

It is important that the assembly area is well varnished and even waxed so that any excess adhesive knocks off when it's set. The surface must be flat for testing the legs of chairs and tables. Fix a shelf above this space for adhesive and glue spreaders, and keep paper towels nearby for cleaning up any spills.

To get the most glue possible, turn tubes upside down when not in use.

An assembly table makes gluing projects enjoyable and accurate.

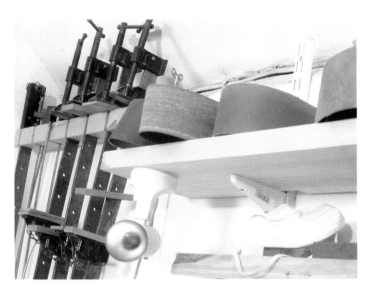

Bar clamps need to be readily available and are best stored on a rack.

Keep smaller clamps near the bench for holding jigs.

Machines to fit your workshop

Arranging machines around the workshop is an art in itself. As much as anything, you have to consider the direction and length of lumber that will be passed across the machine, and don't forget to consider where you will stand. Try to use varying machine heights creatively, since you may be able to position some equipment below the table height of another. Here are some of the key considerations.

Band saws. Band saws are often used to cut narrow lengths of lumber rather than sheets, and so the important factor is carry. I've found that band saws sit well in doorways. Since you need to have only half the machine protruding, it shouldn't get too much in the way. The table on a band saw is often quite high relative to other bench-mounted machines, and you might be able to position a router table nearby without too much interference. Long boards being cut on the band saw will pass over the router table.

Radial-arm saws. These types of saws suit long, thin workshops, while saw tables are better in square areas that have plenty of space in the center. The radial-arm saw only needs length but isn't as good for ripping boards as the saw table, which, since it needs both width and length, is space hungry.

Jointers and planers. In Europe, where workshop space is often more limited, planer thicknessers are popular because they make such efficient use of the direction of work. If you are lucky, you can position a power planer and jointer at right angles, with the boards traveling underneath the outfeed or infeed table of the jointer. This has certainly worked for me, but I'm fortunate to have an L-shaped workshop.

Lumber. Store lumber in the roof space if you can, since this will utilize otherwise dead space; however, remember that lumber is heavy and can be difficult to manhandle up and down. If possible, keep boards of the same species together so that you can find them more easily, especially if they are rough sawn and hence tricky to identify.

You need to store boards flat, with plenty of support to ensure they don't sag, and in a well-ventilated space away from dampness. Check your stock from time to time for mold and insects. You don't need to separate dry boards with sticks as you do when they are seasoning, but make sure you don't let oak and some other species touch iron or steel fittings, since this can lead to staining of the wood.

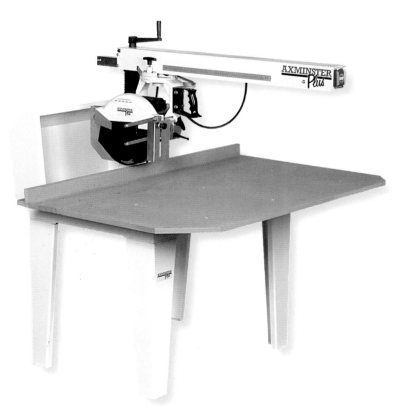

Small scraps are useful for padding when assembling projects, though I prefer permanent pads on my bar clamps.

Shelves for offcuts and short lengths of lumber are valuable, especially if they can be compartmentalized by species.

As your woodworking progresses, you will amass a growing stock of offcuts. These are very valuable and need to be easy to access for quick jobs like making jigs around the shop. However, offcuts can easily overwhelm a workshop, and it is important to have an area dedicated to them that doesn't overflow into the rest of the workshop. Once your offcut storage is full, you can probably start burning some of it.

That said, keep hold of even the smallest bits of valuable exotic species. I have some exquisite Cuban mahogany—which is now impossible to buy—recycled from an old wardrobe, and I refuse to throw out even the tiniest piece.

Sharpening. Dedicate an area to sharpening. Ideally, this should be close to the workbench but in an area where water and metal filings won't contaminate projects that you are working on. You need especially good light for sharpening and a work surface a bit higher than the bench.

Dust. All machines and power tools need extraction, but while this can be achieved with small vacuum extractors for tools that only produce dust or fine chippings, the jointer and power planer need proper extraction for shavings. The best solution is to site this outside the workshop by running ducting from the machines through the walls. There are many systems that can achieve this using flexible hose, soil pipe, or metal tubing.

If you have more than one machine connected to the same extraction unit, you will need to fit blast gates at each source; otherwise you will lose too much pressure. These can be relatively simple affairs or electronically controlled by a central command box. When laying out the ducting, try

to keep the bends to a minimum, since these will undermine the flow.

If you are particularly concerned about dust, you might also consider an ambient filter, which works on a similar principle to the kitchen extractor except that it filters dust within the workshop without ejecting it outside. The advantage of this, especially over the extractor housed externally, is that there is no need for air to come in from outside, which can have an effect on your heating system.

Heat. Though you have to take care with the obvious fire risks, wood-burning stoves are probably the most effective and economical way of warming a workshop, especially if you live in the countryside. Gas isn't as good, since it produces water vapor, but electric heating works well. Obviously, in a garage connected to the home, you may be able to run central heating to the workshop and potentially add a dedicated pump and circuit so that you are only warming that room during the day when everyone is out of the house.

A wood-burning stove gives fabulous heat in the workshop.

Finishing. It is easy to forget the importance of finishing in woodwork, and yet this is often what separates the really good woodworkers from the ordinary. Invariably, when I've been a judge of amateur woodworking competitions, it is the quality of the finish that is the deciding factor, especially for wood-turning and carving. You need an area clear of clutter and dust, where you can apply finishes to your projects. It could even share space with your sharpening area, where you may not be producing too much dust.

Foam applicators are cheap and good for applying many finishes.

Tools. When it comes to storing tools, accessibility is the important thing, though rustproofing comes a close second. I have problems with dampness in my workshop, but I don't like to store my tools in sealed cupboards, preferring to have them close at hand. To be honest, I'm not that well organized, but I do like tools to be in a logical place, with bar clamps hanging beside the assembly table and chisels at hand behind the bench. Storing all the rarely used tools I've collected over the years has always been my big challenge until the day I put them all in a big cardboard box and shoved them to the back of a cupboard.

Lighting. Successful woodworking depends on good lighting. Daylight is obviously excellent, but many workshops won't have this luxury, so other solutions are necessary. Striplights are good for ambient light, but

A small portable and powerful lamp is excellent for checking finishes.

nothing beats a number of spotlights directed at the area where you work. Use a light with a strong weighted base that takes a high-voltage bulb to illuminate your work.

Materials

All about wood—dealing with defects

Knots can add character to any project, but they are difficult to deal with, since the grain changes direction around the defect and there is a risk that the knot will fall out. It's often a case of judging whether you think the knot will survive and if it will get in the way of joints or profiles. Positioning knots in the center of the board, rather than near the ends or edges, is important. You may well need to use a scraper (see page 117) to finish the knot, and you might consider filling any gaps with epoxy resin to hold it in place. Try adding color to the resin for contrast.

Advanced adhesives

You can't underestimate the value of good glue for woodworking, and for most tasks, white cabinetmaker's adhesive (PVA) is ideal. However, there are many others to choose from that can be used for specific jobs.

Polyurethane adhesives

Polyurethane glues react with the moisture in wood (or any other material) and foam as they escape the joint. They come in a couple of types, notably distinguished by the speed of set, with some fixing in no more than five minutes. What you gain in speed you lose in glue line, and the fast-set polyurethane adhesives tend to leave a white crystaline deposit. Slower-setting types are usually stronger, and the best have a darker glue line that can't be seen once you apply a finish.

Advantages

Excess glue can be knocked off the surface after assembly, especially if you've applied a finish first. The glue doesn't dull blades and cutters, and is easy to work. They are simple to apply.

Disadvantages

The glue can go off inside the bottle, with a thick film forming. Your fingers will end up black or brown with dried glue, though this can be removed with acetone.

Yellow glue

Once you get into woodworking more seriously, you will soon discover yellow glue, which is essentially an improved version of white glue. Many of the properties are the same, but it tends to set faster and is stronger. These aliphatic glues are more water-resistant than white glue but are very easy to use.

Advantages
Easy to spread and use.
Relatively inexpensive.
Strong.
Fast setting.

Disadvantages
It sets a yellow color, but
not noticeably unless the
glue line is obvious.
In hot weather it may give
you only a few minutes to
complete an assembly.

Two-part epoxy

Two-part resins are commonly used around the home for
household repairs, but some woodworkers also use them
for projects. Their selling point is that you can build them
up to fill gaps, and there is the opportunity to add color or
fillers. They set quickly and are very hard. I use them for
some repairs and occasionally for laminating because they
are easy to apply with a brush and you can adjust the mix
of catalyst and resin for a longer open time.

Advantages
Quick drying.
Can fill gaps and be mixed
with colors or fillers.
Very strong.

Disadvantages
Expensive.
Can be brittle, and don't
always adhere well in
dusty conditions, so watch
out when using them
for repairs.

Cyanoacrylates

Usually referred to as Super Glue, cyanoacrylates are
designed to bond quickly but are not necessarily chosen
for longevity. They tend to be fairly brittle and can
survive pull stresses, but are often easily broken with
sheer pressure. It is worth buying the more expensive
brands, and you can find some that set more slowly and
are also less brittle. This sort of adhesive is useful in the
workshop when you need to make jigs or hold something
temporarily. You can also use them alongside longer-
term adhesives when clamps won't work. The
cyanoacrylate holds the pieces together long enough for
the other glue to set for a permanent bond.

Advantages
Set fast.
Very strong, at least in the
short- to medium-term.
Various types available.

Disadvantages
Too brittle for long-term use.
Can easily stick fingers to
wood! Make sure you have
a bottle of debonder.
Expensive.

Hot glues

Dispensed from a heated gun, hot glues set very quickly
and are very useful for temporary fixtures. Some people
use them all the time, but I've found that the glue sets so
fast that you don't always have time to complete the job.
Turners swear by them for holding wood on the lathe.
These glues certainly have their uses, and it's worth
buying an inexpensive gun, but don't expect to be using
it every day.

Advantages
Quick setting.
The glue has some
flexibility.
Low wastage.

Disadvantages
Delay waiting for gun to
heat up.
Glue can set too quickly.
Glue is only ever a
temporary fixture.

Hide glue

Traditional hide glue used to be kept warm in a pot,
emanating the most horrible stench. It was used by
furniture makers, and some antiques restorers and
repairers still employ it for authenticity. However, these
days you can buy a sanitized and improved version in a
bottle. It takes a long time to set and is very strong, with
the same honey consistency of traditional hide glue.

Advantages
Traditional.
Adheres well to almost
anything.
Long open time for
adjustments.

Disadvantages
Slow drying.
Very vulnerable to damp.

Contact adhesive

Some woodworkers use contact adhesives for applying
veneer. It is certainly strong but tends to be messy to use
and takes time.

Many woodworkers favor contact adhesive for gluing down veneer.

Project **Sideboard 1**

For the hallway

This sideboard can be used in many rooms around the house, but the drawer is ideal for phone directories in the hallway. The pine here is reclaimed, and the project is a good opportunity to practice tenons and mortises. Next lesson we will make the drawer.

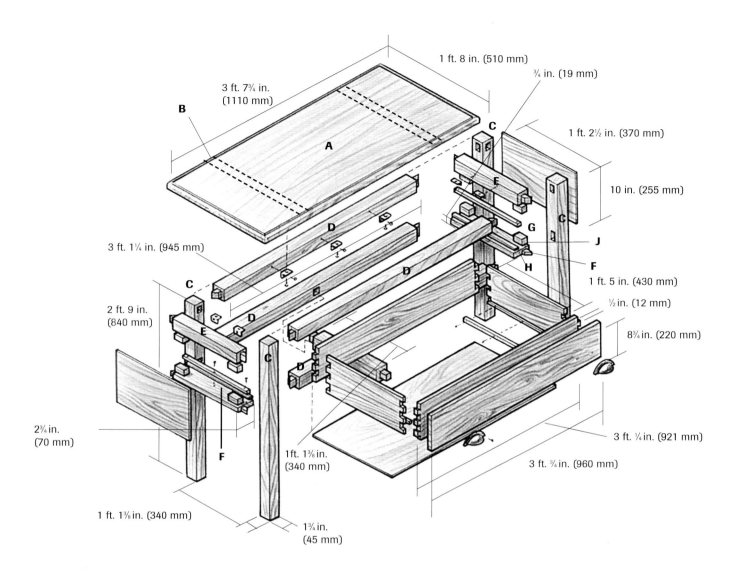

1 ft. 8 in. (510 mm)

3 ft. 7¾ in. (1110 mm)

¾ in. (19 mm)

1 ft. 2½ in. (370 mm)

10 in. (255 mm)

3 ft. 1¼ in. (945 mm)

1 ft. 5 in. (430 mm)

½ in. (12 mm)

2 ft. 9 in. (840 mm)

8¾ in. (220 mm)

2¾ in. (70 mm)

1ft. 1⅜ in. (340 mm)

3 ft. ¼ in. (921 mm)

3 ft. ¾ in. (960 mm)

1 ft. 1⅜ in. (340 mm)

1¾ in. (45 mm)

Cutting list

Part	Material	Quantity	Dimensions thickness, width, length	Part	Material	Quantity	Dimensions thickness, width, length
A Top	softwood	1	¾ x 20 x 43¾ in. (19 x 508 x 1110mm)	**F** lower side rail	softwood	2	¾ x 2¾ x 15¾ in. (19 x 70 x 400 mm)
B Top bearer (not shown)	softwood	3	¾ x 1½ x 17 in. (19 x 38 x 430 mm)	**G** drawer guide	softwood	2	¾ x 1¾ x 13⅜ in. (19 x 45 x 340 mm)
C Leg	softwood	4	1¾ x 1¾ x 33 in. (45 x 45 x 840 mm)	**H** drawer runner	softwood	2	⁵⁄₁₆ x ⅜ x 19¼ in. (2 x 10 x 489 mm)
D Front/ back rail	softwood	4	1 x 1¾ x 39⅝ in. (25 x 45 x 1006 mm)	**I** side panel	softwood	2	¼ x 10 x 14½ in. (6 x 254 x 368 mm)
E Side rail	softwood	2	1 x 1¾ x 15¾ in. (25 x 45 x 400 mm)	**J** block support	softwood	2	⅞ x ⅞ x 2 in. (21 x 21 x 50 mm)

1 Surface the components for the framework, including the legs, rails, drawer guides, and drawer runners.

Cut the mortises in the legs (**C**) for all the rails, taking care not to break the grain where the mortises meet (see page 194).

Cut the tenons on the rails, including the lower side rails (**F**), noting that each tenon is 1³/₁₆ inches (27 mm) long. Make sure the distance between the shoulders is consistent. Do a test fit of all the joints; then glue the front and back frames, followed by the whole thing.

2 Nail and glue the drawer runners (**H**) to the lower side rails.

3 Clamp the drawer guides (**G**) to the lower side rails so that the guides are flush with the inside face of the legs. Mark the position and drill screw holes in the lower side rails. Then glue the drawer guides in place, screwing up from below.

4 Glue the blocks (**J**) in place so that they are flush with the outside of the legs.

5 Glue the side panels (**I**) to the rails.

6 The top (**A**) can be made from stripwood, bought ready-planked at a home center, or by gluing up narrower boards, then planing or belt-sanding the top smooth. Stop the top from cupping by screwing three cleats (**B**) to the underside, ideally elongating the holes in the cleats so that the top can move a little (see page 184).

7 Rout a profile around the edges of the top, using a bearing guided cutter or with the side fence attached to the router. Make sure you rout the end grain first (see pages 137 and 181).

Lessons learned

- Cutting accurate joints requires a flat bench top.

- You can't have enough clamps.

- Complex assemblies are best done in stages.

Lesson 3
Tails and Pins

Getting started

I recall making my first dovetails as a boy at school, encouraged to build a toolbox from 1-inch (25-mm)-thick utile. It was too heavy to carry when empty, let alone when full of tools. The real error was that between myself and my teacher, we managed to position the dovetails the wrong way around, so that all the weight was held by the pins instead of the tails. Thanks to good glue, it didn't fall apart, but that was something of a miracle.

When to use a dovetail

The dovetail is the most decorative of woodworking joints, as well as one of the strongest, relying very little on the glue line. Perhaps only the wedged or draw-bored mortise-and-tenon joints are inherently stronger without adhesive. While the mortise-and-tenon is the joint of choice when connecting square or nearly square section components like rails and legs, the dovetail is most useful for joining boards, restricting any tendency for the wood to cup and also providing good strength.

Dovetails are most commonly used in the construction of boxes, drawers, and other high-quality casework. The visibility of the joint is something of a statement of ability in itself, especially now that there are so many quicker alternatives, like the biscuit joint (see pages 138 and 140) and the locked miter (see page 149), which are just as good. Unlike the mortise-and-tenon, which hides the vital parts of the joints within

itself, the dovetail lets everything hang out and any inaccuracy is highly conspicuous.

Basic principles of the dovetail

Though there are now many different types of dovetail jig that can cut the joint quickly and accurately, there is a satisfaction in being able to produce a tight-fitting dovetail by hand. It isn't that hard, either; it just takes patience and care.

Throughout the lessons so far, we've been debating the benefits of cutting joints so accurately that you don't need to pair them off. Huge amounts of time can be saved by developing the skills that allow you to fit any tenon into any mortise when, for instance, constructing the underframe of a table. With dovetails it's best to start afresh and assume that each joint is unique, at least until your experience and confidence grows. Without using a jig, it is very difficult to repeat a series of tails or pins, and one of its attractions is that each joint is slightly different.

Most woodworkers will cut the tails first. These are the fan-shaped parts that give the joint its name. On the other board you cut the pins, which fit between the tails. You use the tails on the first board to mark up the pins on the other. Usually you will have an equal number of tails and pins to the joint, though often you will start and finish with half pins, one at each end of the joint.

How you lay out the tails and pins and how you vary the spacing are very much matters of style. Visually it looks more interesting to have slightly wider tails than pins, and the finest work will usually have the thinnest pins, though the pins and tails can be roughly the same width. The angle of the tails, however, is important and depends on the strength of the lumber you are using. For softer species you need a higher angle, while the hardest woods are strong enough to cope with a shallow angle. One common rule is that you use an angle of about 1:6 for softwoods and 1:8 for hardwoods.

Variations of the dovetail joint

There are fewer variations on the dovetail than for many other joints, but they are all useful for different kinds of joinery. Here are some examples you may use:

Lesson planner

Key techniques	Key tools and materials
• Choosing a dovetail • Marking up a dovetail • Cutting dovetails • Making boxes	• Quarter-sawing lumber • Lumber for drawers • Dovetail templates • An engineer's square

The through dovetail. The basic joint is for both the tails and pins to be visible, like interlocking fingers clasped together. This is used in boxmaking, casework, and for the joint between drawer sides and the drawer back.

Making a clean, workable through dovetail takes a great deal of practice and skill, but it is essential for casework and items with drawers.

The blind, mitered dovetail. Often referred to as the secret mitered dovetail, this is a joint too advanced for many woodworkers, combining two of the trickiest joints to cut and being very difficult to achieve with jigs. This joint has to be cut by hand, and it is no coincidence that it isn't used very much. Anyone who claims to have employed the blind mitered dovetail ought to be censured to prove it because, of course, it is entirely hidden. What it achieves, however, is a mitered joint that is locked together, which almost no other technique can claim.

The tapered dovetail. Also known as the sliding dovetail, this joint is effectively a dado or housing but has the advantage of being self-tightening, so it is ideal for the construction of items too large to manage with bar clamps. A dovetailed dado or housing is cut in one component, tapering gradually to match a taper on

a dovetailed tenon cut on the other piece. Only as the two pieces are slipped together do you discover the success of the joint, by which time it may be too late to get it apart again. It is not widely used these days but has its place.

Of course, you can also produce dovetailed dados that aren't tapered, which just slide together and rely on glue for the final bond. These won't pull the components together as tightly as the tapered dovetail, but they are useful for inserting shelves into the sides of bookcases and similar pieces. You can work a dovetail on one or two sides of the shelf.

The half-blind or lapped dovetail. Used particularly in drawer construction to hide the ends of the pins when looking at the front of a drawer, the half-blind dovetail shows the end of the pins and sides of the tails, but hides the ends of the tails. Surprisingly, it can be easier to cut because half the joint is hidden, though extracting the waste from the sockets between the pins can be awkward. Some commercial woodworkers get around this by cutting a normal through dovetail and then sticking a false front to the drawer, as, in fact, we've done in this Sideboard lesson.

Unlike the through dovetail, half of this lapped dovetail is hidden. It is still a tricky operation, particularly extracting the waste from the sockets.

Having marked the depth line, use a dovetail template to mark the tails.

Put the board at an angle in the vise to cut down the tail vertically.

Shade the waste so that you cut to the waste side of the lines.

Cut the half pins at each end, taking care to cut vertically to the line.

Marking up a through dovetail

Because you cut each joint individually unless you are using a special jig (**D**), the marking up is especially important. It really is up to you how you divide up the tails and pins, and you have to experiment a few times to discover the effect you like. But always start by marking out the tails, using a dovetail template and small engineer's square to mark down the board and then across the end grain. A marking gauge sets the depth, though you can set this a fraction deep so that the tails are a little overlong and can be sanded back later.

Once you've cut the tails, which we'll explain later, you can use them to mark the positions of the pins. Initially it's a good idea to shade the waste areas you are removing!

Cutting the through dovetail

Whether you start with the tails or pins (and hundreds of pages have been written on the dilemma) is a matter of personal habit. I tend to cut the tails first.

1 Cut down the tails, obviously cutting to the waste side. To get the angle consistent, it's a good idea to cut all the angles that slope one way, and then all the ones

that slope the other. The same is true with the pins. This enables you to build up a muscle memory, and you are more likely to keep the angle consistent. Stop just short of the depth mark.

2 Use a coping saw to remove the waste between the tails, taking care not to cut below the depth mark. Removing the waste relieves the pressure when it comes to cleaning up the line with a chisel. You will need a very sharp bevel-edged chisel for paring end grain. While the first cuts can be done with a mallet, the last ones are best done solely with arm pressure, with your hand guiding the edge into the scored depth mark.

3 Clean up the tails. Then place the other part of the joint in a bench vise, with the end grain flush with the top of the bench. Lay the tails on top and mark across the positions. Mark the depth and then down the pins with the engineer's square.

4 Cut the pins and remove the waste as you did for the tails. Then you can start testing the fit, which always takes a bit of time. You want the fit to be firm without being too tight. The softer the lumber, the tighter the fit because the fibers will compress a little.

Let the little half pin fall away and do the other one.

Use a coping saw to remove the waste from between the tails.

Chop down to remove the waste from between the tails.

Use the finished tail piece to mark off the pins on its neighbor.

Cut down the pins and remove the waste with a coping saw. Then chop away the waste with a chisel.

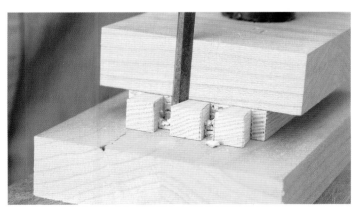

The packing piece also supports the chisel to keep it vertical.

biscuits, and dowels. Miters are also popular for boxmaking, since they too don't require much thickness and the corners are neat. They are not particularly strong, and will probably need some reinforcement (see page 76).

Generally, boxes are made from four sides, a base, and a top, though you don't have to look far to find exceptions. The base is usually held in grooves that are routed into the sides. The same is often true of the top, depending on the design. It may also be glued into rabbets or simply to the top of the sides. Or the top could be an independent frame and panel that are simply hinged to the back. The possibilities are endless, and boxes are a good opportunity to have a go at veneering and even marquetry.

Cut fingers in an offcut to clamp up a dovetailed joint, allowing the pins to protrude. They can be sanded back later.

To strengthen a long miter joint, rout cavities for keys into the miters.

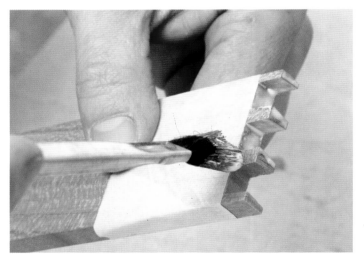

Use a brush to apply adhesive to the dovetails before assembly.

Assembling the through dovetail

The only important trick when it comes to assembling the dovetail is that you cannot exert pressure on the corners, since the tails or pins might protrude. Instead, you need to position the clamps farther in, away from the joint, but as close as possible so that you don't bend the components.

How to make a box

Boxmaking has become very popular over the last 15 years, with some remarkable designs produced. As a speciality, it has the advantage of not taking up much space or lumber, and everyone has a use for a box. However, it usually requires great accuracy, since boxes are inspected with microscopic degrees of curiosity.

Dovetails are often used for making a box because they hold the components in place. Another advantage is that with dovetails you can use thinner stock than for almost any other joint, since it is strong and you don't have to insert one piece into the other, as is the case for tenons,

The block stops the cavities from being routed too deeply.

Boxmaking tips

1 It's a good idea to make the box as a complete unit and then cut off the top after it is assembled. This can be done with a fine-blade table saw (see page 218) or with a narrow cutter in a router table. The trick is not to cut through the sides, but to stop just short. This way the top doesn't loosen, and you can make the final cut with a craft knife.

Put a thin cutter in the router table to separate the box from the lid.

Make light cuts, gradually working your way around the box.

Ensure the lid isn't caught in the cutter when separated from the box.

2 You often don't need heavy clamps to assemble the box: Rubber bands and masking tape will do to hold the components while the glue sets.

If accurately cut, mitered boxes can be glued up with decorator's tape.

3 Lining the inside of the box offers the opportunity to introduce another type of lumber—perhaps even using an aromatic species—and it also helps to align the top and sides of the box. The linings can be mitered inside the box, protruding just a little above the side to guide the top into position.

Use a mitered liner to achieve a better fit for the lid.

The lining needs to have a neat finish to match the rest of the jointing.

Tools

Dovetail templates

You can make your own dovetail template easily enough, but they are usually inexpensive to buy and are very useful. There are various designs, often offering two ratios to cope with softwoods and hardwoods.

Engineer's square

A small metal engineer's square is useful in many instances not only for setting up machines but particularly when it comes to marking up dovetailed joints. The blade needs to be only about 3 inches (76 mm) long. Still, check that it is square, both for the inside and outside edge of the blade.

Japanese saws

More and more woodworkers are using Japanese saws, sometimes to complement a tenon saw or to replace it entirely. Characterized by a long handle, fine blade, and teeth that usually cut on the pull stroke, the Japanese saw is ideal for cutting dovetails because it produces a particularly thin cut.

The long handle tucks neatly into your elbow for superb control, but I've found that some of the thinner blades have a tendency to wander and have less control than a fine dovetail or gent's saw. They take a bit of getting used to when starting the cut into end grain, since the teeth have a tendency to bite into the fibers and don't ride over the lumber as smoothly as a Western tenon saw.

Japanese saws have no kerf and are ideal for dovetailing.

There are many types of Japanese saw, and you won't regret buying one to experiment with. For dovetailing, you'll probably need a saw with about 24 tpi.

Materials

All about wood—aromatic lumber

The bottom of a drawer is traditionally made from an aromatic lumber, like cedar of Lebanon or incense cedar, to ward off insects and for the delicious smell as you pull the drawer open. These drawer bottoms are often left unfinished so as not to inhibit the aroma.

Quarter-sawing a log or a board

Drawer sides, which are sometimes known as drawer linings, are traditionally made from quarter-sawn lumber.

1 By cutting up yew branches on a band saw, you'll soon learn how to quarter-saw a log.

2 Cut it into strips, perhaps 1 inch (25 mm) wide.

The description derives from the technique of dividing a log into quarters along its length and then cutting boards with the growth rings at 90 degrees to the face. Because wood shrinks more from the center outward (radially) than around the circumference (tangentially), this is the most stable cut. There is also less opportunity for the growth rings to "straighten," which leads to the cupping of plain-sawn boards.

It can be difficult to find quarter-sawn boards, since most logs are plain-sawn. The most you will find is some quarter-sawn sections on a board, usually toward the edges. It is, however, very simple to convert a plain-sawn board into a quarter-sawn example.

3 You can see from the reassembled log how the grain on each board is at 90 degrees to the surface. This is the most stable cut.

Project **Sideboard 2**

For your paperwork

A good deep drawer is superb in the hallway for storing phone books and all those items that don't have a home in the office or the kitchen. Making this drawer is an excellent exercise in dovetailing.

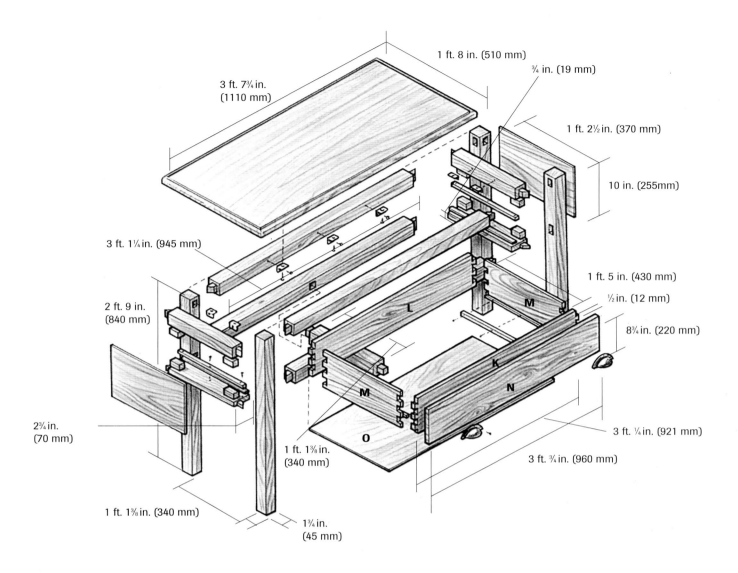

1 ft. 8 in. (510 mm)

3 ft. 7¾ in. (1110 mm)

¾ in. (19 mm)

1 ft. 2½ in. (370 mm)

10 in. (255mm)

3 ft. 1¼ in. (945 mm)

1 ft. 5 in. (430 mm)

½ in. (12 mm)

2 ft. 9 in. (840 mm)

8¾ in. (220 mm)

2¾ in. (70 mm)

1 ft. 1⅜ in. (340 mm)

3 ft. ¼ in. (921 mm)

3 ft. ¾ in. (960 mm)

1 ft. 1⅜ in. (340 mm)

1¾ in. (45 mm)

Cutting list

Part	Material	Quantity	Dimensions thickness, width, length
K Front	softwood	1	½ x 7½ x 36¼ in. (12 x 190 x 921 mm)
L Back	softwood	1	½ x 7⅛ x 36¼ in. (12 x 181 x 921 mm)
M Side	softwood	2	½ x 7½ x 17 in. (12 x 190 x 430 mm)
N False front	softwood	1	⅜ x 8¾ x 36¼ in. (10 x 222 x 921 lmm)
O Base	ply/softwood	1	3/16 x 16½ x 35¾ in. (2 x 419 x 908 mm)

1 Surface all the parts to thickness, and cut and plane to width. There are a couple of points to notice. Instead of cutting lapped dovetails, as an introduction to this most famous joint, we are gluing a false front (**N**) to the drawer after assembly to give the impression of a lapped joint (see page 43). The fact that we've specified a plywood base influences the design of the drawer, although we've actually adapted the traditional approach used when a solid lumber base is fitted to let it move (see page 184), so the back (**L**) is narrower than the sides (**M**).

Rout the groove in the sides and front for the base, ¼ inch (6 mm) from the bottom edge. It is easier to do this now than after you have cut the dovetails, when there's also a risk of taking chips out of the tails in particular.

Mark out the tails on the front or back at whichever corner you want, using a dovetail template to get the angle right (see page 212). Cut the joint.

2 Use the tails to mark up the pins on the sides. Cut the pins and test the fit; do the same for the others.

Cut the plywood base (**O**) to size, and slot it into the sides and front; assemble the drawer without glue.

Glue the drawers, using bar clamps with blocks to pull the joints together. Check the diagonals; then slide the base into the grooves and pin to the bottom edge of the back. You can support the base further with thin bearers glued to the sides and front beneath the groove.

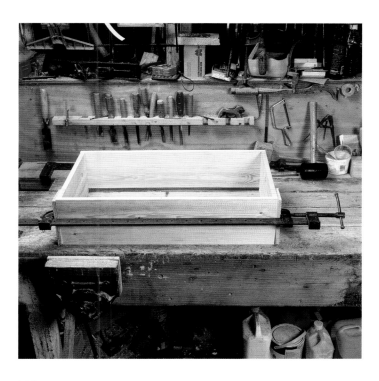

3 Use a block plane or belt sander to trim back the proud pins or tails (see page 206). Then glue the false front to the drawer. Once the glue has set, you can plane the edges and clean up the front.

4 Test the fit of the drawer in the sideboard. There should be no more than a ⅟₁₆-inch (1.6-mm) gap around the outside of the drawer and preferably a bit less. The important thing is that the gap is consistent.

Finish the outside of the drawer and screw the drawer pulls to the front.

Lessons learned

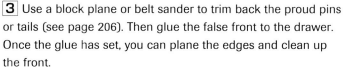

- Dovetails take a lot of practice!

- Don't worry if the pins protrude through the tails, as they can easily be sanded back afterward.

- Experiment with the order of cutting dovetails. You may find you prefer to cut the pins before the tails.

- For the drawer to fit well, the case must be absolutely square.

Lesson 4
Crosscut to Accuracy

Getting started

If you want to convert wide lumber into manageable boards, buy a band saw. But if you want to achieve some really accurate results quickly and repeatedly, go out and get a table saw. When you buy one, though, make sure it's good, since it will soon become your best friend and you'll discover uses for it you never imagined.

There's a bit of a cultural divide about the table saw. In the United States it has become a multipurpose machine, used for many operations. In the United Kingdom the spindle molder (shaper) and the dedicated tenoning machine are favored, and the table saw tends to be used for fewer jobs. Some woodworkers prefer the radial-arm saw or its modern equivalent, the sliding chop saw or miter saw. These are especially suitable for narrower workshops, because the work is laid on the table and the saw is moved. But they are not as useful for ripping lumber and for cutting wide sheet materials.

Using a table saw

I don't believe that a table saw can compare with the band saw, jointer, and power planer, or even the router table as the great leap forward for an improving woodworker, but it is certainly useful. It is also very versatile and has the potential for employment in many jointing jobs. It must, however, be set up very accurately.

Safety is an important consideration when using a table saw because it is a powerful machine. It is essential that you keep the riving knife fitted to the saw, since this keeps the cut open so that the board doesn't bind on the blade

Make sure the saw blade is square to the table.

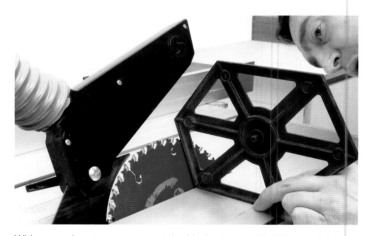
With an angle setter you can set the blade at a specific tilt to cut joints for certain types of geometric angles.

and kick back at the operator. By keeping the guard in place, you ensure that any lumber that flicks up from the saw can't go very far in the air and toward your face. Many top guards also have fittings for dust extraction. There are some operations on a table saw, like tenoning, that can be done safely enough, but you should fit some form of homemade guard to house the blade and limit the consequences of kickback.

Table saws can be improved by fitting a homemade or store-bought insert where the blade projects from the table. When you are trimming small pieces off the end of a board, they have a tendency to fall down into the gap in the insert. If the gap is too wide, say more than $\frac{1}{16}$ inch (1.5 mm), there

Lesson planner

Key techniques	Key tools and materials
• Setting up a table saw • Ripping with a table saw • Crosscutting with a table saw	• The table saw • Alternatives to a table saw • Choosing a sawblade

There needs to be a good angle gauge on the saw to show the tilt of the blade.

It's good to have an off switch you can knock with your knee.

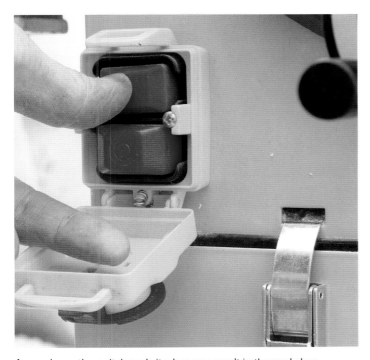

A guard over the switch seals it when you aren't in the workshop.

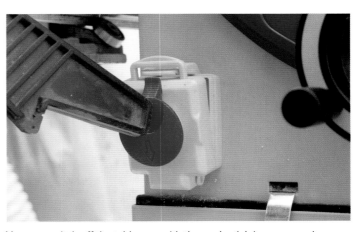

You can switch off the table saw with the push stick in emergencies.

Some saws have a clip for a push stick on the rip fence, which keeps it close.

is a chance that trimmings will catch the blade and throw back toward you. Always wear earplugs when using a table saw—or any machinery and power tool for that matter—and make sure the dust is extracted. I often wear a visor if I'm concerned that an operation might be hazardous.

It is very important that you have push sticks at hand for pushing the lumber across the saw. You need two, one for each hand, but it's a good idea to have more around the workshop, since they always seem to get mislaid. Make sure you have them by every machine, particularly the table saw, band saw, and router table. Get used to using a push stick even when you don't need it—it's a good habit to develop. However, remain aware of the risks you face, and don't assume that you are safe because you are wearing the gear and using a push stick. It is just as important to feel the pressure you are having to exert and

Make sure the power is off when you change the blade.

listen to the sound of the machine, since mistakes and accidents often happen when tools are under load and you are having to work too hard. I've noticed that you use more pressure with a push stick than you might with only your hands, and then when the cut finishes, your hand rushes toward the blade.

Ripping with a table saw

Personally, I cut boards to width along the grain (ripping) with a band saw as often as possible because you lose less wood in the cut. However, the band saw won't always cut beautifully straight, and a home woodworker's band saw is probably not as powerful or as fast-cutting as the home woodworker's table saw.

Usually you will rip with the board against the fence, which you should be able to adjust side to side and forward and back. By sliding the fence forward a little, you can give yourself more lead-in and counter any tendency for the wood to bind against the fence after the cut.

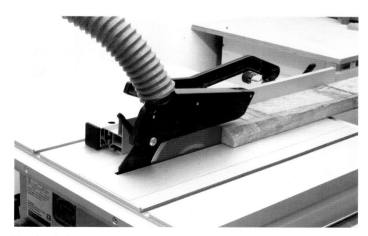

Use the rip fence for cutting along the grain.

When ripping long boards, it is useful to have a roller stand on which the lumber can rest as it leaves the saw. These can be made from a piece of broom handle held in a frame, or you can buy various designs depending on your budget. I have only the most basic metal roller, and not the ball-bearing type, since most of my work is relatively short. But if you do a lot of work with long boards or whole sheets of plywood, it is worth buying a support that is accurate and smooth-running.

Crosscutting with a table saw

I use a table saw for accurate crosscutting operations more than anything else. For this you need a fine-tooth blade and an accurate miter fence. These are the two essentials, but I would also add a flip stop, since it is so useful for repetitive cutting.

If you have a sliding carriage for the miter fence, and I thoroughly recommend you do, it is worth fitting

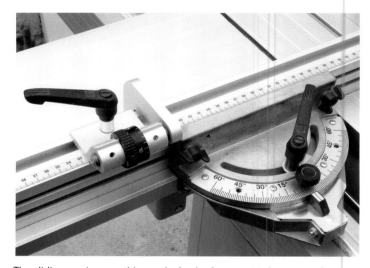

The sliding carriage on this saw locks the fence at 90 degrees and 45 degrees.

With the crosscut fence at 45 degrees, you can cut accurate miters.

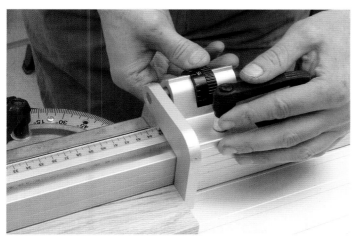

A flip stop is essential for repetitive cutting to length.

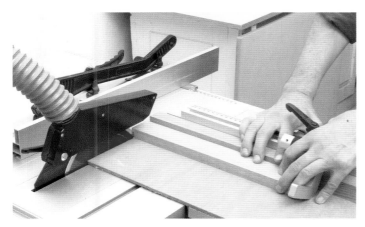

Fix a false table to the crosscut fence to hold the workpiece solidly.

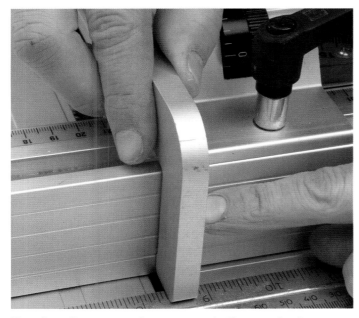

Use a fine adjuster or your finger to move the flip-stop a fraction.

a false "table" that slides back and forth on the carriage. This way you can run the plywood "table" right up against the blade for less breakout, and it also means the join between the carriage and the proper table is bridged because it can be very difficult to level this join on cheaper table saws. The only disadvantage is that you lose a bit of available cutting height.

When it comes to cutting angles with a table saw, it's best to alter the fence, if at all possible, rather than tilting the blade. Resetting the fence afterward is usually far easier than resetting the blade, though it does depend on the saw.

Common tasks for the table saw

There are a number of books that concentrate solely upon the table saw, for it is a versatile machine and can perform many operations.

1 **Tenoning**. The simplest technique is to cut tenon shoulders on the table saw, with the component against a stop on the miter fence. You can then remove the cheeks on a band saw or with a tenon saw. However, you can also produce a carriage for the rail to be tenoned that uses the table saw for cutting the cheeks as well.

2 **Dovetails**. With the blade tilted to the appropriate angle, you can cut the tails. Then with the blade upright and the

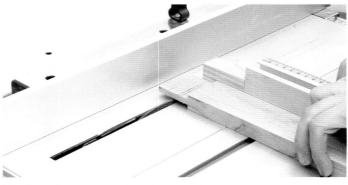

Watch out for the saw binding if you run the tenon against the rip fence while using the crosscut fence.

Set the saw blade to the depth of the tenon.

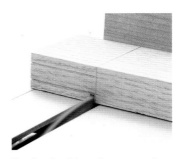

Cut the shoulders of tenons on the table saw, cheeks on a band saw.

With a special jig against the rip fence, you can cut tenons easily.

The notch pushes the workpiece through the saw.

fence adjusted, cut the pins, to remove the bulk of the waste before you clean them up by hand (see page 209).

3 **Tapering.** You can buy adjustable jigs that you fit to the rip fence on the table saw for cutting tapers. Or you can simply cut a piece of 1-inch (25-mm)-thick plywood at the appropriate angle and fit it to the rip fence.

4 **Dados.** Table saws are often used for cutting grooves, though you ought to replace the top guard with a

homemade alternative. Don't remove the riving knife. With multiple cuts you can use the table saw to cut dados wider than the kerf of a single blade, or you can buy kits for stacking blades. The use of wobble blades, which are canted over at an angle as they spin, is frowned upon in some countries.

5 **Miters.** Though the radial-arm saw and the chop saw are often favored by site carpenters for cutting miters, the table saw is still an effective tool for the job.

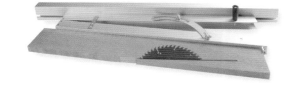

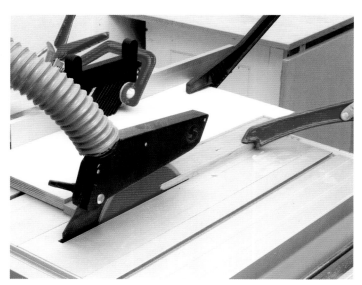

With a homemade jig you can cut tapers with ease using a table saw.

Set the depth of cut with a depth gauge.

Using a drawing like an atlas

Working your way around a drawing is a bit like using a road map to search for identifying details, while using the cutting list for supporting evidence. A good drawing shows the construction clearly, with no doubts about the position and shape of components, and has as few annotations as possible.

Ideally, the cutting list should give you the length of each component, though you may want to add a little to this when roughly cutting up all the parts. Those dimensions that are defined by the cutting list—for example, the width and thickness of a part—don't need to be repeated in the drawing. There are, however, exceptions to this rule, specifically when parts are shaped or tapered, in which case you need to look out for the angle and length of the taper and the final width or thickness. A good drawing should also show the distances between shoulders, such as on the rails of a table, which are not given by the cutting list.

When using a drawing, check the dimensions tally with the cutting list before you start cutting up lumber. Trust me, there can be errors. This not only reduces the number of wasteful mistakes, but it also acquaints you with the construction. Check that dimensions add up. Be particularly cautious when the measurements are given in both metric and imperial, since the conversions may not be correct. Try to establish which measurement was originally used, searching for the most number of "rounded" figures that are a clue to its origins. If you are able to determine this, you can then make your own conversions and check their validity as you proceed.

Making a scratch stock

A great little homemade tool for beading is the scratch stock. Though you can buy one, there is something satisfying about making it yourself. Use an old piece of hacksaw blade for the cutter, which is inserted into a wooden stock, held in a groove by screws. Make very gradual, shallow cuts, slowly extending the blade from the stock. You can sharpen the blade as you might a cabinet scraper (see pages 117 and 119).

Cut a short length of hacksaw blade for the cutter on the scratch stock.

Cut the stock of the scratch stock from a piece of hardwood.

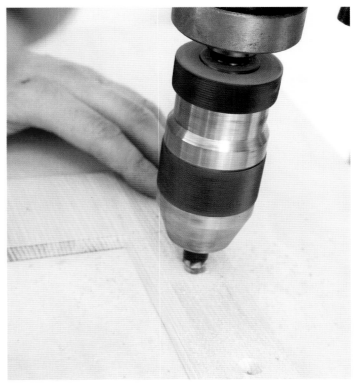

Using a file, work the shape of the cutter on the end of the hacksaw blade.

Drill and countersink the scratch stock halves together and hold the cutter.

Tidy up the scratch stock on a disk sander.

Scratch stocks need to be held tightly, and gradually the bead is formed.

Tools

The table saw

When it comes to choosing a saw table, the first criterion is likely to be the size of blade, with the most common sizes being 8 inches (203 mm) and 10 inches (254 mm) for home woodworkers. Blade diameter often determines the power of the motor, the size and robustness of the machine, and the price. Generally, though, I'd favor buying an expensive, smaller machine over a cheap, larger table saw.

The problem is that an 8-inch (203 mm) table saw cannot cut boards 8 inches (203 mm) thick. The amount of blade protruding through the table will be far less than this, and then you have to take into account how the top guard fits on the riving knife, since this can further inhibit the cut depth. When using the blade on an angle, the depth of cut is restricted even more.

The best saws have cast tables, which are made from either aluminum or iron and ground flat. A good model will have a sliding carriage to make crosscutting easier and far more accurate. Some have extension tables to the sides and back, but a roller stand will do for the latter, and you don't need as much table space as you might imagine. The quality of the saw can also be judged by the type of motor used. The cheaper models are fitted with brush motors, which you can identify by their high-pitched screech. They also tend to start quickly, almost with a jolt. Induction motors are much quieter, which is a major consideration for home woodworkers, and many will have a soft start, thereby taming the beast a bit.

Alternatives to the table saw

The traditional approach to woodworking is to have a solid table saw that is used for ripping and crosscutting,

Trade secret

Marking out a curve from two halves

When marking out a curve for cutting on a band saw, you need to draw only half the shape on a piece of card or paper. Transfer that curve twice onto a piece of thin plywood to create a template that you use for marking all components. Don't be tempted to mark the first piece and then use this for the next and so on, since you are likely to alter the shape as you cut each piece.

but there are alternatives or additions you might consider since they are better for some jobs.

1 **Radial-arm saw.** Favored by anyone who rarely rips boards and who often cuts to length. If you have a band saw for ripping boards, the radial arm might be a good choice, especially if you have a long workshop with plenty of work-surface space, but perhaps not so much free space in the center. Table saws, in comparison, are best in square shops, where there is plenty of space in the center for both cross-cutting and ripping. Radial-arm saws are not brilliant for cutting up sheet materials, since the length of cut is limited.

2 **Chop saws.** Also known as the miter saw and used extensively on-site, the chop saw is very similar to the radial arm, but usually has more sophisticated adjustments for cutting miters. It also has a much shorter length of cut, so is more likely to complement a table saw than replace it. Like the radial-arm saw, you need plenty of wall space. Excellent if you are cutting loads of miters. Some miter saws now have a table over the top for ripping.

3 **Contractor's saw or saw site.** A lightweight version of the traditional table saw, the contractor's saw is usually relatively inexpensive for the cut it offers. It is certainly worth considering, and the flip-over version offers options for using the machine like a traditional table saw or chop saw.

Beading tools

Obviously you can use a router for beading, but sometimes for small jobs it's quicker and more satisfying to do it by hand. You can either make a scratch stock yourself (see page 223) or buy a beading tool with ready-formed cutters.

Materials

Choosing a saw blade

Get used to changing the saw blade in the table saw, since the choice of blade has a significant impact on what you can achieve with the machine. It is certainly worth buying a good blade because the table saw lives and dies on the quality of the cut.

The number of teeth is probably the main consideration when buying a saw blade. Though there's a temptation to select a general-purpose blade, say 32 teeth for an 8-inch (203-mm) blade, this tends to fall short for both ripping and crosscutting. A finer blade, say 48 teeth for the same blade, will crosscut beautifully to a finish you can joint, while still being able to rip reasonably. I'd also buy a rip saw of 16 teeth for a much more aggressive cut to cope with the longer fibers when ripping. With fewer teeth, there are wider spaces for the dust to be ejected, but don't use this blade for crosscutting, since it will tear the wood.

You won't find a huge range of kerf widths when it comes to choosing a saw blade. Most are about ⅛ inch (4 mm), but you can find finer. The majority of the teeth have relatively similar shapes, but some have what is known as negative rake for a finer cut and less chance of grabbing occurring in a miter saw.

Cleaning and storing saw blades

If you have more than one saw blade, make sure they are stored safely so that their brittle tungsten teeth don't chip in your own holder or a bought one. Keep them well oiled to stop rusting.

It is an easy mistake to think that a saw blade is blunt, when it is often just caked in resin. Ironically, cutting softwoods can do more damage to a saw blade than hardwoods. However, it is short-lived, since the buildup of dirt can be treated with a cleaning spray, which can also be employed for router cutters.

All about wood—abrasive lumber

Some species are famously abrasive and dull blades faster than others. This isn't always because they are harder or heavier than others, since some lumber contains abrasive particles that wear down an edge more quickly than others. Oak, for instance, can be abrasive, but it is the exotic species that are likely to be worst for this.

Project **Cherry bookcase 1**

For the living room

Though it looks large, this bookcase is no more than casework, to the front of which is attached a frame and doors. The casework can be joined together with a biscuit jointer.

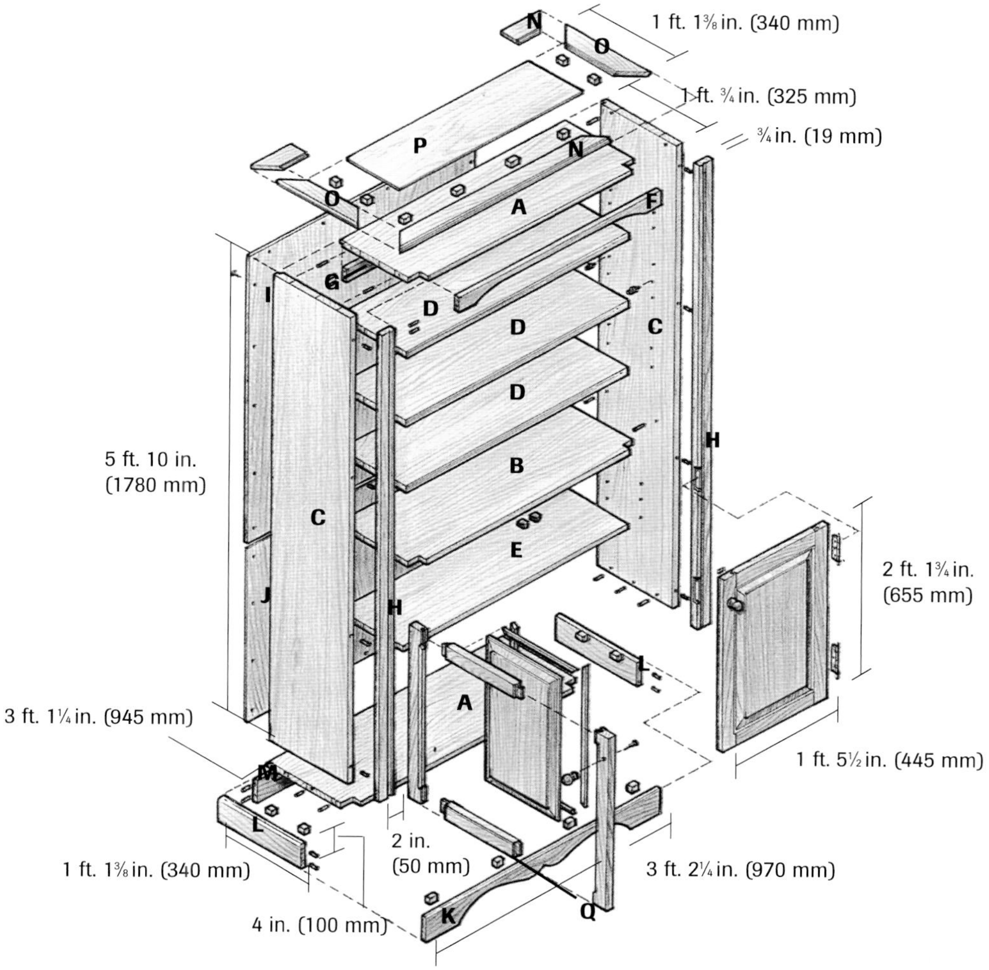
1 ft. 1⅜ in. (340 mm)
1 ft. ¾ in. (325 mm)
¾ in. (19 mm)
5 ft. 10 in. (1780 mm)
2 ft. 1¾ in. (655 mm)
3 ft. 1¼ in. (945 mm)
1 ft. 5½ in. (445 mm)
2 in. (50 mm)
1 ft. 1⅜ in. (340 mm)
3 ft. 2¼ in. (970 mm)
4 in. (100 mm)
A
B
C
D
E
F
G
H
I
J
K
L
M
N
O
P
Q

Shopping list

Extra tools for the job

Brass shelf supports and lug supports (sixteen of each)
Beading cutter or beading tool

Cutting list

Part	Material	Quantity	Dimensions thickness, width, length
A Top/ bottom	cherry	2	¾ x 13½ x 36¾ in. (19 x 343 x 933 mm)
B Pot shelf	cherry	1	¾ x 13¼ x 36¾ in. (19 x 335 x 933 mm)
C Side	cherry	2	¾ x 12¾ x 70 in. (19 x 324 x 1778mm)
D Shelf	cherry	3	¾ x 12¾ x 36¾ in. (19 x 324 x 933 mm)
E Cupboard shelf	cherry	1	¾ x 11¼ x 36¾ in. (19 x 286 x 933 mm)
F Front top rail	cherry	1	⅝ x 4 x 34¼ in. (16 x 102 x 870 mm)
G Back top rail	cherry	1	¾ x 2 x 36¾ in. (19 x 51 x 933 mm)
H Upright	cherry	2	¾ x 2 x 70 in. (19 x 50 x 1778 mm)
I Ply bookcase back	plywood	1	¼ x 37½ x 42⅝ in. (6 x 952 x 1083 mm)
J Ply cupboard back	plywood	1	¼ x 37½ x 26⅝ in. (6 x 952 x 676 mm)
K Plinth front	cherry	1	¾ x 4 x 38¼ in. (19 x 102 x 972 mm)
L Plinth side	cherry	2	¾ x 4 x 13⅜ in. (19 x 102 x 340 mm)
M Plinth back	cherry	1	¾ x 4 x 36¾ in. (19 x 102 x 933 mm)
N Cornice front/back	cherry	2	¾ x 2⅝ x 38¼ in. (19 x 67 x 972 mm)
O Cornice side	cherry	2	¾ x 2⅝ x 13⅜ in. (19 x 67 x 340 mm)
P Ply dustboard	plywood	1	¼ x 10 x 34 in. (6 x 254 x 865 mm)
Q Glue block	cherry	20	¾ x ¾ x 1³⁄₁₆ in. (19 x 19 x 27 mm)

1 Start by preparing the main components of the casework, namely the sides (**C**), the top and bottom (**A**), the pot shelf (**B**), and the back top rail (**G**). You can probably make do without the final part. Cut all the parts exactly to length and drill the sides for the shelf supports. Notice that the pot shelf is ¼ inch (6 mm) narrower than the top and bottom (**A**) to account for the thickness of the ply back (**I** and **J**), which is rabbeted into the sides, top, and bottom.

2 Joint the horizontal parts (**A**, **B**, and **G**) to the sides (**C**) with dowels or biscuits depending on your equipment and preference.

3 Rabbet the back edges of the sides, top, and bottom for the ply back. With such long components, it's easier to do this hand-held with the router than by using a router table (see page 136).

4 Cut the notches from the front of the top and bottom to accommodate the uprights (**H**).

Cut out the two pieces of ply for the back, making sure the cuts are accurate. Check the diagonals to test for square.

Glue up the casework using bar clamps to draw the sides to the horizontal parts. You'll need six bar clamps: two per shelf, front and back. Check the diagonals and screw the back in place to add support.

Prepare the lumber for the uprights and front top rail (**F**). Notice that the front top rail is slightly thinner than the uprights to make up for the beaded profile along the inside edge of the uprights.

5 Use a router, scratch stock, or a combination plane to shape the bead down the upright (see page 146).

6 If you choose to join the rail to the uprights with a mortise-and-tenon, the rail will have to be a bit longer for the tenon.

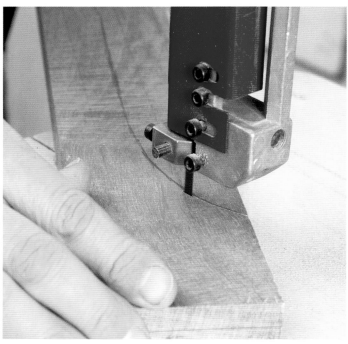

7 Cut the curved recess from the top front rail with a jigsaw or band saw, having marked it up with a template.

8 You can glue the rail and uprights now; then fix them in position with dowels (see page 54), or wait until the doors are ready next lesson and cut the hinge recesses first.

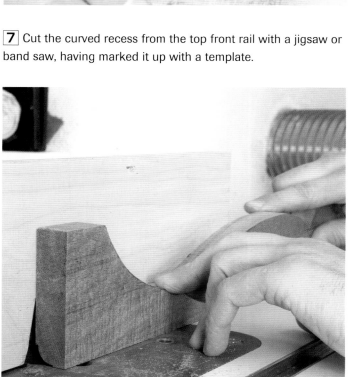

9 Prepare the parts for the plinth (**K**, **L**, **M**). For strength, this is best constructed with reinforced butt joints (see pages 54 and 138), but it would be tidier if mitered, in which case you might need to screw or glue right-angled corner blocks inside the corners. If you rout the profile along the top edge of the plinth after you have assembled it, the fact that the corners aren't mitered will hardly be noticeable.

10 Cut the shaped lower edge of the front plinth rail (**K**) using a template as a guide. Using a halved template is useful here (see page 58). Assemble the plinth. If you can do so, dry with the bookcase on its back so that you can test the fit of the plinth against the casework. The bottom of the bookcase should fit neatly on blocks screwed and glued to the inside of the plinth.

11 Rout the profile on the cornice components (**N** and **O**) and also rout a rabbet on the top inside edge to take the plywood dustboard (**P**).

Lessons learned

- Large assemblies are daunting, but actually not always as difficult as you might imagine.

- Miters are one of the most difficult joints to get right, especially when they are as long as the ones on the cornice.

- Finishing shaped components is much more difficult than finishing straight parts.

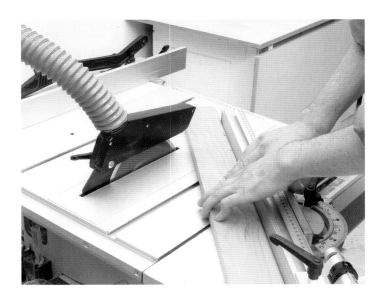

12 Miter the cornice parts and assemble with a band clamp, screwing the dustboard in place for support. You can screw or dowel the cornice to the top when you are ready. Prepare the lumber for the other shelves (**D** and **E**) and insert on the support. Now you are ready to make the doors.

Lesson 5
Frames and Panels

Getting started

Medieval furniture was characterized by being made from solid boards in a simple style. An evolution of this approach has been to hold panels within a frame. This saves on wood and gives the piece greater strength and stability. However, making a frame and panel needs jointing cutting skills and equipment.

I've always loved making panels. There is something very satisfactory about machining up all the parts and then jointing the components together. With so many options for ornamentation and decoration, you can stamp your individuality on a design and try out different effects. You will also need to experiment with more advanced techniques, and the accurate jointing puts greater emphasis on the integrity of your work, so your tools have to be razor sharp and working well.

Panels can be made from plywood or MDF for economy, but the excitement comes from producing solid woodwork. More care is needed to allow the wood to move, but you can experiment with various styles of cutter to produce different raised and fielded paneling.

The principles of frame-and-panel construction

One of the most important developments in furniture design was the evolution of frame-and-panel construction, which replaced the use of simple solid boards for the doors and "bodywork" of cabinets and chests. Holding a panel within a frame makes better use of lumber, is more stable, and provides more opportunities for decoration and individuality.

Today it means we can use man-made sheet materials in projects while retaining a sense of craftsmanship. This is economical, saves time, and makes the frame even easier to construct, though it may inhibit the potential for ornamentation.

The frame-and-panel offers the woodworker so many chances to make his mark. You can alter the dimensions

When rails are molded, you may need to meet profiles with a miter.

The solid wood panel fits into a groove in the frame components.

Lesson planner

Key techniques	Key tools and materials
• Basic frame-and-panel • Adjusting the mortise-and-tenon to suit • Veneering	• Router cutters for jointing • Drilling jigs for shelves • Moisture meters • Figure in wood

of the rails and stiles in relation to the panel, with some of the arts-and-crafts designers doing this with spectacular results. The frame edges, particularly those facing inward, can be profiled with any molding, though it is the lack of any such decoration that distinguishes Shaker furniture. Study furniture of different ages to see how these small details help define the age.

In almost every case, the posts and rails are tenoned and mortised, with tenons worked on the horizontal rails and mortises cut in the posts. In this lesson we will look at some of the variations of the joint and discuss how they can be made by machine or power tool. There are any number of ways you can deal with the panel. Usually it is inserted into grooves routed into the rails and posts, though you can also use a rabbet and bead. The panel

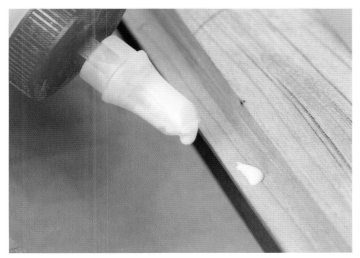

When gluing a solid wood panel into a frame, apply only a dab of glue so that the panel can move.

Trade secret

Judging the sizes of tenons

In deciding the depth of the mortise, you are trying to compromise the need for a long tenon to give the joint strength, without weakening the posts. I'd go for a mortise between half and two-thirds the width of the post. The same compromise applies when marking out the haunch. For a 2-inch (50-mm)-wide rail, the groove for the panel is likely to be up to ⅜ inch (10 mm) deep. The haunch is about ½ inch (12 mm) wide, and the tenon proper is 1⅛ inch (30 mm) wide.

itself can be flat, or raised and profiled, sometimes known as fielding.

Making the basic frame-and-panel

The simplest frame-and-panel has no molding on the rails and posts, and the flat panel is fitted into a groove, which is the same width as the mortise. In these circumstances the panel will usually be plywood or veneered board and can be glued into the groove to help strengthen the assembly.

If, the panel is made from solid lumber you must give it room to move, so the grooves in the posts (assuming the grain runs up and down) are cut deep enough to give the panel some extra space. In this instance you fix the panel in place by using glue in the groove down one post or using a dab of adhesive at the center of the groove on each rail. With the first technique, the panel can expand and contract across its whole width toward the unglued post, while with the latter technique the panel moves both sides away from the center.

Making a simple frame-and-panel

1 **Leave a horn** of at least 1 inch (25 mm) on the end of each post and cut the rails exactly to length. Extending the mortise to the end of the post would weaken the lumber, so instead the tenon has a haunch to fit into the groove, which is routed the full length of the post. The haunch stops the rail from twisting.

2 **Chop out the mortises first.** Then rout the groove for the panel along the inside edge of both the posts and rails. It is easier to cut the mortise before the groove is worked, basically because you can see the marks more clearly, and the cutter isn't deflected. It doesn't matter that you cut the groove in the rails before cutting the tenons; in fact, it reduces the amount of work you need to do.

3 **Cut the tenon,** with the haunch fitting neatly in the groove. This has to be accurate for doors, since the top of the rail and post will be visible.
Tip: If you don't want the haunch to be visible on the top of the post but need the benefits a haunch provides (no weakness in the post and no twisting of the tenon), you can slope the haunch. You cut it just as you would any other tenon.

4 **Cut the panel to size.** If it is made from solid lumber rather than sheet materials, you need to leave at least ⅛ inch (3 mm) for movement.

5. Assemble the frame-and-panel before you cut off the horns on the posts. You can apply a finish to the panel and the inside edges of the frame before assembly, but leave all the others unfinished to be tidied up after the glue has set.

Check for square when clamping up a frame and check the diagonals.

Decorating the simple frame-and-panel

In Shaker furniture the simple frame-and-panel was left entirely unadorned. However, you may want to add a profile on the inside edge of the rails and posts. There are a couple of ways to do this.

1 **The stopped chamfer.** The simplest solution, which gives a piece a country look and feel, is to chamfer the inside edges but stop short of the joints. If you use a router to do this, the end of the stopped chamfer will be slightly scalloped, which can be left like that, but is a telltale sign of this modern technique. For a more traditional look pare back the ends of the chamfer.

2 **A bearing-guided router.** With the frame assembled dry, but without the panel in place, you can use a router with a bearing-guided cutter to shape a profile. The only problem is that the molding narrows at the joints, though you can hide this with a little careful scribing by hand.

You may notice on some budget furniture that there is sometimes a V-section groove along the line of the joint. This is used to hide any inaccuracy in the joint and make finishing easier, since you don't have to worry about cross-grain scratching.

Variations of the mortise-and-tenon

How the mortise-and-tenon is marked out and cut depends on two main factors. The first, as we've seen, is how the panel is held in the frame, which is most tidily done with a groove. Fitting the panel into a rabbet presents other challenges. And proper decoration of the frame can be done more effectively than the compromises we've explored so far.

1 **Rabbeted frame.** Some panels, particularly thicker ones, are best held in a rabbet, with pins or with a bead. This has consequences upon the way the mortise-and-tenon are laid out. The solution is to have offset shoulders so that one tenon shoulder is longer than the other to fit into the rabbet.

2 **Mitered moldings.** The traditional and most effective way to join a post and rail that have a molding along the inside edge is to miter the profile at the mortise. This takes some care, but isn't as difficult as you'd imagine. The best solution is to make a jig to guide the chisel at 45 degrees to pare the miter. Rout the molding first, and the panel groove or mortise; then cut the mortise, just as you would normally. To miter the moldings, cut the edge of the post to the depth of the molding and then miter the end of the profile.

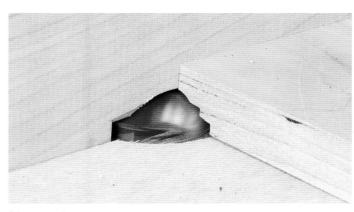

A horizontal panel molding cutter is large and must run slowly.

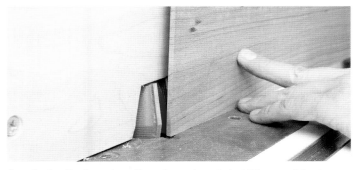

A vertical cutter is easier, although you have to hold the panel firmly.

Producing panels

There are many options for decorating the panel. The most traditional is with a long bevel, usually stepped at the top. This can be done with a plane, specifically a shoulder plane. Router catalogs are full of more complex shapes you can try, though the cutters are very expensive and need to be used in a router table. The least expensive and easiest to use are vertical panel cutters, as opposed to much larger horizontal cutters.

Making the panel

First, though, you have to make the panel. Normally you will have to do this by gluing a number of boards with butt joints to produce a panel that is wide enough and stable enough. Very rarely will you find a single piece of lumber that can be used as a panel over, say, 8 inches (203 mm) wide without incurring some risk of the board cupping, though this does depend on the thickness of the panel. Very thin solid wood panels, of ¼ inch (6 mm) or less, shouldn't have the strength to do any damage if they start to cup.

Assembling a panel from thinner strips is also economical, since you don't have to rely on wider boards. But it does mean you have to spend more time arranging the lumber, joining the boards, and cleaning up.

1 Start by surfacing and edging the boards, at least ⅛ inch (4 mm) thicker than the final thickness. Once you become better at judging the grain of wood, you will often find that you have to edge only the boards and leave the faces rough-sawn from the band saw until they have been glued as a panel. This way you don't end up surfacing sides twice, before and after they have been glued.

2 When it comes to arranging the strips, you must check from the end grain that the growth rings alternate, to diminish the consequences of the boards cupping. If they do start cupping because of a change in conditions, they should cup in opposite directions, resulting in a wavy line but not major damage.

3 Once you have this in mind, you also need to arrange the boards for visual effect. For a start, ideally you want an odd number of boards so that there isn't a conspicuous center line. Then it's a case of looking for boards that match and also avoiding joints that certainly don't match. Watch out for knots or defects that have been cut in half, since these will show up clearly along a join line. When the grain on one board is curving or the rings are far apart, you don't want to put it next to another that has very straight grain with close marking. Remember you are trying to re-create the effect of a real board and doing your best to hide the lines.

With panel boards, find an arrangement that has an even grain pattern.

4 Glue up the board. I use polyurethane adhesive for this job because it is very strong, but also because it is much easier to pare off once it has set than most other types of glue (see pages 89 and 200). You shouldn't need to reinforce this sort of joint with biscuits or dowels, but if you do, plan them carefully so that you don't reveal one when it comes to fielding the panel.

5 Glue the panel, using bar clamps above and below if necessary to stop it from bowing.

6 Once the glue has set, clean up the joints and plane. If the panel is very wide, you may need to surface it by hand, though horizontal drum sanders can take much wider panels than most power planers and jointers, but they are expensive (see page 238). This is when it's good to have learned excellent hand-planing skills.

TIP: When assembling panels wider than your jointer or planer can cope with, it is worth considering producing the panel in halves. Surface both halves and then join them together, perhaps using biscuits or dowels to ensure they are level. Then you'll have far less hand planing or belt sanding to clean up the panel.

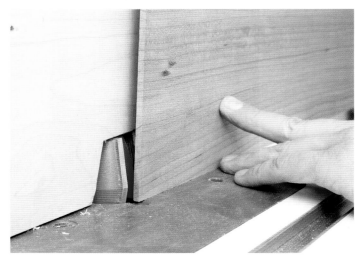

Always rout across the end grain first with the vertical molding cutter.

Conditioning panels
To be sure that panels won't bow, it is a good idea to leave them a day or so before surfacing and cleaning up. In large workshops, you will often find a stack of panels, glued but rough. This gives the boards time to do any moving and also means that you have plenty of panels to surface to the same thickness at the same time.

Preparing for movement
There is a very good chance that any solid wood panel will shrink inside its frame once it is in the centrally heated home. This is why some woodworkers condition wood under the bed to get it well acclimatized. Given that the panel will contract, it is very important to apply finishes to the panel before inserting it in the frame, especially stains. Otherwise, when the panel contracts, a contrasting line will be exposed.

Tools

Matched router cutters
The modern solution to mass-producing doors is to use matched router cutters that mold and groove the rails and posts, and can then be used to cut an exact reflection of the molding and groove on the end of the rails. This overcomes the need to miter the molding and also means you don't need to cut mortises-and-tenons, but the technique can only be used for smaller doors that don't take too much wear and tear. They are designed for use in a router table.

With matched cutters, where accuracy is important, hold the workpiece firmly.

When cutting across the end of a rail, support the rail with the miter slide.

The joint works well for small doors because the panel sits in the groove.

A shelf-drilling jig is set up very easily by holding the two runners on a purpose-made bar clamp.

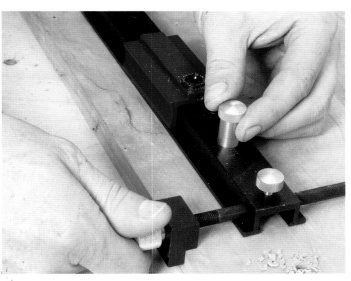

By using a special lug, you can move the whole assembly for further drilling.

You can change bushes in the mechanism of the jig for different drill bits.

Make a drilling jig from plywood, using a collar on the drill bit for depth control.

Drilling dowel holes for shelves

The dowel joint may not be as popular now as it was 20 years ago, but dowel jigs are superb for laying out repeat holes for fitting shelves and the like. Alternatively, you can make your own by simply marking up a length of plywood and drilling holes in the appropriate places to create a template.

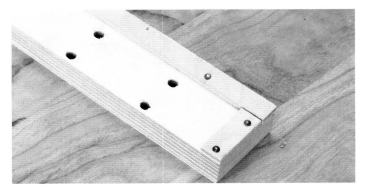

The homemade drilling jig has guides underneath for accurate positioning.

Moisture meters are ideal for testing the condition of boards.

Moisture meters

Once you start making panels for furniture, you will need to start considering the moisture content of the lumber you are using. Because the boards can be wide, any movement caused by changes in temperature or humidity will be amplified and could damage the piece you are making. Moisture meters cost anywhere from $40 to $300, and you can choose one with spikes or one that measures the resistance through electromagnetic waves. It is important, though, that the scale goes down below 10 percent moisture content, since lumber used in projects in hot, dry homes will need to be down to 9 percent.

Horizontal drum sanders

Growing in popularity is the horizontal drum sander. This has a moving rubber conveyor that feeds a panel or board beneath a spinning drum, covered in abrasive. Not only are they extremely accurate and can remove tiny quantities of waste at a time, but they are also open-ended, so that you can pass a panel through the sander two ways, doubling the available width. A typical small sander may be 16 inches (406 mm) wide, so can thickness or surface a panel 32 inches (813 mm) wide.

The sanding drum is raised or lowered within a frame, with the weight of the motor acting as a balance or cantilever so that the drum doesn't dip at the open end. That said, I have seen some woodworkers who fit a secondary support at the open end to nullify the tendency for cheaper models to dip. Generally speaking, though, these machines are so accurate that you can use them to produce your own veneers and even to tidy up marquetry panels.

Materials

Veneer and veneering

For centuries, since the first exotics were imported from the tropics, woodworkers, particularly cabinetmakers, have been using thin veneers to produce panels. The savings in expensive lumber are obvious, and there can even be a saving in time, since the veneer needs only light sanding after gluing to the core. Of course, veneered panels cannot be fielded or molded, though I've seen some startling designs that reveal the layers of veneer and core, and make a feature of this.

Originally, cabinetmakers would apply veneer to a softwood core, but today we tend to use plywood or MDF, which are both perfectly flat and need no preparation. You do, however, need to apply veneer to both sides of the core because the veneer is stronger than you imagine and will try to bow the core unless it is counterbalanced. The balancing veneer is often invisible within a project and doesn't have to be the same quality or species.

Traditionally, cabinetmakers used animal glue to stick down veneer. If you are doing a lot of gluing, you will probably use yellow glue, though you could use liquid hide adhesive. For small projects, contact adhesive is excellent. It is quick to use and the veneer is fixed immediately, with some limited opportunity for adjustment.

Veneers are cut in all sorts of ways to reproduce the effects of plain-sawn or quarter-sawn boards, with the bulk of veneers peeled from the log to produce the wide grain patterns of a plain-sawn board. Most veneers are sliced to between 0.6 and 1.0 mm thick, though you can also buy constructional veneers up to 2.0 mm, which are especially useful for laminating. Veneers come into their own when you start working, with the amazing burls and figure that are found in some lumber.

All about wood—figure

You will sometimes hear woodworkers talking about the figure of a board. This has two meanings. Generally, the word refers to the grain patterning, a well-figured board having an interesting pattern created by the growth rings. More specifically, figure refers to unusual effects that are found in some boards, but are not created by the arrangement of the growth rings. The acer family of species, which includes maple, sycamore, and plane, is famous for the subtle rippled, mottled, and curly figure you find in some boards, as well as the extraordinary bird's-eye maple that resembles the explosion of a firework.

Apply contact adhesive to the ground, making sure it is only a thin layer.

Then apply a coat of contact adhesive to the veneer.

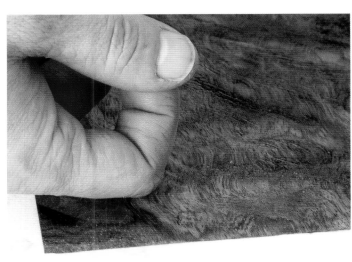

Test the tackiness with the back of a finger.

Glue the veneer down with a roller.

Project **Cherry bookcase 2**

For the finest doors

In the last lesson we studied the construction of the casework for the bookcase, and now we are going to make the doors. Quantities given here are per single door: Obviously, you will need to double this for two doors. Length given for the rails assumes a tenon 1½ inches (38 mm) long. Length and width given for the panel assume the panel is set ⅜ inch (10 mm) into the grooves in the rails and stiles.

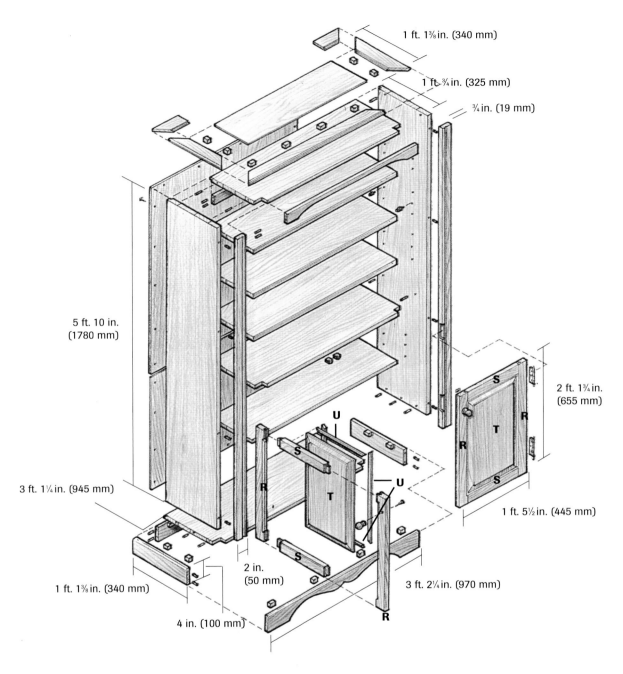

1 ft. 1⅜ in. (340 mm)

1 ft. ¾ in. (325 mm)

¾ in. (19 mm)

2 ft. 1¾ in. (655 mm)

5 ft. 10 in. (1780 mm)

1 ft. 5½ in. (445 mm)

3 ft. 1¼ in. (945 mm)

2 in. (50 mm)

1 ft. 1⅜ in. (340 mm)

3 ft. 2¼ in. (970 mm)

4 in. (100 mm)

Cutting list

Part		Material	Quantity	Dimensions thickness, width, length
R	Stile	cherry	2	¾ x 2 x 25¾ in. (19 x 51 x 654 mm)
S	Rail	cherry	2	¾ x 2 x 16½ in. (19 x 51 x 419 mm)
T	Panel	cherry	1	¾ x 14¼ x 22½ in. (19 x 362 x 571 mm)
U	Beading	cherry	1	¼ x ¼ x 72 in. (6 x 6 x 1829 mm)

Shopping list

You will also need

Brass butt hinges 1 pair
2 in. (51 mm) per door
Turned doorknob
Magnetic or ball catches

Extra tools for the job

The doors can be made by using paired profile router cutters, which are excellent for quickly producing doors that don't need the strength provided by a mortise-and-tenon. You will need to use them in a router table (see page 146).

1 Prepare the two stiles (**R**) and two rails (**S**) for each door. Start by cutting the mortises on the stiles. Notice that the tenons are haunched. Mark up the tenons on the rails.

Rout an ovolo profile along the front of the rails and stiles.

2 You can either rout a groove along the rails and stiles for the panel (**T**), or cut a rabbet around the back and hold the panel in place with beading (**U**). We've chosen the latter option.

3 Cut the tenons on the rails.

4 Miter back the molding on the stiles and rails where they meet. Check the fit of the tenons in the mortises.

TIP: Make a jig for paring the moldings at 45 degrees by creating a sandwich with 45-degree ends that you hold over the rail or stile for mitering the molding.

5 Test-fit the frame and check the diagonals for square. Once satisfied, you can glue it.

Glue boards for the panel (see page 84) and then plane and sand smooth.

6 Use a raised-panel molding cutter in a router table to shape the panel, working across the end grain first.

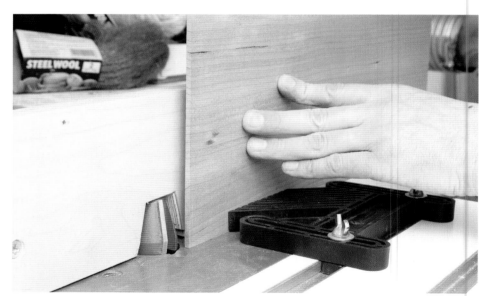

7 Fit the panel in the door frame, and pin the beading to the frame so that the panel can move as the ambient humidity changes. Drill a hole for the doorknob and fit.

8 Cut the hinge recesses in the door and screw in place. Offer the door up to the bookcase upright and mark off the positions of the hinges. Cut the recesses and screw in place.

Clean up the completed door and finish. Fit the catches to the door and the underside of the pot shelf.

Lessons learned

● Even with a router table, it takes a lot of effort to work an even molding around a panel. Often you will need to clean up with a shoulder plane.

● Make sure the doors are a snug fit inside the casework. Sloppiness here will be highlighted, and the gap must be consistent around the door.

● Fitting hinges takes much practice. Your first ones often look untidy, but gradually your technique will improve.

● Experiment with cutting mortises-and-tenons on components that are grooved, rabbeted, or profiled, or a combination of them all. Understanding the layout is difficult and has to be done through trial and error.

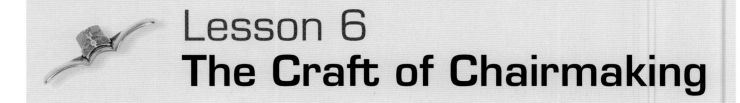

Lesson 6
The Craft of Chairmaking

Getting started

Chairmaking

Of all the woodworking skills, chairmaking is perhaps the most advanced, though it doesn't have to be so. The principle distinction from most other types of woodworking is the need to cut joints at various angles, and not just the 90 degrees for which so much of our equipment is designed. This requires an ability to set up machines and marking devices accurately, and/or having a very good eye for angles and good coordination. The fact that chairs take more stress, especially from tilting, than most projects further complicates the issue.

Formal chairs that are largely produced from square or rectangular section rails, legs, and stretchers require very accurate jointing, usually with mortises-and-tenons. These angled joints need careful planning and accurate marking up. More informal country chairs, like this lesson's project, have greater margin for error and usually employ round mortises-and-tenons, the latter being lined up by eye or with a jig.

More often than not, country chairs have a solid seat, into which are drilled holes for the legs, back, and arms. More formal chairs have framed seats, with the comfort provided by cane or upholstery. A compromise is the rushed or woven seat that has rails, but these are largely hidden and are usually drilled into the legs.

Angled mortises-and-tenons

Look at the seat of most chairs and you can't help but notice that it splays out from back to front. Look from the side and you'll see that the back support is laid back at an angle for comfort, and the seat is often tilted upward a little to force the sitter's lumbar region into the chair and to stop your bottom from sliding forward. As a result, the mortise-and-tenon is often angled.

To cut an angled mortise-and-tenon, you have to decide how you want to arrange the angles. To produce the splay of the seat, you would normally cut the shoulders of the rail at the appropriate angle. You'd also cut the tenon at the same angle. This way, the mortise on the legs would be cut "square."

The shoulders are quite easy to cut at an angle, but cutting the tenon at an angle can be tricky, as well as undermining the strength of the joint because the grain may be "short" in the angled tenon. This is certainly the way you would always do it for the front leg. However, you will sometimes find chairs that have the rear legs twisted outward at the same angle as the splay. Here, the joint between the side rail and the back leg is normal and square, but the joint between the back rail and back leg is at an angle. Chances are that with chairs the angles will get you somewhere!

Marking and cutting an angled mortise-and-tenon

In some cases, when the angle is very slight and the leg into which you are mortising is quite sturdy, there may be space to angle the mortise, keep the tenon straight, and angle only the shoulders, but it's six of one and half a dozen of the other.

1 Set the adjustable square to the appropriate angle for the splay. Make sure the wing nut that fixes the square doesn't interfere, since you may well need to use both sides of the blade and stock.

2 Mark up and cut the mortise either in the leg or in an offcut to use as a test piece.

Keep an offcut

1 One of my rules of woodworking is to always keep an offcut of every component in a project, either as a

Lesson planner

Key techniques	Key tools and materials
• Bending wood • Basic turning • Drilling angled holes • Ergonomics of a chair	• Sharpening turning tools • Grain direction • Chair making tools • Finishing turned parts

complete extra piece or just the waste that's cut off the end. Write on the offcut which piece it is; then use it for setting up marking gauges and machines, and for testing joints. By trialing each joint first, you reduce the margin of error, and by actually cutting the first joint on a piece of scrap, you've hopefully made the mistakes that are bound to happen on an offcut and not on the real thing. Cutting a preparatory joint prepares you for what will happen and how the tools or machines will react, and it builds up your muscle memory of the operation. The last joint of a batch the woodworker cuts is always the best, and the first is usually the worst—so I've always wondered why we don't cut the last one first!

Keeping a few offcuts from parts of a project helps when it comes to setting up machines.

Use a sliding bevel to guide freehand drilling of angled holes.

2 Use the adjustable square to mark up the shoulders on the rail.

3 Mark up the angle of the tenon itself along the grain (or at least at an angle to the grain). When it comes to selecting lumber for the rails, this is a time when a piece with grain that curves at the end can be ideal, providing added strength to the tenon. Mark the position of the tenon on the shoulder line, and then use the adjustable square to mark up the angled tenon. It's certainly worth doing a trial joint first and potentially using this as a template.

4 Cut the tenon as you would normally.

Drilling angled holes

In the making of country chairs, holes have to be drilled at angles for the legs and other parts to splay. You can do this with one or two adjustable squares (or templates) with a cordless drill or brace and bit by eye, or you can set up an angled table on a bench drill. This will certainly speed things up, especially for repetitive drilling, but according to some chair makers, it isn't necessarily in the spirit of chairmaking.

This sort of jig can be very simple, no more than a piece of plywood with a batten underneath to raise it to the appropriate angle. If you get seriously into chairmaking you could make an adjustable drilling jig, with a screw raising and lowering the table for variable angles.

A simple jig for a bench drill makes angled drilling so simple.

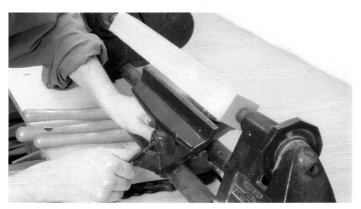

Set up the tool rest roughly level with the center of the workpiece.

Honing can be done on a slow grinder—in this case, with a leather wheel and paste.

Getting started

Chairmaking

Of all the woodworking skills, chairmaking is perhaps the most advanced, though it doesn't have to be so. The principle distinction from most other types of woodworking is the need to cut joints at various angles, and not just the 90 degrees for which so much of our

Turning depends on sharp tools. Make sure you have a good tool rest on your grinder for sharpening turning chisels.

Some slow grinders have a shaped wheel for honing the inside of gouges.

equipment is designed. This requires an ability to set up machines and marking devices accurately, and/or having a very good eye for angles and good coordination. The fact that chairs take more stress, especially from tilting, than most projects further complicates the issue.

Formal chairs that are largely produced from square or rectangular section rails, legs, and stretchers require very accurate jointing, usually with mortises-and-tenons. These angled joints need careful planning and accurate marking up. More informal country chairs, like this lesson's project, have greater margin for error and usually employ round mortises-and-tenons, the latter being lined up by eye or with a jig.

More often than not, country chairs have a solid seat, into which are drilled holes for the legs, back, and arms. More formal chairs have framed seats, with the comfort provided by cane or upholstery. A compromise is the rushed or woven seat that has rails, but these are largely hidden and are usually drilled into the legs.

On a roughing gouge like this, you are aiming for a continuously smooth single bevel for the gouge to run well.

Angled mortises-and-tenons

Look at the seat of most chairs and you can't help but

Skew chisels are difficult to sharpen as the point easily blues, and it is hard to achieve a straight edge and even bevels on both sides.

For roughing, hold the gouge with a hand over the tool for stability.

With a smaller gouge, you can hold the tool gently in your fingers.

Notice how the gouge is held at an angle to the spinning wood.

For a bead, use a small fingernail gouge, twisting the gouge in your fingers as it rolls over the bead.

Mark up any features with pencil.

develop a feel for the bevel by sharpening the turning tool without a rest and purely by feel. Don't do this yourself.

To sharpen, gently pivot the turning tool toward the spinning wheel and feel for the bevel. This is really important. Once the whole bevel is rubbing, any vibration will disappear. Check to see what you have ground on the bevel. Gradually raise your lower hand, which should be at the end of the handle, until the sparks are pouring over the edge. Then you know the tool is sharp.

This is pretty much the same action as you will use for turning: Presenting the bevel until it rubs, and then raising the handle to engage the edge. Turning is really very simple and is based on this principle, so get it right from the beginning and you will always be able to turn. It is entirely a question of touch.

Start with the roughing gouge, which looks like a big U, and present it to a spinning piece of wood until you hear and feel it rubbing against the lumber, without the edge touching. Slowly raise the handle until the edge starts to cut the wood. The higher you raise the handle, the deeper you cut. Tilt the gouge to the left and start cutting toward the left. Then go the other way. Soon you'll get the hang of it,

and after a while you can try a coving gouge, which is sometimes referred to as a fingernail gouge. For a slicing action, like a plane, you use a skew, but cut only with the bottom third of the edge or the tool will jump and catch because the edge isn't supported. The tip of the skew can be used for cutting grooves and lines in the wood.

Advanced turning

Wood turning has become a hobby in itself, with more gadgets and tools produced for turners than any other woodworking speciality. It can be very satisfying, with shapes emerging from beautiful pieces of lumber and heaps of shavings growing around your feet. Spindle-turning is fine for chairmaking, but anyone who gets into turning will soon want to make bowls and other vessels, for which you will need to buy a chuck to hold the blank without support from the tail center.

Bending wood

There are two techniques for bending wood, and both are great fun—in fact, this is possibly my favorite part of woodworking.

1 **Steambending.** The most traditional technique is to use a steaming chest, in which you put the piece to be bent for a few hours. The combination of heat and moisture makes the fibers more pliable. Once it is cooked, you remove the piece and quickly bend it around a former, holding it in place overnight for the fibers to find a new position. You'll need to bend it more than you think because there will be a tendency for the bent wood to spring back a bit.

You can make a steaming box quite easily, perhaps even from a drain pipe if you don't have many pieces to cook at the same time. It needs to be sealed to raise the pressure as far as possible, and you need to insert pegs on which the lumber can rest so that the steam reaches all the parts. Steam can be produced by heating an old drum of water with a rubber hose connected to the steaming box.

The length of time the wood needs in the steamer depends on the species and the dimensions, but expect it to take at least two hours for a 1-inch (25-mm)-square length of ash, which is one of the easiest to bend. Many species can be bent, with varying degrees of difficulty, but the important thing is to ensure the grain is straight, with no weakness or curved grain that is likely to break under pressure.

2 **Laminating.** The principle of laminating thin strips of wood or ply has amazing potential but is more complex than steambending. With steaming you really need only one former, around which you pull the lumber. For successful laminating, you need a male and a female former so that the glue line between the laminations is invisible, though this can be achieved with a strip of metal if you get into laminating in a big way. The beauty of it is that it's quick and you don't need to make a steaming box and wait for the wood to cook. I use the technique for making handles, and it is also used in chairmaking.

Ergonomics of chairmaking

When it comes to designing chairs, there are some principles of the human form that help us define the measurements. For a fuller explanation of chair design and ergonomics, invest in a book on furniture design—I recommend *Designing Furniture* by Seth Stem.

Dining chair

Height of seat: 17¾ in. (451 mm)
Seat slope: max 1 in. (25 mm) front to back
Seat width: (front): 18 in. (457 mm)

Seat width: (back): 15½ in. (394 mm)
Slope of back: 90–95°
Arm width: 19¼ in. (489 mm)
Seat depth: 16¼ in. (413 mm)
Back height: 32 in. (813 mm)

Tools

Chairmaking tools

Some tools used for chairmaking are part of many standard tool kits, but other specialized equipment won't be as easy to find. It may be available only from specialist suppliers, direct from manufacturers, or from secondhand dealers.

Rounders

Lathes are often not long enough for the turning of chair legs, stretches, rails, and backs. This is also a tricky operation, with time needed to prepare the lumber for the lathe, and the long, thin spindles having a tendency to vibrate and the cutting edge to judder. Rounders are designed to convert square-section lumber into round rods, working a little like a pencil sharpener.

Brace-and-bit

The brace-and-bit has largely been replaced by the cordless drill, but when it comes to drilling larger holes, the cordless doesn't always have the torque for the job. That is when the brace-and-bit works so well, and is in many ways easier to control. There is also a beauty in the sound of the bit biting into wood and cutting the fibers.

The sticks in chair backs can be rounded with a spokeshave.

Spokeshave and drawknife

The spokeshave is useful for many woodworking jobs beyond chairmaking and is available with either a curved sole or flat sole. The former is more versatile for shaped work, the flat spokeshave being used for shaving the edges off straight boards. The drawknife is simply a long blade held between two handles and has very little to control the cut, so it tends to be used for more aggressive, freehand shaping.

Adze

In most woodworking workshops, the adze is like a small ax except that the blade is at right angles to the handle and is curved to shape seats.

Choosing a lathe and tools

A lathe needs to be able to perform various tasks so that there is plenty of scope for experimenting with different types of turning. It needs to be long enough between centers to turn a chair leg but with enough space to turn a bowl or platter up to 12 inches (305 mm) in diameter. It doesn't need to be particularly expensive or have more than four or five speeds.

Turning tools are often sold in sets, and this is usually a cost-effective approach. Look for a set with a roughing gouge, parting tool, skew—ideally 1-inch (25-mm) wide—½-inch (13-mm) and ¼-inch (6-mm) spindle gouges, and a ⅜-inch (10-mm) bowl-turning gouge. The latter is machined from a thicker bar to give the edge more support when cutting into the end grain of a bowl.

Materials

All about wood—using grain direction

In wooden boatbuilding and the construction of an old vaulted roof, woodworkers look out for curved boards that could be used for the ribs. This way the fibers aren't disturbed, and the strength of the wood is retained. The same is true for chairmaking, especially when the back legs of a chair are long and curving. Lumber for steambending must be straight, with no weaknesses that might break under pressure.

Finishing turned objects

There are many sanding options for cleaning up turned projects, though a sheet of sandpaper will do to start. Just be careful not to burn your hand when holding the abrasive against the spinning wood or get your fingers trapped against the tool rest. Always wear a dust mask or respirator when sanding at the lathe, since huge quantities of dust are produced. Preferably, keep sanding to a minimum, and work on improving the finish straight from the tool edge. Not only is this

quicker in the long-term, but the finish is cleaner with the fibers less bruised.

The simplest finish to apply to turned items is sanding sealer, either shellac or cellulose, which can be applied on a rag with the item spinning slowly. Do this a couple of times, cutting back with 320-grade abrasive between coats; then hold a stick of carnauba wax against the spinning wood. This hard wax can then be buffed to a high shine.

Wear gloves to avoid the risk of burning your fingers.

Apply sanding sealer with a cloth while the lathe is turning slowly.

Polish with carnauba wax, which is tough and finishes to a good shine.

Project **Kitchen chair**

For your kitchen

Chairmaking is simultaneously the most difficult and the simplest woodworking skill. The angles are tricky to work out, but you need very few tools and a wheel-back kitchen chair certainly requires less accuracy than last lesson's bookcase.

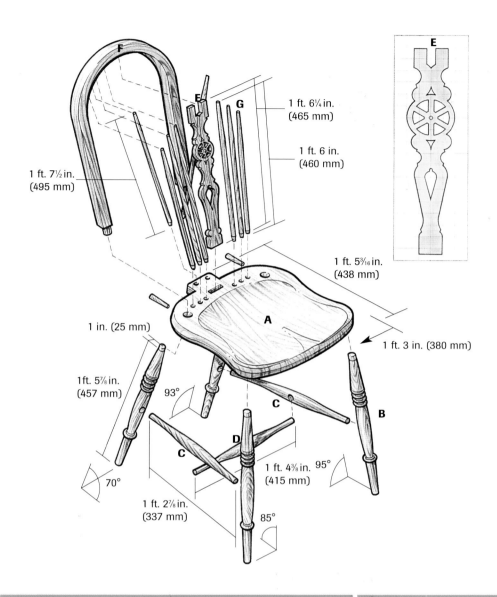

1 ft. 7½ in.
(495 mm)

1 ft. 6¼ in.
(465 mm)

1 ft. 6 in.
(460 mm)

1 ft. 5³⁄₁₆ in.
(438 mm)

1 in. (25 mm)

1 ft. 3 in. (380 mm)

1 ft. 5⅞ in.
(457 mm)

93°

C

B

70°

D

1 ft. 4³⁄₈ in.   95°
(415 mm)

1 ft. 2⅞ in.
(337 mm)

85°

E

Cutting list

Part	Material	Quantity	Dimensions thickness, width, length
A Seat	elm/cherry	1	1⅝ x 15 x 17³⁄₁₆ in. (40 x 381 x 437 mm)
B Leg	ash/beach	4	1¾ x 1¾ x 17⅞ in. (45 x 45 x 454 mm)
C Stretcher	ash/beach	2	1⅛ x 1⅛ x 14⅞ in. (30 x 30 x 378 mm)
D Center rail	ash/beach	1	1⅛ x 1⅛ x 16⅜ in. (30 x 30 x 416 mm)
E Splat	ash/beach	1	⅜ x 4⅛ x 18¼ in. (10 x 105 x 464 mm)
F Back bow	ash/beach	1	1⅛ x 1¼ x 49 in. (30 x 32 x 1245 mm)
G Stick	ash/beach	8	⅝ x ⅝ x 19½ in. (16 x 16 x 495 mm)

Extra tools for the job

Steaming box
Chairmaking tools:
Spokeshave and
drawknife and **angle**
grinder

1 Plank up boards to make the seat (**A**), ideally using a very strong polyurethane glue, or whatever you've come to trust most. Use biscuits to strengthen the joint. Preferably use an odd number of boards to make up the seat (see page 84).

Cut the seat to shape and "bottom" the top. You can do this traditionally, or by using an angle grinder with a wood-carving disk attached. It takes time to get the seat right, and each seat should be better than the previous one.

2 Drill the 1-inch (25-mm)-diameter holes for the legs, using an adjustable square to help you judge the splay. The splay is 95 degrees back and front and 85 degrees to the sides. Make sure you don't drill through the seat, though the legs on many such chairs do protrude the whole way through and are wedged. Alternatively, drill the holes using a bench drill, with a sloped jig setting the angle.

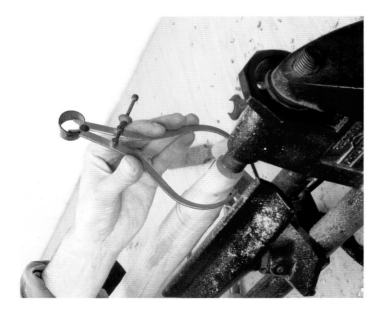

3 Turn the legs (**B**), stretchers (**C**), and center rail 90 degrees (**D**).

4 Fit the legs into the seat and mark the position for the stretcher holes.

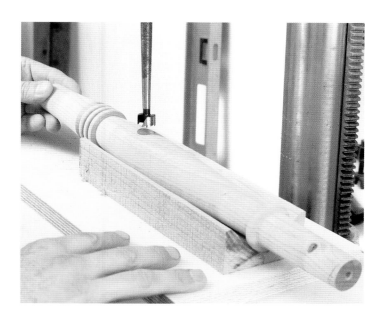

5 Drill and assemble the underframe; then do the same for the center rail.

6 Make a note of which part of the underframe fits where and then glue, adjusting the parts until the legs wobble as little as possible. You can always trim them later.

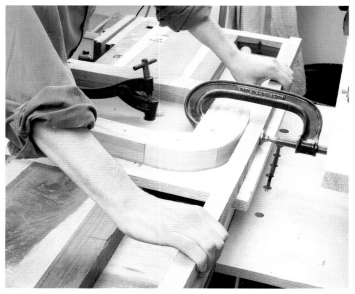

7 Drill the 1-inch (25-mm)-diameter holes in the seat for the bow back (**F**), either using adjustable squares as sighting guides or by using a jig in the bench drill.

8 Make a former slightly tighter than the radius of the bow back. Put the piece in a steamer for at least two hours; then bend around the former and hold in place with C-clamps and bar clamps. Alternatively, laminate thin lathes with glue around a former, but you will need a male and female former for this job.

9 Next day, clamp the bow in a vise and mark off the length of the tenons at the ends. Cut around the shoulders and cut off the corners. Then pare back the tenon to a circle, checking the fit with a suit hole drilled in an offcut (rather than offering up the whole seat).

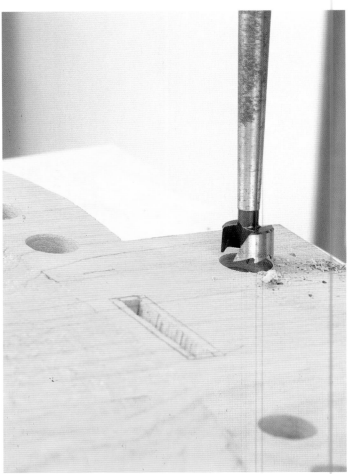

10 Check the fit of the bow in the seat. Then drill the ⅜-inch (10-mm) holes for the sticks (**G**), and chop out the mortise for the splat (**E**). Once again you can do this by eye with an adjustable square or by using an angled jig.

11 Cut the sticks roughly to length and offer up to the bow to line up the holes. Then drill the ⅜-inch (10-mm) holes in the bow. Use a couple of offcuts to measure the length of each stick. Before you round the full length of each stick, test the fit in the bow and seat: You don't want to waste time getting a stick perfectly round and then make a mistake cutting it to length!

13 Use a coping saw or fretsaw to shape the splat and check its fit in the seat. Then cut a corresponding pair of mortises in the bow. Attach the turned roundel to the splat.

12 Round the sticks with a spokeshave, which I prefer. Sand smooth.

Lessons learned

- Chairmaking is all about accurate drilling. Notice how any gaps will be seen, but the tapered components can often be pushed in tight.

- Turning identical components is very awkward and requires loads of practice. But remember that chair legs are farther apart than you might imagine, and many people won't notice any differences.

- It's best to make chairs one at a time, as they are so difficult to replicate. There is a time saving in batching parts, but it's still a challenge to make the match.

14 With all the parts cleaned up, you can assemble the chair, though many chairmakers will recommend you do all the finishing, right up to the wax, before assembly.

Lesson 7
Making Tables

Getting started

Tables always impress people. Non-woodworkers don't realize that they are one of the easiest of constructions to produce. A wide expanse of gloriously finished wood looks fantastic and any deficiencies in the underframe are usually hidden away, as long as it doesn't rock. Many tables are so heavy that they won't budge anyway.

The greatest challenge when making a table is usually, for the home woodworker, assembling the whole thing and clamping up wide panels like the top. This isn't a worry for small side tables, but kitchen and dining tables are often quite large. One option is to use bolts to draw the end frames together, or you could look back to our technique of draw-boring tenons (see page 128). Or you could make your own long bar clamps by acquiring some special clamp heads that are fitted to a wooden bar.

The thing is that by this stage, woodworkers should be thinking for themselves and starting to devise their own solutions to the challenges they face. That is one of the measures of success, and a sense of independence is one of the rewards of building up a stock of skills and tools.

Making a table
Compared to producing chairs, designing and making tables are intriguing and fortuitously simple. Though tables may be large and the top can be challenging to finish, the construction is, at least in principle, relatively straightforward. It's a question of choosing the appropriate underframe and then devising a shape and style for the top. And few projects offer the woodworker quite the same opportunity to display the beauty of wood.

Options for the underframe
The most common design for a table is to position four legs at the corners and join them with four rails. This is a good design for dining tables because it gives you plenty of space to place the chairs and for diners to stretch their legs. The downside is that such underframes have inherent weakness because their legs are not supported or reinforced with lower rails.

One way to get around this is to use deeper rails, to lengthen the join line between the rails and the legs and reduce the tendency for the legs to pivot. This, however, can interfere with the legs of anyone sitting at the table, and there is a tricky compromise between the height of the tabletop and the height above the knees of the rails. This problem can be nullified by shaping the rails so that they are narrower at the center than at the joints. Another option is to use thicker material for the rails, thereby increasing the joint strength.

Many old tables have four low rails near the feet, but the result is heavy-looking and more restrictive. A compromise is to join the legs low down at the ends and then use a full-length rail (or stretcher) to join the end rails. For desks, which are used from only one side, you can offset this central rail so that it doesn't interfere; indeed, it becomes a perch for the sitter's feet.

To produce a slender, elegant design, table legs are often tapered on any of the four faces, with contrasting results depending on which side is tapered. The two outside faces are the most commonly tapered, but it doesn't have to be done like this. Legs can be round, square section, hexagonal, octagonal, or rectangular. They can curve or splay. The options are endless. You can even support the top on a single pedestal, which is great for small round tables, especially if they are made to tilt. On larger dining tables the pedestal is both hidden and potentially unstable.

Lesson planner

Key techniques	Key tools and materials
• Designing a table • Proportions of a table • Tapering table legs • Cutting a sliding dovetail	• Skew chisels • Trammel bars for cutting circles • Locks and fitting them

Options for the top

The proportions of the top depend largely upon the space it has to fill and the table's purpose. Round tables are welcoming but waste space because so much of the top is a dead zone in the center. Rectangular tops are the most efficient, though I've always loved elliptical tables because the sitters can all see each other, there is very little wasted area, and the changing curves are intriguing. My father once produced a fabulous range of coffee tables, with a Christmas theme, only to discover that the downside of a holly-shaped top is laddered stockings and bruised shins.

Solid wood tabletops are often cleated at the ends, with a loose tongue joining the cleat to the end of the boards. This stops the boards from cupping but allows them to move across their width. I made the mistake of joining the cleat to one tabletop with dowel rods, only for the top to split terribly when it couldn't move at the center.

Ergonomics of a table

Based on the average dining chair being about 18 inches (457 mm) high, the lower edge of the rail or apron needs to be about 24½ inches (622 mm) above the ground, with the average tabletop 29 inches (737 mm) high. Ideally, the tabletop should overhang the rails by about 9 inches (229 mm).

How many people can sit at a table depends largely upon the arrangement. For instance, a 50-inch (1270-mm)-diameter table can sit six people, while eight people can sit at a 48-inch (1219-mm)-square table. You need to give each person about 26 inches (660 mm) space around the circumference of a round table, which can be converted into the diameter by multiplying the number of people by 26, and then dividing by 3.14. Sitters at square or rectangular tables need only 24 inches (610 mm).

Use a jig to taper table legs on a table saw.

Five ways to taper table legs

With most of these techniques, you taper adjacent sides with some form of jig first, and then remove the jig to taper the opposite faces.

1 **The table saw.** You can buy a tapering jig, but it's just as simple to cut a piece of 1-inch (25 mm) ply to the appropriate angle and clamp it to the rip fence. With a fine blade, this will need only a little finishing.

2 **The band saw.** Some band saws have fences that can be set at any angle to the blade. If yours does not, then simply clamp a wooden straightedge to the table and use it to cut the taper. The finish from a band saw isn't that great, but it is a good way of removing waste.

3 **The thicknesser.** Just as for the table saw, you need to insert a carriage into the thicknesser to taper boards. The jig can be designed for tapering along the length or across the width of a piece of wood. It gives a good finish, but takes more time to set up than on the table saw.

With a template you can taper with a router table.

4 **The router table.** It doesn't help to angle the fence on a router table, since the cutter will still produce a straight edge. A simple solution is to make a plywood template of the tapered leg (which is a good idea anyway for marking up) and fix it to the board with double-sided tape or hot glue, and then use a bearing-guided trimming cutter to rout the taper. Work with the grain by starting at the wide part of the leg and rout toward the foot.

A slightly more complicated method, but quicker once it is set up, is to make a jig that slides in the groove for the miter fence. By holding the workpiece at an angle to the groove with stops and toggle clamps, you can easily taper the leg.

Use a router table to cut a tail on a board for a sliding dovetail.

Tools

Skews

When it comes to cutting lapped dovetails, one of the greatest challenges is cleaning up the corners inside the sockets. You can buy skews specially designed for the job, or you can take an old bevel-edged chisel and grind it to a sharp angle. Unfortunately, you will need two because the operation is "handed."

Trammel bars

Trammel bars are used for cutting or routing circles with a router. A simple version can be made easily enough from a length of plywood screwed to the base of the router and then pinned or screwed to the center of the workpiece. Often you will need to use a trammel bar from underneath the tabletop, or whatever you are cutting, so that the fixing mark isn't seen. If fixing on the top face cannot be avoided, it's a good idea to temporarily glue a block to the workpiece, to which you can fix the trammel.

5 **By hand.** Of course, you could taper the leg by hand, in which case all you need to do is mark the top and bottom points and plane away the waste.

How to cut a sliding dovetail

The dovetailed dado is a useful joint for attaching rails, as we are doing with the center rail on this lesson's project. It is also commonly used for making compartments within drawers, since it is naturally strong and helps to reinforce the construction. A stopped version makes sure you can't see the joint. The basic joint has parallel sides and is best produced by routing the "tenon" on a router table, and the "housing" with the router hand-held.

A more complicated version is the sliding dovetail, which is self-tightening. Both the socket and the tail are very slightly tapered along their length so that they tighten only right at the end. Tapering the socket with the router hand-held is simple because you only have to move the straightedge you are using as a fence fractionally. But to taper the tail, you will need to make a carriage for the rail, sliding in the router table's groove for the miter fence. This sort of jig takes time to produce but is worth it in the long run.

Keep aside any jelly jars because they make an excellent home for tiny screws and fittings in your workshop.

Adjustable trammel bars, which fit in the fence-bar sockets of the router's base, are available from various manufacturers. When using a trammel, watch out for changes in grain direction as you work around the circle. You need to work against the rotation of the router cutter, which means there will be times when you will be routing against the grain. Make very light cuts at those stages.

Use the best brass fittings; they will certainly improve your project.

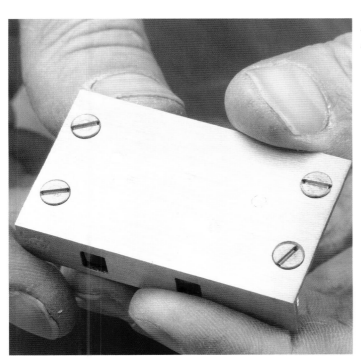

Screw heads that aren't lined up in a lock will look untidy.

Materials

Locks and fitting them

There's no great secret to fixing locks in place, but care is needed to make the job tidy. The keyhole can be very awkward to shape tidily, but an escutcheon hides any inaccuracies. For the best finish, use brass slotted screws, and try to get the slots all lined up in one direction, or leave them proud and then grind them back to look like rivets.

All about wood—the mighty oak

Oak is probably the finest of all hardwoods, with various species offering subtly different effects. White oak is superb: It incorporates an even grain and good patterning that make it easy to use, has little wastage, and is a warm medium-brown color. Red oak is richer in color and cheaper, but doesn't have quite as interesting grain. European oak is wilder than both of them, with amazing flamelike medullary rays and a richer honey-brown color. Diseased oak turns brown, to varying degrees, and tends to be softer. Japanese oak is the palest of the species, while Tasmanian oak is coarsest of all.

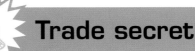

Trade secret

The beauty of screws

There are a couple of really unexpected uses for screws. Grind a notch out of the head of a flathead screw and you can make it into an improvised scratch stock, fixed into a small block. When you don't have wide enough bar clamps, you can use a screw to draw the joint together, though not as you might expect. The trick is to insert the screw into the edge of one board and then drill a corresponding hole in the edge of the adjacent board. From the hole, elongate a groove beneath the surface, with only a gap for the screw's shank. By adjusting the depth of the screw, you can loosen or tighten the joint as the screw slides in the slot.

Project **Cherry dining table**

For the dining room

This table will sit four to six people and has a neat drawer at one end. The tapered legs lighten the design. In this case it is made from cherry, but you can use whatever you have.

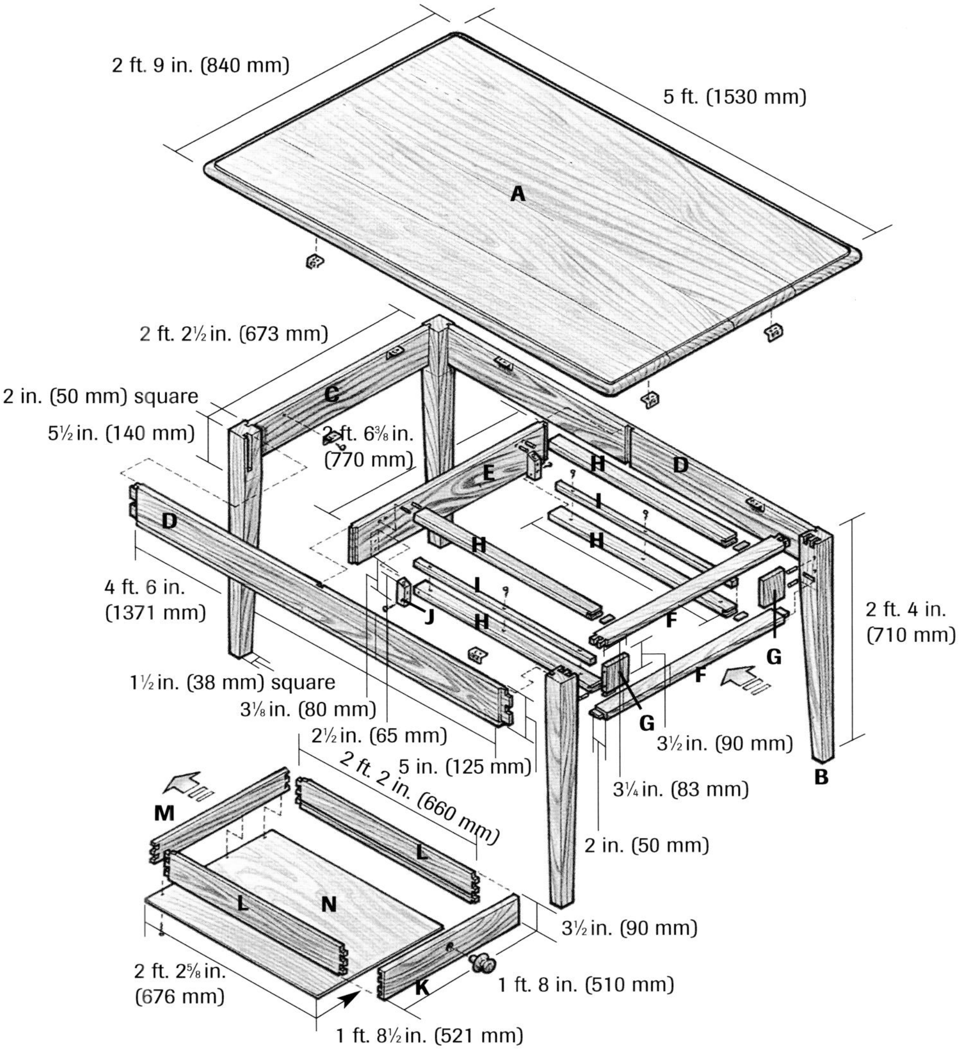
2 ft. 9 in. (840 mm)
5 ft. (1530 mm)
A
2 ft. 2½ in. (673 mm)
2 in. (50 mm) square
5½ in. (140 mm)
C
2 ft. 6⅜ in. (770 mm)
E
H
D
I
H
D
H
I
4 ft. 6 in. (1371 mm)
J
H
F
G
2 ft. 4 in. (710 mm)
F
1½ in. (38 mm) square
3⅛ in. (80 mm)
G
2½ in. (65 mm)
3½ in. (90 mm)
5 in. (125 mm)
B
2 ft. 2 in. (660 mm)
3¼ in. (83 mm)
M
L
2 in. (50 mm)
L
N
3½ in. (90 mm)
2 ft. 2⅝ in. (676 mm)
K
1 ft. 8 in. (510 mm)
1 ft. 8½ in. (521 mm)

Shopping list

Extra tools for the job

Drawer knob
Dowels 5/16 in. (8 mm)
Right-angled expansion brackets to fit the top: 8

Cutting list

Part	Material	Quantity	Dimensions thickness, width, length	Part	Material	Quantity	Dimensions thickness, width, length
A Top	cherry	1	⅞ x 33 x 60 in. (22 x 840 x 1525 mm)	**H** Runner/ kicker	cherry	4	¾ x 1¾ x 25⅝ in. (19 x 45 x 651 mm)
B Leg	cherry	4	2 x 2 x 28 in. (50 x 50 x 711 mm)	**I** Drawer guide	cherry	2	¾ x ¾ x 25⅝ in. (19 x 19 x 651 mm)
C End rail	cherry	1	¾ x 5 x 29 in. (19 x 125 x 737 mm)	**J** Runner block	cherry	2	⅞ x 1 x 3⅛ in. (21 x 25 x 79 mm)
D Side rails	cherry	2	¾ x 5 x 56½ in. (19 x 125 x 1435 mm)	**K** Drawer front	cherry	1	⅝ x 3½ x 20 in. (16 x 90 x 508 mm)
E Center rail	cherry	1	¾ x 5 x 31⅜ in. (19 x 125 x 797 mm)	**L** Drawer side	cherry	2	⅝ x 3½ x 26 in. (16 x 90 x 660 mm)
F Drawer rail	cherry	2	¾ x 2 x 28½ in. (19 x 50 x 724 mm)	**M** Drawer back	cherry	1	⅝ x 2⅞ x 20 in. (16 x 73 x 508 mm)
G End fillet	cherry	2	¾ x 3¼ x 3½ in. (19 x 83 x 89 mm)	**N** Drawer bottom	cherry	1	¼ x 20½ x 28⅜ in. (6 x 521 x 721 mm)

2 Cut the top drawer rail (**F**) to length and mark out and cut the double blind dovetail.

1 The subframe of this table looks a bit daunting, but you should realize by now that the way to go is splitting it into two end frames, which you assemble first. Only when they are glued and tidy, do you attempt to join them with the side rails (**D**). The center rail (**E**) slides into place later, when you also fit the kickers (**H**).

Prepare the legs, but don't yet taper them. Mark up and cut the mortises (see page 99) for the side rails and the end rail, and the mortise for the lower drawer rail. Notice that the mortises aren't centered on the legs but offset toward the outside so that there is a ¼-inch (6-mm) return on the legs.

3 Use the tails on the top-drawer rail to mark out the sockets on the top of the legs (**B**). Drill the holes in the legs for the end fillets (**G**) that fill the space on either side of the drawer.

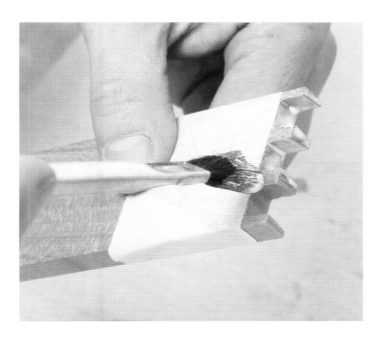

TIP: Apply glue to the dovetails with a small brush so that it gets into all the difficult-to-reach corners. When not in use, keep the brush in a solvent or water, depending on the type of adhesive you are using.

5 Cut the dados in the side rails (**D**). These go the whole way across the rail and can be cut like sliding dovetails if you prefer, which will hold the side rails in position better.

Rout ¼-inch (6-mm) grooves along the inside edge of the drawer rails (**F**). These take a loose ¼-inch (6-mm)-thick plywood tongue, which makes it easier to assemble the kickers (**H**) and center rail (**E**). Work the bead along the bottom edge of the side rails, using either a router hand-held, a router table, or a scratch stock (see page 223).

4 Taper the leg (see page 222) on a table saw to 1½ inch (38 mm) square at the bottom. Clean up with a bench plane.

Prepare the materials for all the rails. Cut the tenons and check the fit. You will probably need to pair off the joints (see page 75) for this project because the joints are all quite complex, and there isn't a huge amount of repetition.

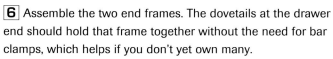

6 Assemble the two end frames. The dovetails at the drawer end should hold that frame together without the need for bar clamps, which helps if you don't yet own many.

Clean up the end frames once the glue has set. Then join them together with the side rails, which will probably be too long for any bar clamps that you own. This is when the technique of draw-boring (see page 128) is an advantage, since you don't need clamps.

7 Prepare the center rail and all the components for the drawer runners, kickers, and guides. Cut the ¼-inch (6-mm) dados in the outer ends of the kickers and runners; then drill the dowel holes in the ends of the kickers. It's hardly worth setting up a jig for this, so you can use dowel center markers (see page 57) to mark these positions on the center rail.

8 Fit the center rail and the kickers to the underframe. Screw the drawer guides (**I**) to the runners and the blocks (**J**) to the center rail.

Cut the end fillets to length and drill for the dowel holes. Glue in place. Then screw brackets to the underframe to attach the top.

10 Clean up the top with a try plane or belt sander and cabinet scraper. Round the corners and run an ovolo cutter around the edges, guided by a bearing. Screw to the underframe, making sure the brackets allow for movement in the tabletop (see page 184).

9 Make the drawer by the usual technique (see page 212), cutting the tails first and then the pins. In the drawing, we've shown ply being used, with the grain running from front to back. If you use solid wood, position the grain running side to side. Drill the drawer front (**L**) for the knob.

Glue the boards for the tabletop (**A**). We've shown four boards on the drawing, but I'd favor three or five, since odd numbers look more interesting (see page 85). To make the joints more accurate and to reduce the amount of cleaning up, use biscuits (see pages 138 and 140).

Lessons learned

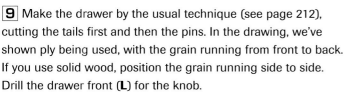

- The use of dovetails helps to hold the end frames together and reduces the need for long clamps.

- With a little ingenuity you can taper table legs very easily and accurately.

- A bench drill is superb for accurate drilling.

- Neatly fitted locks and hinges work better and look more professional.

Lesson 8
Onward and Forward

Getting started

So here we are, the final lesson. It's been an interesting ride, and I hope you've enjoyed it all. I've tried to convey the many possibilities and sow some seeds to act as a springboard for anyone wanting to take up woodwork. You'll find books that tell you more about the detail of joint cutting and tool fettling, but I hope you will have got a sense of the fun that can be had by learning how to make your own furniture and the pride you'll feel in developing your own workshop.

A couple of lessons ago we explored turning, and that is just one of many paths you might take. I've come across all sorts of woodworkers in my time as an editor of woodworking magazines, and they're constantly changing direction, testing new techniques, and challenging their skills. The arrival of a new jig might spark a new idea, and in this lesson we will be studying the most modern jigs you can buy.

The thing is that woodwork was never designed to be easy. You'll "waste" boards' worth of timber from misjudgments, but that's all part of the process, and if you're not making mistakes, you're not trying hard enough. Then again, woodwork doesn't have to be difficult, and usually more challenging projects only seem daunting because of their size. Once you break them down into manageable bits, the fear diminishes. As many famous philosophers have said, a journey of a thousand miles starts with a single step. I hope your woodworking journey has been rewarding so far and is ever so into the future.

Chest construction

The Shaker cabinet is a superb example of how to make a chest of drawers. These days, with so much sheet material being used, it is pleasing to see casework built around a frame. It is also an example of how gradually a construction becomes stronger and stronger as more components are added.

The rails at the front are jointed into the sides, as are the top and bottom back rails. Along the sides are runners to support each drawer, acting also as kickers to stop the drawer from tipping forward. The top edge of the drawer at the back is sometimes beveled slightly so that it only tips forward just before it is fully open. A stop fixed to the underside of the front rails stops the drawers from falling out, though by beveling the bottom back edge of the drawer a little, you can lift up the drawer front enough to get the drawer in and out. The dustboard fits into a groove in the runners/kickers and rails. It is ever so simple and yet very effective.

Each part reinforces the construction further, from the rails to the dustboards and then the top and the back and the plinth. Screw holes must be elongated wherever appropriate to allow for expansion and contraction.

Specialized options

With our course almost over, it's time to look ahead and explore some of the avenues for future woodworking!

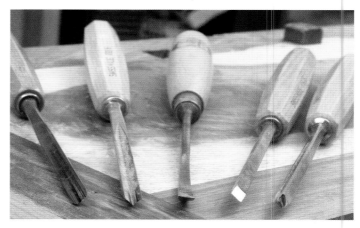

Carving tools with octagonal handles won't roll off your surface!

Lesson planner

Key techniques	Key tools and materials
• Chest construction • Wood carving • Marquetry and scrollwork	• Dovetail jigs • Joint-cutting jigs • Drilling jigs

Wood carving

You need very few tools, but plenty of skill and hard work, to take up carving. A band saw is useful for cutting out blanks, and a solid bench and holding device are essential. Only a few tools are needed to get going, perhaps a shallow gouge and a straight chisel, but you will very quickly discover what suits your projects. There are also various rotary burrs and sanding devices that can be fitted into miniature drills and grinding tools.

Micro carving chisels are useful for getting into awkward corners.

To hold a small carving, glue a round disk to the bottom to be held in a vise.

There are so many types of carving burr to fit in a rotary tool.

Use the burrs in a rotary tool, of which there are many.

Carving by hand is very rewarding work.

Hone carve chisels on the leather wheel of a slow-turning grinder.

Many people start with chip carving because it is the most regimented, a bit like carving out a house name, but with greater potential for creativity. Chip-carving tools are pretty cheap, and you don't need many. Relief carving puts images into three dimensions, normally cut from a relatively thin board, whereas carving in the round is nearer to sculpture and is probably the most difficult.

Marquetry

It is easy to become intoxicated by veneers and the amazing woods that you can sample for low cost. Making them into images takes patience and a good eye but needs little more than glue and a craft knife, at least to start. Suppliers offer plans and kits of veneer. Ambitious practitioners dye their own veneer and shade it with hot sand to give it a three-dimensional look. Pyrography is also popular for adding burned details to marquetry pictures, or for producing scenes of their own.

A development of marquetry is the assembly of veneers as a pattern into a block. By cutting the block in different ways, extraordinary effects can be produced. This is known as parquetry.

Scrollwork

Many books have been written for woodworkers using a scroll saw and looking for projects to make with it. The scroll saw is certainly a versatile machine, and it can be used for marquetry as well as intarsia, which combines marquetry and low-relief carving to produce three-dimensional scenes from contrasting pieces of wood.

Finding out more about woodwork

Magazines are superb sources of information for woodworkers, not least because many of them are full of advertisements. Poring over a catalog is an excellent way to learn which tools do what and to pick up some of the jargon. The best magazines test tools and equipment and give honest assessments of their performance, but watch out for those publications that can never find anything wrong. The Internet has some woodworking sites and is valuable as a forum for woodworkers stuck alone in their workshops. It is a very useful tool for finding out details about suppliers and techniques from other woodworkers.

Tools

Dovetail jigs

Dovetail jigs come in various designs, almost all of them employing a router to cut the pins and tails, though I have a very old Arcoy dovetailing jig that is powered by

The fingers on the Leigh dovetail jig guide the router cutter to cut.

For the pins, you use a straight cutter that is guided by angled fingers.

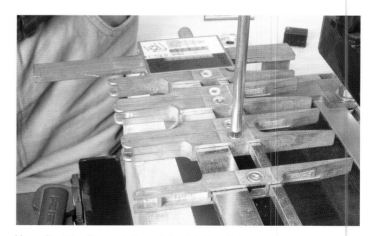

You adjust the fingers to lay out the joint in whatever pattern you want.

an electric drill. The majority of dovetail jigs today have an arrangement of metal fingers that guide a bush attached to the router base. Most use a dovetail cutter for the tails and a straight cutter for the pins, and both can cut through lapped dovetail joints.

The cleverness of a dovetail jig is that you simply turn the comb of fingers over to cut the other half of the joint.

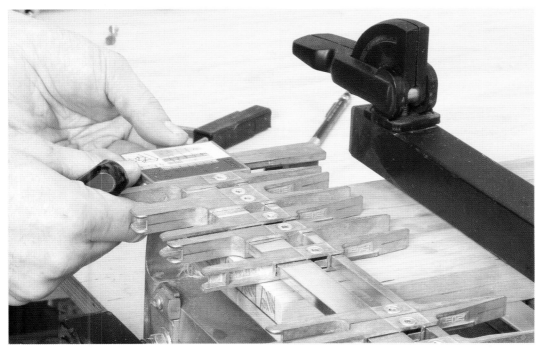

You can fine-adjust the jig to adjust the fit.

The best dovetail jigs have variable fingers that can be adjusted to produce whatever spacing you desire. Make sure you check if they can be used for cutting small dovetails if you are into boxmaking or even drawermaking. And find out what else they can do. Some can be employed for many of the jobs you'd use a router table for, or even as a drilling jig for dowel joints or to space shelf supports. Others can cut sliding dovetails and dados.

Woodrat

If you are making a series of dovetail joints, as in the Shaker cabinet this lesson, and want to explore small-scale batch production, a dovetail jig will soon earn its keep. Do plenty of research to discover the machine or jig that suits you best. There are some intriguing jigs these days that work on a router table, which is very simple and cheaper than some of the more sophisticated equipment.

The Woodrat routing center is used for dovetails and jointing techniques.

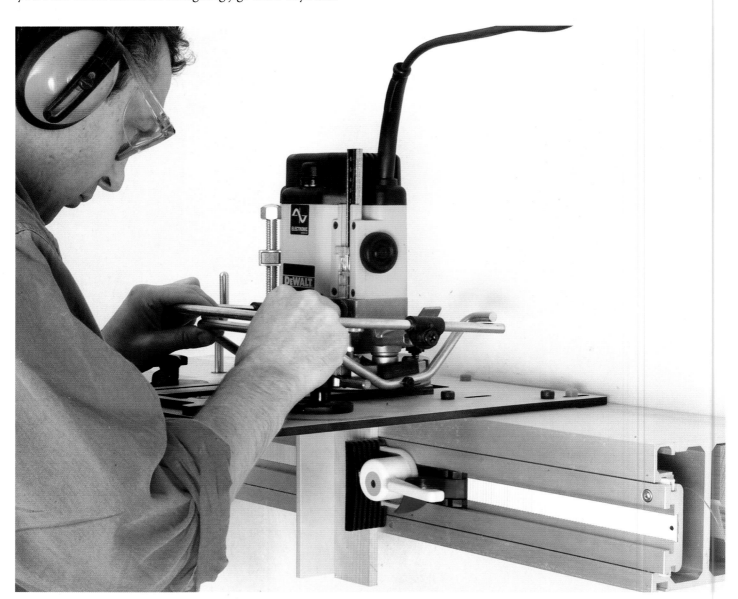

The Woodrat mechanizes the methods you would use to cut dovetails by hand and utilizes a rack to use one half of the joint to cut the other.

Underneath you can see how the dovetail cutter creates the tails.

Once cut, the tails are held at the left-hand end of the Woodrat.

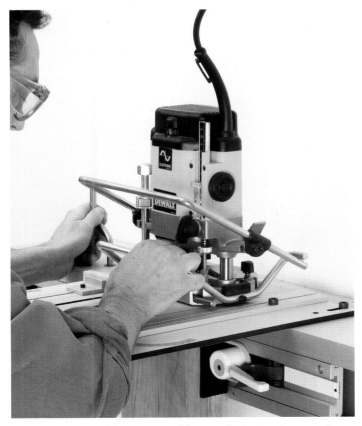

The Woodrat is used for tenons, moldings, and other routing operations.

Innovation for joints

Over the last five or ten years there have been various innovations in the cutting of joints to make them stronger and easier to work. After years of the router dominating innovation in tools and equipment, there has been something of a return to the drilled joint but in a completely new form.

1 For years, woodworkers have used drills to remove the waste from mortises, but we've all experienced the drill bit sliding out of control when it hits the previous hole. With a jig, however, you can drill holes as close together as you like and use a special loose tenon to fit perfectly into the wavy mortise. The "tenons" are supplied as a strip of molded hardwood, looking like a piece of child's modeling clay. Alternatively, you can make your own tenon with a special router cutter.

A Miller dowel acts as a wooden screw but is decorative and obviates the need for a wooden bung.

A special drill bit is used to make the right holes for a Miller dowel.

2 One of the challenges of woodworking is that there are few options for assembling a project without mechanical joints and adding the reinforcement later. Screws and nails are a compromise because you will invariably be fixing them into end grain, which isn't satisfactory, because the fibers are forced apart without binding. The screw or nail will usually pull free.

The modern solution is a ribbed and stepped dowel, which is inserted into a stepped hole that is drilled after assembly using a special bit. The dowel acts as a wooden nail, with the holding qualities of a screw, except that it can be glued into the end grain effectively. Depending on your view, the downside or upside is that the end of the dowel is visible, though some woodworkers make a feature of this by doming the head. As the dowels are available in various hardwoods, you can probably find one to match most common lumber.

Tap the Miller dowel home, and it pulls up any gap.

The Kreg jig, and similar pocket-drilling devices, cuts an angled cavity in a board with a clearance hole for a hidden screw.

Various designs of pocket drilling jig are available, with different combinations of hole. Notice the depth stop on the bit.

3 To overcome the problems of screwing into end grain, the pocket-screw jig also enables the woodworker to add fixings to a joint after assembly. The smaller portable jigs can be clamped to a rail using the stepped-drill bit to make a cavity for the screw head and a pilot hole for the thread. It isn't one of the strongest joints, but it is very useful for utility purposes around the workshop in the making of jigs and stands.

It's a good idea to make a rack for bar clamps so that they are stored safely but are ready for action.

Project **Shaker cabinet**

For the bedroom

A multiple-drawer cabinet, like this one in Shaker style, is ideal for storing clothes and oddments. If you can complete a project like this, you can do anything, and it is only complicated by the many frames you have to produce. Planning is essential.

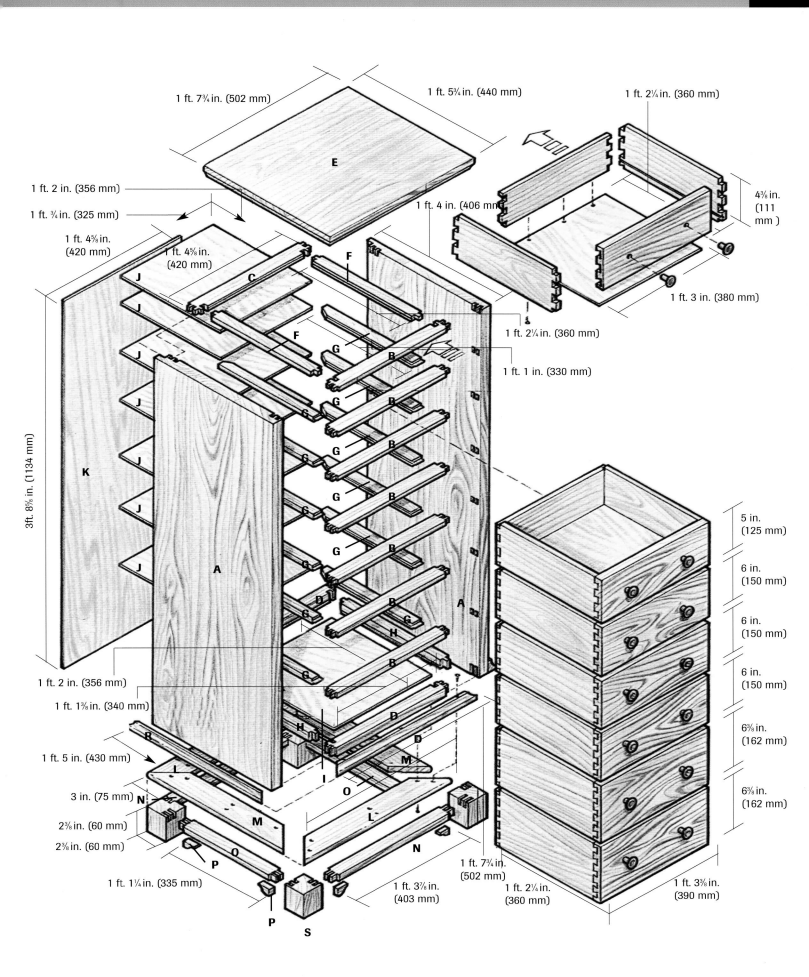

1 ft. 7¾ in. (502 mm)

1 ft. 5¾ in. (440 mm)

1 ft. 2¼ in. (360 mm)

4⅜ in. (111 mm)

1 ft. 2 in. (356 mm)

1 ft. ¾ in. (325 mm)

1 ft. 4 in. (406 mm)

1 ft. 3 in. (380 mm)

1 ft. 4⅝ in. (420 mm)

1 ft. 4⅝ in. (420 mm)

1 ft. 2¼ in. (360 mm)

1 ft. 1 in. (330 mm)

E

J

J

C

F

F

J

G

B

G

B

J

G

B

J

G

B

K

G

B

J

G

B

J

A

A

G

H

B

3 ft. 8⅝ in. (1134 mm)

5 in. (125 mm)

6 in. (150 mm)

6 in. (150 mm)

6 in. (150 mm)

6⅜ in. (162 mm)

6⅜ in. (162 mm)

G

D

1 ft. 2 in. (356 mm)

1 ft. 1⅜ in. (340 mm)

H

D

D

R

M

1 ft. 5 in. (430 mm)

L

I

O

3 in. (75 mm)

N

M

2⅜ in. (60 mm)

L

L

2⅜ in. (60 mm)

M

N

O

P

1 ft. 7¾ in. (502 mm)

1 ft. 1¼ in. (335 mm)

P

1 ft. 3⅞ in. (403 mm)

1 ft. 2¼ in. (360 mm)

1 ft. 3⅜ in. (390 mm)

S

Cutting list

Part	Material	Quantity	Dimensions thickness, width, length
A Side	cherry	2	1⅛ x 16 x 44⅝ in. (30 x 406 x 1133mm)
B Top front rail	cherry	7	⅝ x 1⅛ x 16⅝ in. (16 x 30 x 422 mm)
C Top back rail	cherry	1	⅝ x 1⅛ x 16⅝ in. (16 x 30 x 422 mm)
D Bottom front/back rail	cherry	2	1¹⁄₁₆ x 1⅛ x 16⅝ in. (27 x 30 x 422 mm)
E Top	cherry	1	1⅛ x 17⁵⁄₁₆ x 19¾ in. (30 x 440 x 502 mm)
F Top runner/kicker	cherry	2	⅝ x 1 x 14¼ in. (16 x 25 x 362 mm)
G Middle runner/kicker	cherry	12	⅝ x 1 x 13 in. (16 x 25 x 330 mm)
H Bottom runner/kicker	cherry	2	1 x 11¹⁄₁₆ x 14¼ in. (25 x 281 x 362 mm)
I Plywood bottom	plywood	1	¼ x 13⅜ x 14 in. (6 x 340 x 356 mm)
J Plywood dustboard	plywood	7	¼ x 12¾ x 14 in. (6 x 324 x 356 mm)
K Plywood back	cherry	1	¼ x 16⅝ x 44⅝ in. (6 x 422 x 1133 mm)
L Plinth front/back mitered rail	cherry	2	⅝ x 2¾ x 20¼ in. (16 x 70 x 514 mm)
M Plinth side mitered rail	cherry	2	⅝ x 2¾ x 17½ in. (16 x 70 x 444 mm)
N Plinth front/back rail	cherry	2	⅝ x 1⅛ x 17⅞ in. (16 x 30 x 454 mm)
O Plinth side rail	cherry	2	⅝ x 1⅛ x 15¼ in. (16 x 30 x 387 mm)
S Plinth leg	cherry	4	2⅜ x 2⅜ x 2⅜ in. (60 x 60 x 60 mm)
Q Front plinth molding	cherry	1	⅝ x ¾ x 19¾ in. (16 x 19 x 502 mm)
R Side plinth molding	cherry	2	⅝ x ¾ x 17 in. (16 x 19 x 430 mm)
P Plinth supports	cherry	6	⅝ x ¾ x ¾ in. (16 x 19 x 19 mm)

The drawers are designed to cascade, with the top drawer 5 inches (125 mm) deep, the next three 6 inches (152 mm) deep, and the bottom two 6⅜ inches (162 mm) deep. The sides and backs are the same respective depths, so for brevity's sake, we've listed only the lengths and thicknesses of the parts. Notice that each drawer back is narrower than its drawer front by the distance from the bottom edge of the drawer front to the top of the groove for the drawer bottom. This should be about ½ inch (12 mm).

Cutting list

Part	Material	Quantity	Dimensions thickness, width, length
T Drawer front	cherry	7	¾ x 15⅜ in. (19 x 391 mm)
U Drawer side	cherry	14	⅜ x 14 in. (10 x 356 mm)
W Drawer back	cherry	7	⅜ x 15⅜ in. (10 x 391 mm)
X Drawer bottom	cherry	7	¼ x 15 x 13¾ in. (6 x 381 x 349 mm)

Shopping list

You will also need	Extra tools for the job
Drawer pulls 14	**Bar clamps** lots **Dovetail jig** **Skew chisels** for cleaning out lapped dovetails

1 Prepare the sides (**A**). There's no harm in leaving them 2 inches (51 mm) overlong at this stage, to make cutting the bottom and top mortises easier, with less risk of breakout. Mark out the mortises to correspond with the cascading depth of the drawers. It's a really good idea to do a trial mortise-and-tenon on scrap to test the technique and the fit.

2 Cut the mortises by hand or with a mortiser, making sure they are identical.

3 Surface and thickness all the rails (**B, C, D**) and runners/kickers (**F, G, H**). Cut the fingered tenons at the end of each rail (see page 195) and check to see that they fit in the mortises, testing that any tenon fits in any mortise. By now, you should be able to repeat cuts like this without having to pair up each joint.

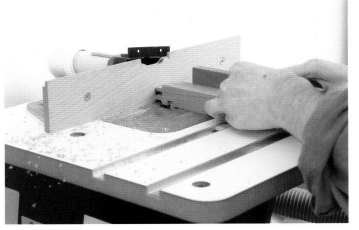

4 Groove the rails and runners/kickers for the plywood dustboard (**J**). The middle runners/kickers have a ¼-inch (6-mm)-thick stub tenon that fits into that groove at the front. The bottom and top runner/kicker (**F** and **H**) are joined to the front and back rails with either a vertical tenon or with a dovetail.

5 Assemble the seven frames one at a time, checking the diagonals and that each frame is identical.

With all the frames assembled, do a test fit of fitting the sides to the frames. This is probably best done with the case on its back, using a bar clamp level with each front rail. If you have enough bar clamps, raise the assembly off the ground and insert bar clamps underneath as well.

6 Screw the plywood back (**K**) into place to add rigidity to the case, though with quite so many frames it shouldn't be that important.

Glue the boards for the top (**E**). Smooth and cut to size. Then rout the edges with a decorative molding, working the end grain first.

Now start working on the plinth, first by cutting the short legs (**P**) to length. Mark up and cut the mortises and then cut corresponding tenons on the rails.

Cut the mitered rails (**L** and **M**) to length, and drill the screw holes to attach them to the plinth rails.

Assemble the plinth rails and legs, and screw the mitered rails in place to hold it all together. Afterward you can add the little supports (**S**), which are in fact short lengths of the molding.

7 Prepare the parts for the drawers (**T**, **U**, **W**, **X**), making them in batches—start with the single top drawer, then the next three down, and finally the bottom two, though you can groove all the parts at the same time for the drawer bottom. You can do this on a router table, though some woodworkers favor the table saw (see page 218).

Cut the tails on the sides, marking them out so that they are a fraction (no more than 1⁄32 inch/0.8 mm) overlong (see page 208). Cut out the tails; then use these to mark up the tails on the front and back. This is when a dovetail jig is so useful (see page 270).

Cut the drawer bottom to size and test the fit. If you make the drawer bottom from solid lumber—and incense cedar is the favorite—you will need to have the grain running across the drawer so that the bottom can expand and contract underneath the drawer back. Drill the drawer fronts for the pulls, and fit and finish.

Lessons learned throughout this book

By now you have the skills and equipment to do almost anything as a woodworker. Here, though, are some of the key lessons I've learned and would recommend you follow:

- When cutting joints, always prepare too much wood so you have spare components in case of mistakes. Also, make sure you have offcuts that can be used for testing cuts and marking up.

- Buy some disposable latex gloves for gluing and finishing. They keep your hands clean and make the whole process easier.

- Don't panic that your workbench isn't exactly flat or that your vise doesn't work perfectly. It will never be good enough, and you will be able to improve your kit and tools as the improvement in you skills demands. I have a rule that if you have a choice between doing something that needs to be done today and another that will help tomorrow, do the one for tomorrow first: You can always work late into the night to finish the job, and you will gain more and more by investing ahead.

- Always do a dry run of any assembly, and prepare all your clamps ready. Always check the diagonals on frames and cases. The moment glue is introduced, it will become twice as complicated.

- Check the grain direction carefully before any planing, especially if it is a final cut. Never plane a finished piece without checking the depth of cut on your plane.

- Connect dust extraction to all your machines.

- Level your workbench to ensure there is no rock.

- Enjoy your woodworking and be flexible with your deadlines!

Conversion Charts

This book was researched and written with both Canadian and U.S. markets in mind. Since both countries—at varying rates of speed and with varying degrees of success—are converting to the metric system, we've included both metric and standard (also referred to as "imperial," "English," and "U.S.") systems for most measurements and weights. But old habits die hard. There are products, materials, and practices so steeped in the old "non-metric" terminology that in many cases, only the "standard" terminology and measurements are used.

Case in point: A 2x4, which actually measures 1-½ x 3-½ in., is still called a 2x4 in both countries. Very few people refer to it as a "38 x 89." Pipe, drill bits, plywood, nails, tile, insulation, doors, and many other building materials and products, at the time this book was printed, continue to be referred to (and sold) by their "standard" names. As an offshoot of this, the materials lists and estimating information are occasionally listed only as "standard" measurements.

When in doubt about converting from metric to standard and vice versa, consult the information on these charts.

English system to metric system

To Change:	Into:	Multiply by:
Inches	Millimeters	25.4
Inches	Centimeters	2.54
Feet	Meters	0.305
Yards	Meters	0.914
Miles	Kilometers	1.609
Square inches	Square centimeters	6.45
Square feet	Square meters	0.093
Square yards	Square meters	0.836
Cubic inches	Cubic centimeters	16.4
Cubic feet	Cubic meters	0.0283
Cubic yards	Cubic meters	0.765
Pints	Liters	0.473
Quarts	Liters	0.946
Gallons	Liters	3.78
Ounces	Grams	28.4
Pounds	Kilograms	0.454
Tons	Metric tons	0.907

Metric system to English system

To Change:	Into:	Multiply by:
Millimeters	Inches	0.039
Centimeters	Inches	0.394
Meters	Feet	3.28
Meters	Yards	1.09
Kilometers	Miles	0.621
Square centimeters	Square inches	0.155
Square meters	Square feet	10.8
Square meters	Square yards	1.2
Cubic centimeters	Cubic inches	0.061
Cubic meters	Cubic feet	35.3
Cubic meters	Cubic yards	1.31
Liters	Pints	2.11
Liters	Quarts	1.06
Liters	Gallons	0.264
Grams	Ounces	0.035
Kilograms	Pounds	2.2
Metric tons	Tons	1.1

Fractions and Metric Equivalents

Inches (in.)	1/64	1/32	1/25	1/16	1/8	1/4	3/8	2/5	1/2	5/8	3/4	7/8	1
Feet (ft.)													
Yards (yd.)													
Millimeters (mm)*	0.40	0.79	1.0	1.59	3.18	6.35	9.53	10	12.7	15.9	19.1	22.2	25.4
Centimeters (cm)*								0.95	1	1.27	1.59	1.91	2.22	2.54
Meters (m)*													

Inches (in.)	2	3	4	5	6	7	8	9	10	11	12	36	39.4
Feet (ft.)											1	3	3-1/4†
Yards (yd.)												1	1-1/12†
Millimeters (mm)*	50.8	76.2	101.6	127	152	178	203	229	254	279	305	914	1,000
Centimeters (cm)*	5.08	7.62	10.16	12.7	15.2	17.8	20.3	22.9	25.4	27.9	30.5	91.4	100
Meters (m)*											.30	.91	1.00

*Metric values are rounded off. † Approximate fractions.

(actual size)

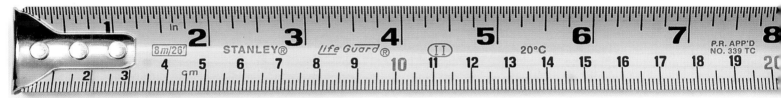

Temperature

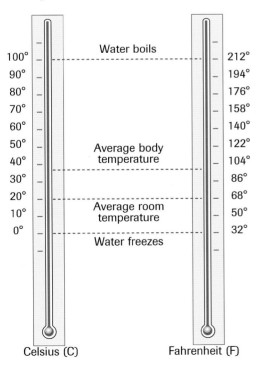

Celsius (C) Fahrenheit (F)

Water boils — 100° / 212°
90° / 194°
80° / 176°
70° / 158°
60° / 140°
Average body temperature — 50° / 122°
40° / 104°
30° / 86°
Average room temperature — 20° / 68°
10° / 50°
0° / 32°
Water freezes

The two systems for measuring temperature are Fahrenheit and Celsius (or centigrade). To change from degrees Fahrenheit, used in the United States, to degrees Celsius, subtract 32, then multiply by 5/9. For example: 68°F - 32 = 36; 36 x 5/9 = 20°C. To convert degrees Celsius to degrees Fahrenheit, multiply the degrees by 9/5, then add 32 to that figure. For example: 20°C x 9/5 = 36; 36 + 32 = 68°F.

Nails

Nail lengths are identified by numbers from 4 to 60 followed by the letter "d" which stands for "penny." The imperial and metric equivalents are listed here.

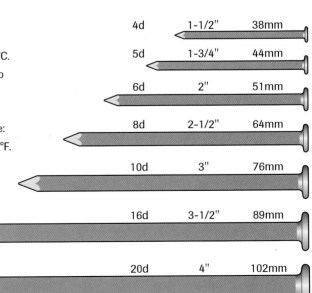

4d	1-1/2"	38mm
5d	1-3/4"	44mm
6d	2"	51mm
8d	2-1/2"	64mm
10d	3"	76mm
16d	3-1/2"	89mm
20d	4"	102mm

Index

Acknowledgments

The Complete Illustrated Woodworking Course was written over a period of months in 2004 and 2005. The book could not have been produced without the nudging and care of Miranda Sessions at Collins & Brown, the photographic and woodworking skills of Michael Wicks and doubtless other designers and creatives I haven't met or have forgotten to mention.

I'd also like to thank Martin Godfrey for supplying a Woodrat (www.woodrat.com), Keith at BriMarc (www.brimarc.com) for the Leigh dovetail jig and other bits of kit, and Stanley Tools for sending us a box of tools (www.stanleytools.com). Axminster Power Tool Centre also supplied us with photographs.

Obviously the book would never have been produced without the tolerance and support of my family—Tina, Lara, and Sasha—who all had to cope with the disruption of late nights and photoshoots. And finally a big thanks to Jude Adam and Jane Gazzo from BBC 6 Music for their entertaining radio show.